MASTERING THE ART OF
LONG-RANGE
SHOOTING

WAYNE VAN ZWOLL

Published by

Gun Digest® Books, an imprint of F+W Media, Inc.
Krause Publications • 700 East State Street • Iola, WI 54990-0001
715-445-2214 • 888-457-2873
www.krausebooks.com

To order books or other products call toll-free 1-800-258-0929
or visit us online at www.gundigeststore.com

ISBN-13: 978-1-4402-3465-1
ISBN-10: 1-4402-3465-5

Edited by Jennifer L.S. Pearsall
Cover Design by Al West
Designed by Elizabeth Krogwold

Printed in China

OTHER BOOKS BY WAYNE VAN ZWOLL

Mastering Mule Deer

America's Great Gunmakers

Elk Rifles, Cartridges and Hunting Tactics

Modern Sporting Rifle Cartridges

The Hunter's Guide to Ballistics

Elk and Elk Hunting

The Hunter's Guide to Accurate Shooting

The Gun Digest Book of Sporting Optics

Bolt Action Rifles

The Complete Book of the .22

Deer Rifles & Cartridges

Hunter's Guide to Long-Range Shooting

Leupold & Stevens: The First Century

Shooter's Bible Guide to Rifle Ballistics

Gun Digest Shooter's Guide to Rifles

■ ■ ■

TABLE OF
CONTENTS

ABOUT THE AUTHOR

A full-time journalist for the outdoors press, Wayne van Zwoll has published nearly 3,000 articles and twice that many photographs in more than two-dozen magazines, including *Field & Stream, Outdoor Life,* and several NRA titles. Once editor at *Kansas Wildlife*, he has also edited other periodicals having to do with hunting, shooting, and conservation. His "Rifles & Cartridges" column in *Bugle* is now in its twenty-second year—the longest-running feature of the Rocky Mountain Elk Foundation's flagship magazine.

Wayne has authored 15 books on firearms and their use afield. He has garnered several prestigious honors, including Leupold's Jack Slack and *Gun Digest's* John T. Amber awards for excellence in gun writing. A Life Member of RMEF and the NRA, Wayne has served on the board of the Outdoor Writers Association of America, and he has taught English and Forestry at Utah State University, where, in 2000, he earned a doctorate studying the effects of the post-war hunting motive on wildlife policy. This academic background in natural resources led Wayne to work with the Bureau of Land Management and the Washington Department of Game. He served as a contract photographer for the U.S. Forest Service, then became one of the Elk Foundation's first field directors. He has guided hunters in Utah and Wyoming, and has hunted on five continents, and he is also a professional member of the Boone and Crockett Club.

Since competing on the Michigan State University rifle team, Wayne has qualified for the final Olympic tryouts and won two state prone titles. A volunteer Hunter Education instructor in five states, he taught marksmanship for 14 years at Safari Club International's summer camps. Wayne has introduced and taught the National Archery in the Schools Program in Bridgeport, Washington, where he also serves on the School Board. He started and still directs his High Country Adventures program, to acquaint more women with traditional field sports. HCA Camps in Utah and Wyoming led, eight years ago, to annual HCA hunting safaris in Namibia.

Wayne lives in Bridgeport, Washington, with his wife, Alice. A marathoner, Wayne has run four times at Boston, but now finds a busy writing and speaking schedule eating deeply into his exercise routine.

ACKNOWLEDGMENTS

Having now logged nearly 40 years behind keyboards and firearms, I'm indebted to both for putting rice and beans on the table. But I'm much more beholden to the many people who have kept me on task and taught me about priorities I might have overlooked. My late parents, Neil and Ruth van Zwoll, told me to put education first. Good advice still. Earl Wickman loaned me the best DCM .22 in the rack, because he saw I was serious about shooting. Earl just turned 90. He'd still like to see me shoot better. My wife, Alice, has patiently wielded a camera when I needed a photo of myself, though she abhors cameras. She has also typed for me, fed me, borne my children, and taken care of the yard when I had to write. She has not yet changed the oil in my Suzuki; we're working on that. I'm also mighty thankful to the many, many people in the firearms industry who make this not only a wonderful community to join, but who have selflessly shared their time and expertise so I could write and photograph more intelligently. I can't begin to name you all, so won't. Thank you for your friendship, too. It is most valuable.

—Wayne van Zwoll

Beginning with the Norman invasion, in 1066, the bow and arrow shouldered its way into the culture of the British Isles. With it, kings defended the realm and extended its boundaries, routed much larger forces and, by threat of the "grey goose wing" alone, kept aggressors at bay. Royal edicts required able men to become proficient with the longbow. Edward IV ordered "Every Englishman or Irishman dwelling in England" to have his own bow "of his own height, made of yew, wych or hazel, ash, auburn, or any other reasonable timber." Fines were levied on citizens who failed to hone their skills regularly—and at *distance*!

The bow didn't replace the spear, the pike, or the sword, it made them less relevant. An army that became bled out by arrows before it came within pike's reach was unlikely to prevail. In 1542, an English Act dictated that no man of 24 years of age or more might shoot any mark at "less than 11 score distance"—that's more than 200 meters, a long shot for many rifles!

The lethality of arrows lay partly in their great numbers, partly in their mesmerizing arc. Loosed to fall accurately on a line of troops at a given distance, they skewered soldiers *en masse*. Their descent put them into unarmored shoulders and down onto the heads, backs, and rumps of cavalry horses. The steel bodkin, driven by a 100-pound bow, could penetrate mail and light plate. The longbow was truly a long-range weapon.

The first firearms couldn't match the bow for reliability or reach and, so, were slow to supplant it. But five centuries after the English had loosed a half-million shafts at Crecy, a young man working in his father's forge, in upper New York State, fashioned a rifle. Eliphalet Remington's muzzleloader had no unique features, but it was well built and accurate. On it, Remington founded a dynasty.

During the rifle's early growth, other American inventors (and their counterparts in Europe) developed stronger mechanisms of better steel. Sharps and Browning came up with falling-block actions that, with Remington's Rolling Block, replaced the famed Hawken on the Great Plains and triumphed in shooting matches to 1,000 yards. The advent of smokeless powder, and then jacketed bullets, flattened trajectories. Refinement of optical sights further extended reach. Hunters and soldiers who make "the long shot" these days are hardly limited to 200 meters. Some hits have been verified beyond 2,000.

As this is written, the current distance record for a shot made against an enemy soldier is held by an unknown Australian sniper, of the Delta Company, 2nd Commando Regiment. He made the killing hit, in 2012, during Operation Slipper, in Afghanistan. A GPS unit measured the range at 2,815 meters, or 3,079 yards. The shooter is unknown, because two fellow snipers fired at the Taliban commander simultaneously. One bullet struck.

Having fired at targets a lasered mile away—a mere 1,760 yards off—I am awed by this shot. It is, of course, exceedingly difficult to land a bullet in a target, one perhaps 18 inches wide, at even a mile. You can barely afford a minute-of-angle error; make that half a minute at 3,000 yards. No matter how sleek or fast your bullet, its parabolic arc at such range is so steep, you must know the range *precisely*. Know, too, that that bullet will likely meet multiple air currents *en route*. The gentlest breeze, unnoticed or poorly judged, can move the missile many inches, even feet, off course.

This book won't ensure you'll hit more often far away. But the rifles, ammunition, and techniques described here can help you do just that. Better hardware matters less than better marksmanship, so you'll not buy your way to proficiency at distance. It's the shooting that may get you there. Long shooting at steel plates in practice, and at paper in competition, is great fun. It gets you in touch with your bullet's arc and confirms what you might already know about drop and drift. It tests your shooting positions and trigger control. Shooting at distance is valuable, because it makes short shots easier, too.

As regards hunting, a close shot trumps a long one; *your odds of missing and crippling increase with yardage*. In my view, stalking closer not only adds excitement to the hunt and makes its conclusion more memorable, it is an imperative for any sportsman. When someone boasts of making a long shot on game, this consolation comes to mind: "Don't be embarrassed. You'll get closer next time." Indeed, the long poke is often evidence you didn't have the initiative or the skills to narrow the gap. Yes, you might also have run short of time or faced terrain that made an approach truly impossible. But, in my view, long shooting at game is properly a last resort and, likely as not, one to be declined. Until I'm 90-percent sure of a killing hit with the first bullet, there's no shot.

Except in war, shots so far as to be uncertain are best kept to targets that don't bleed.

—*Wayne van Zwoll*

PART 1:
BEYOND
ARM'S
REACH

IT'S NOT INTUITIVE. PERHAPS THAT'S WHY THE BOW RANKS AMONG THE GREATEST HUMAN INVENTIONS!

Ned Frost slept in a tent with a wrangler named Phonograph Jones. In the middle of the night, a grizzly entered their tent and stepped on Jones, peeling the skin off his face "by the rough pressure of his paw." The man awoke with a yell, whereupon the bear broke his lower ribs with a swipe of its paw. Frost, unarmed, hurled his pillow at the beast. The grizzly bellowed and snatched up Frost, still in his sleeping bag, its great teeth piercing the man's thighs.

In a thicket of jack pines a hundred yards off, the bear shook his prey so violently, Frost's thigh muscles were torn out and he was hurled free. He landed, half-naked and badly crippled, in the undergrowth. Painfully he pulled himself up into the branches of a pine.

■ ■ ■

The longbow is still deadly, but today's hunters shoot short, not in volleys at distance.

Saxton Pope (left) and Art Young hunted game as big as grizzlies and lions with arrows.

Ishi, of the Yana tribe, appeared in 1911, died in 1916. He taught Dr. Saxton Pope about the bow.

The most memorable encounters afield are up close. Ned Frost had killed his first grizzly at age 14. By the time Saxton Pope and Art Young engaged him to guide their 1920 expedition into Yellowstone National Park, he'd reportedly taken 500 more. One, chased for miles by a pack of hounds, made its stand at the base of a cliff. There it dispatched all but two of the dogs; when Frost arrived, only one was ambulatory. Ned fired at the bear. It charged, covering the 40 steps between them as fast as Frost could lever five rounds through his rifle. Anchored by deep snow, he couldn't dodge as the bear lunged—and collapsed dead on his chest.

No one was better qualified than Ned Frost to guide hunters to a grizzly. But this would be no ordinary hunt. Museum permits from the California Academy of Sciences, in San Francisco, would allow Dr. Pope and his colleague to shoot grizzlies inside the Park. And they would use only bows and arrows.

Collecting bears for a diorama could have been done more certainly with bullets. But Pope was keen to use his homemade arrows. He was not a rifleman, or even, by upbringing, a hunter. Years earlier, as an instructor in surgery at the University of California, he'd tended a Yana (or Yaki) Indian found starving on the outskirts of Oroville. That encounter changed his life.

Indians had been assumed gone from the Deer Creek drainage. Then, in 1908, linemen, surveying for a power dam, were suddenly confronted by a naked red man brandishing a spear. They fled. Next day they came looking for him. At the base of a rockslide, two arrows whistled past. Nothing more was seen or heard of this phantom warrior. Then, three years later and 32 miles away, a butcher's boy followed his barking dog to an emaciated Indian huddled in the corner of a corral. An armed posse captured him.

Locked up, the man cowered, refusing to eat or drink. He understood neither English nor Spanish— nor the dialects of Indians brought to visit him. T.T. Watterman, of the University's Department of Anthropology, arrived. On a hunch, he tapped the wooden edge of the cot on which they sat and spoke one word in the lost Yana tongue: *siwini*. Pine. The wild man's mouth twitched. Clothed and fed then taken to San Francisco, he said his name was Ishi—"strong, straight one." Physically, he was well proportioned, with "beautiful hands and unspoiled feet." He knew nothing of shoes, cloth, metal, horses, or roads.

Quick to parlay Stone Age skills into the artful use of knife, axe, hammer, file, and saw, Ishi could not so readily adopt Caucasian immunities to disease. Dr. Pope became his physician. He found Ishi "kindly, honest, cleanly, and trustworthy"—and a superb hunter. Pope learned from him how to make and shoot the Yana bow and arrow. Ishi contracted tuberculosis and died in 1916. He left his friend Pope with the bow.

These days, it's commonly called a longbow. But Ishi's *man-nee* was more properly a flatbow, fashioned from a broad stave of mountain juniper. At 42 inches, it was more maneuverable in cover than the English longbow. The limbs, 2½ inches wide near mid-point, had much in common with the osage flatbows of the plains Indians, who used these from horseback to kill bison. Ishi's bow pulled about 45 pounds at his draw length of 26 inches (excluding the weighted fore-shaft). He insisted that no one step over it, no child handle it, and no woman touch it. Such actions would make a bow shoot crooked, he said.

Witch hazel was Ishi's first choice for arrow shafts, which he lopped to 32 inches and shaved to a diameter of about 3/8-inch. He straightened each over hot embers, stoned each to an even finish, then cut them to 26 inches. Binding one end of a shaft with a buckskin cord to prevent splitting, Ishi secured a sharp bone between his toes, then twirled the shaft on its point. The resulting hole received the spindle of the fore-shaft, a six-inch dowel of heavier wood glued in place and wrapped with sinew. With an obsidian shard, he notched both ends of the shaft to receive the obsidian head and the string. Feathers from turkeys or raptors were split, stripped of their pith, and bound with wet sinew to the shaft to serve as fletching.

When Saxton Pope and Art Young hunted grizzlies in Yellowstone, their bows and arrows were little more advanced than Ishi's, though their bows hewed to English design and pulled 75 pounds, and their 144 hand-finished shafts wore heads of tempered steel. It would be weeks before the archers found the bear to test that equipment.

After a month afield, with arrows claiming two small bears, but Frost stopping one with his rifle, Pope and Young had their guide pack up "bed rolls, a tarpaulin, and a couple of boxes of provisions" to the head of Cascade Creek. They scouted in Dunraven Pass and found 11-inch tracks. Nearby, the bowmen "fashioned a shelter of young jack pines, constructed like a miniature corral, less than three by six feet in area." They waited there all night, "permitting ourselves one blanket and a small piece of canvas." Over the next days, rain pelted camp and blind.

The great bear of Dunraven Pass showed up later that week, an hour after a frigid midnight. Four other grizzlies materialized, too. "I whispered to Young, 'Shoot the big fellow.' [Then] I drew an arrow to the head, and drove it at the oncoming female. It struck her full in the chest. She reared, threw herself sidewise, bellowed with rage, staggered and fell … ." As for the big bear, "Young discharged three arrows at him. I shot two. We should have landed, he was so large. But he galloped off … ."

After skinning the female by flashlight, the hunters waited for dawn, then scoured the ground for arrows. One of Young's was missing! They took the track of the big bear, but the spoor soon petered out.

"We made wide circles … . We cross-cut every forest path and runway … . He was gone. For five hours we searched in vain, and at last, worn with disappointment and fatigue, we lay down and slept … ."

Near sundown they awoke, ate, and resumed the search, climbing to view the slope from above. Letting themselves down by hand- and toehold, they came upon a hidden ledge.

"There lay the largest grizzly in Wyoming … . By flashlight, acetylene lamp, candle light, fire light and moonlight, we labored. We used up all our knives … ."

Pope weighed the body parts, which came to 916 pounds in sum.

"We cleaned the pelts, packed them on our backs and, dripping with salt brine and bear grease, staggered to the nearest wagon trail."

■ ■ ■

Arrowheads date back 50,000 years, well into the last glacial period. The earliest have been found in Tunisia and Algeria, and in Morocco. While no bows or arrows have survived that long, cave paintings from the Mesolithic Period (20,000 to 7,500 B.C.) show archers in action. Likenesses of their bows suggest some were of composite construction. Digs in the near and Far East have turned up bows with bellies of horn and backs of animal sinew—wood, after all, is not everywhere available.

The bow is hardly an intuitive thing. If you'd been whelped in a cave and taught to kill with rocks and clubs, many moons might pass before you struck upon the idea of a stick, bent by a taut cord, hurling a shaft guided by feathers. Even if you'd been tutored by community geeks and abandoned the stone for the spear, the leap to arrows wouldn't have come quickly. In treeless places, making a shaft was hard enough. Who would have conceived a bow stave? Bows from desert climes are indeed remarkable!

By the second-century B.C., the Chinese had designed bows for mounted archers and charioteers. Homer's Greeks lived by the bow, as did the fearsome Mongols. The Turkish recurve design may have resulted from efforts to put more power in limbs short enough for cavalry. These and other compact bows had flatter profiles than did the famous English longbow, its limbs D-shaped in cross-section and round at the belly. The term "longbow," incidentally, derives not so much from stave length, but from the measure of draw. Early European archers drew to the breast. By the time English

Wayne's laminated bamboo/fiberglass longbow, by John Schultz, is after a Hill design.

arrows skewered French troops at Crecy, the King's archers anchored at the mouth, cheek, or ear. Longer bows permitted this shooting style with less stacking of pull weight. Of course, arrows also had to be longer than those drawn to the chest.

Many types of wood have become bow staves. Late in Europe's Stone Age, archers chose yew for its cast, though they'd evidently not learned to marry heartwood with sapwood. As English yew couldn't match Spanish yew for purity and straightness, bowyers in the British Isles imported staves from southern Europe. Fearful that one day its army might feel the sting of English bodkins, Spain shut off the sale of yew. The English skirted this ban by demanding a bundle of staves with each shipment of Mediterranean wine!

Roger Ascham, tutor to Edward VI and Queen Elizabeth I, wrote in his *Toxophilus* of the Saxons subduing Britons with "their bow and shaft." At the Battle of Hastings, October 14, 1066, Norman archers played a major, if not a decisive role. William drew up his army in three ranks. Archers, crossbowmen, and probably slingers arrayed themselves ahead of the armored foot soldiers and mounted knights. King Harold, foiled by Norman scouts in his attempt to hurry south from Yorkshire and surprise the invaders, had set up a hasty but formidable defense. When the initial Norman assault faltered, the King's troops counterattacked. It was a piecemeal response. In the midst of his fleeing army, William tore off his helmet. "Look at me!" he cried. "I am alive, and with God's help I will conquer!" His forces took heart, rallied, and drove Harold's men back. Twice thereafter the Normans feigned a withdrawal, only to turn on their pursuers and mince their ranks before the English could retreat. Harold's troops bled.

According to Guy, Bishop of Ariens, arrows and bolts finished the Anglo-Saxon army. "The foot soldiers ran ahead to engage the enemy with arrows. … [T]he bands of archers attacked and from a distance transfixed bodies with their shafts, and the crossbowmen destroyed the shields as if by a hail-storm … ." The Bayeux Tapestry, which illustrates the battle, shows many archers and Harold's demise. "The whole shower sent by the archers fell around King Harold, and he himself sank to the ground, struck in the eye."

For all the romance it shares in the legend of Robin Hood, the English longbow secured its place in history by killing people. In the centuries after the Norman invasion in 1066, the bow remained the preeminent weapon in the British Isles. Royal edicts required able men to practice archery, notably at what modern bowmen might consider extreme range. Arrows were shot nearly to the limit of the bow's cast, so the troops could rain volleys, accurately, as far as possible. Shooting long bought the English more time before they had to enjoin hand combat. More time meant more arrows in the air, more enemy casualties.

Even well-armored troops were vulnerable to the feathered shaft. Chain and steel plate impeded movement and throttled a soldier's advance. Archers then had the luxury of loosing arrows repeatedly at joints in the metal of their slow-moving targets. On hot days, armor cooked its wearer—woe to the knight who hoisted his helmet for a breath of air.

As the war bow evolved, England's Edward I deemed it indispensable. He paid handsomely those archers in the King's service. He even pardoned poachers who would wield bows in defense of the realm; this was no small concession, as the common penalty for poaching was prompt hanging with the offender's own bowstring. Meanwhile, the King required much of his subjects to actually *supply* the army. For a royal expedition in 1359, "The Tower" exacted 20,000 bows, 50,000 bowstrings, and 850,000 arrows from the counties.

No battle more clearly showed the longbow's lethality than that waged near the French village of

> Archers had the luxury of loosing arrows repeatedly at joints in the metal armor of their enemies. On hot days, armor cooked its wearer—woe the knight who hoisted his helmet for a breath of air.

Crecy-en-Ponthieu, August 26, 1346. That Saturday morning, Edward stationed 12,000-odd men to defend the Crecy-Wadicourt ridge. Fewer than half were archers, drawn up in wedge-shaped formations that flanked staggered units of soldiers equipped for hand combat. The mile-long line faced King Philip's French force of 36,000 to 40,000—Philip's cavalry by itself matched in number the entire English army!

But nature took a hand. In mid-afternoon, a murder of crows, portent of bad weather, flew over the French ranks. Aware events would soon escape his control, Philip ordered his Genoese crossbowmen forward. Black clouds burst above them, as these troops scrambled to firing positions. Rain drenched their strings (which no doubt stretched, reducing cast); but the storm soon passed, and bright sunshine shot from behind English lines into the eyes of the Genoese. At this moment, Edward's longbowmen, who'd kept their strings and bows under cloaks, loosed their first volley. So devastating was the swarm of arrows descending upon them, many of the French mercenaries cut their strings, dropped their crossbows, and fled back toward their army. About the same time, French knights keen to enter the fray gave their horses rein and charged. In heraldic splendor, they galloped over the Italians, now frantic to escape the English shafts relentlessly raining one barrage after another. In this melee, some knights fell to crossbow bolts.

No one would have counted then, but a practiced archer in Edward's army could send 10 shafts per minute to 240 yards with good accuracy. If heavy horses in battle trappings took 90 seconds to cover the 300 yards to the English front, they, and the troops astride, would have endured a hail of 7,500 arrows from a wedge of 500 archers. The 5,000 bowmen in this epic brawl probably had on hand 100 shafts each.

The French cavalry struggled up a slope bloodied with dead and writhing foot soldiers. They met an unimaginable rain of steel. Arrows skewered horses and perforated chain mail. Wrote longbow scholar Robert Hardy:

The archers nocked and drew, closing their backs, opening their chests, pushing into their bows, anchoring … letting fly [and] grabbing the next arrow from ground or belt or quiver, to nock and draw and anchor and loose, in deadly unrelenting repetition."

French knights, unbelieving, came on, wave after wave. Men-at-arms followed; as many as 16 charges failed. Archers running low on arrows ran forward, pulled them from the ground and the dead. By moonlight, the battle raged. At sunup "the flower of the chivalry of France lay dead upon the field.

Ten years later, on September 19, at Poitiers, more than 2,000 French soldiers died at the feet of English archers; still, the conflict most often cited as won by the bow is Agincourt.

The battle of Agincourt followed the ascendancy of Prince Henry to the English throne. At age 25, he became Henry V and quickly revived hostilities with France. On August 15, 1415, he sailed south in the 500-ton *Trinity Royal*, leading an armada of 1,500 ships ferrying 10,000 men (8,000 of whom were archers!) and almost as many horses. Entering the Seine on the eighteenth, Henry's fleet anchored near Harfleur. Unloading took days. The march north, ordered against the counsel of the Kings' advisors, was as much for show as conquest. Pushing 15 miles a day in deteriorating weather, Henry's forces lost their shine and enthusiasm.

Meanwhile, the French were losing patience. At Maisoncelles, a swelling French force camped within a mile of Henry's. Early on Friday, October 25, the armies arrayed themselves against each other on a plain called Agincourt. By this time, Henry counted only 6,000 combatants; *le Dauphin* boasted 10 times that many. The English advanced first, across muddy ground. They halted just within arrow range, bows braced.

The French army's response doomed both cavalry and infantry. Across plowed furrows they charged. But the poached ground bogged them down, pulling horses and men to its bosom as a hailstorm of English arrows arced into them. The very size of the French force now worked against it. A tide of men piled forward against the stalled advance, while Henry's archers poured death into their ranks. Two woods funneled the French into a front just 900 yards wide. There, slain soldiers fell in heaps high as a saddle. In three hours, 10,000 men—"half the nobility of France"—died. Henry ordered the prisoners killed.

The family who owned and farmed the Agincourt plain five and a half centuries later wrote to a student of the battle:

Don Ward fashioned his own modern longbow and took this Colorado elk at nine yards.

We defended our fields in 1415 and in 1915, in 1939 again, and often in between.

■ ■ ■

Across the Atlantic, during this same time, native hunters had adopted the bow. Almost surely it came with the migration of people from Asia across the Bering-Chukchi Isthmus. The diaspora refined bow design to suit local materials and conditions. Arrowheads fit the quarry. Contrary to common assumption, big heads were used on small game. They required less chipping and didn't slide easily under grass. Losses during knapping were less than with smaller heads, which became more fragile with each flake. Smaller heads made sense for big game, as they penetrated hide and muscle more easily.

Their thin edges cut with less drag; the keen blades of steel heads have nothing on the edges of well-knapped obsidian, essentially volcanic glass. Doctor Saxton Pope shot steel and obsidian heads through cow's liver contained in a box wrapped in deer skin. The steel-tipped shaft drove 22 inches past entry, the obsidian point 30 inches!

For decades after firearms became available on our frontier, many American Indians stuck with the bow. It was lighter in hand and could be repaired, replaced in the field. Arrows could be made from natural materials. The bow was lightweight, quiet, reliable. Plains Indians could shoot arrows more accurately than bullets, from a galloping horse. The bowman pushed as he pulled, easily maintaining his balance. Most mounted Indians drew to the chest, shy of the arrowhead. A 24-inch arrow pulled 20 inches, stacked enough thrust from a stout bow

The rattlesnake skin here is decorative, but a backing of sinew has long been used to enhance the cast of wood-core longbows.

to drive through bison. Raised nocks helped the horseman ready arrows without looking; he could loose several during the time needed to charge a muzzleloader once. Texas Ranger "Bigfoot" Walker observed, "[Indians] can shoot their arrows faster than you can fire a revolver, and almost with the accuracy of a rifle at … fifty or sixty yards." Even Sharps rifles, deadly at long range, often lay untouched behind Indian raids. Reason: the cartridges were hard to find! Carbines in .45-70 and .44-40 had more appeal, because ammunition was more common and likely to turn up in plunder.

The evolution of North American bows and arrows may owe something to Europeans. During the reign of Henry II, Welsh bowmen pestered England's monarchy. Around 1170, a group of Welsh, under Prince Madoc, is said to have sailed for the Americas. Traces of their language and culture—even their physical appearance—carried into the nineteenth century, until smallpox decimated the Mandan people on the upper Mississippi. The bow didn't formally arrive on our Eastern seaboard until hundreds of years later, when firearms controlled battlefronts and had begun to empty game fields worldwide.

Saxton Pope undertook flight tests of various North American bows, tapping the Department of Anthropology at the University of California for examples from 17 native tribes. He used a 30-inch, 310-grain bamboo arrow for each trial. Pope's friend Will Compton—bowyer, hunter, and "a very powerful man"—shot each bow at least six times, loosing the arrows at 45 degrees. Pope recorded distance. "We spared no bows because of their age, and consequently broke two … ."

A 65-pound English flight bow of yew hurled an arrow 300 yards, in Saxton's trials. A longbow of

Bow origin	Draw weight, pounds	Flight distance, yards
Alaskan	80	180
Apache	28	120
Blackfoot	45	145
Cheyenne	65	156
Cree	38	150
Esquimaux (Eskimo)	80	200
Hupa	40	148
Luiseno	48	125
Navajo	45	150
Mojave	40	110
Osage	40	92
Sioux	45	165
Tomawata	40	48
Yaki	70	210
Yana	48	205
Yukon	60	125
Yurok	30	140

some age and 75 pounds draw sent it 250—quite remarkable, as wood limbs lose cast over time. Pope was surprised at the anemic performance of a heavy Tartar bow from China. Composite Turkish bows shot farthest, but only with lightweight arrows. Pope tested the cycling rate of his longbow by flinging arrows skyward. He was able to put seven arrows aloft before the first touched the ground.

Leaning again on the good graces of colleagues, Pope borrowed a shirt of chain armor from the University's museum, to test arrow penetration. A curious attendant offered to don the 25 pounds of steel and stand for a shot from Pope's longbow. The good doctor demurred and put the armor on a wooden box padded with burlap to simulate the human form. From seven yards he loosed a bodkin-tipped shaft of the type used by English archers against the French. The steel point penetrated the thickest part of the back armor, drove through an inch of wood, and bulged the chain on the breast side. The attendant turned green.

In those halcyon days, when you could hunt grizzlies in Wyoming, and test bows from museums, Pope had no access to the electronics and high-speed photography of now that measure and show projectile flight. He timed arrow speed by stopwatch (150 feet per second for a lightweight shaft from his 75-pound yew bow). He determined striking energy by comparing arrow penetration in paraffin with that caused by falling weights (25 foot-pounds at 10 yards). He determined rotation of arrows in flight by nocking two at once on a bow, the shafts connected by fine silk thread. In flight, one arrow paid out thread as the other spooled it up! He found his fletching rotated an arrow six times every 20 yards, about 15 times a second.

Pope investigated the properties of sapwood and heartwood, noting that England's longbow, in its most advanced form, incorporated both. He found sapwood (outside, white) excelled in tensile strength, but heartwood (center, red) trumped it in compression strength and resiliency. A longbow with a belly of heartwood and a back of sapwood best combined the properties of both.

Afield, Pope and Young are best known for big-game hunts, but they shot small game to test their skills.

"I recall one day when Young and I got 24 squirrels with the bow … . Young by himself secured 17 in one morning; the last five were killed with five successive arrows."

These early archers didn't dote on the kill. They seemed beguiled by the bow, as had been their predecessors, Will and Maurice Thompson.

"So long as the new moon returns in heaven a bent, beautiful bow, so long will the fascination of archery keep hold of the hearts of men."

Maurice Thompson, born in 1844, grew up hunting with brother Will, five years his junior. Civil war drew the Thompson brothers to the front lines. They returned to the Cherokee Valley to find the family home destroyed by Sherman's march through Georgia. Though Will had dodged injury, Maurice suffered from a chest wound inflicted at the Battle of Cold Harbor. Penniless, weakened by their long walk, and denied firearms, both young men faced a grim future. Salvation came from an unlikely quarter.

The Thompsons began hunting with handmade bows and arrows. Maurice started to write:

The humanities grew out from Archery as a flower from a seed. No sooner did the soft sweet note of the bow-string charm the ear of genius than music was born ... .

His words found a market—oddly enough, on the eve of smokeless powder. Repeating rifles had already, it seemed, made bows and arrows obsolete. Perhaps the prose took readers from war's pain and loss, still keenly felt. Maurice deftly attached the bow to the romance of storybook times and made the simple act of drawing a bowstring a lyrical event.

During the next decade, after a move to Crawfordsville, Indiana, Maurice wrote in earnest about nature and about hunting with the bow. His essays appeared in prestigious magazines, beginning with *Harper's*, in 1877. Archery offered the Thompson brothers both purpose and income.

Though deadly at distance, the Thompsons insisted that "point-blank range at an absolute center is what calls out the bowman's finest powers." Wrote Maurice:

I have, with my hunting arrows, broken 37 of 50 Bogardus glass balls (the predecessor to clay shotgun targets) thrown into the air toward me at 12 yards.

He recounted hitting a pencil five times in succession at 10 yards.

In 1879, Maurice Thompson was chosen president of the just-formed American National Archery Association. Thompson's T*he Witchery of Archery*, published 1877, became a classic book on the bow. Will, himself a gifted poet, became an attorney. He outlived Maurice, later politely declining an invitation to hunt with Saxton Pope, Art Young, and Will Compton:

No one can know how I have loved the woods, the streams, the trails ... . How often the fierce arrow hissed its threat close by the wide ears! How often the puff of lifted feathers has marked the innocuous passage of my very best arrow!

The longbow's romance—and its effective reach—came vividly to life again in post-Depression America, when a young archer named Howard Hill mesmerized audiences with exhibition shooting and hunting films. Born November 23, 1899, in Wilsonville, Arkansas, Hill first picked up a bow at age four. Uncommonly athletic, he grew to excel in other sports, too. At Auburn, he played golf, baseball, football, and basketball. Maurice Thompson's writings fanned his passion for the bow; he began making his own longbows and winning tournaments.

In 1928, in Miami, he set a flight record of over 391 yards. Then Hill brought his skill to Hollywood, where he shot for Errol Flynn in the 1938 film *The Adventures of Robin Hood*. He produced 23 reels on archery for Warner Brothers. In my youth, television matinees featured Hill shooting coins out of the air. His shafts arced into targets so distant as to challenge riflemen. Hill's bow was so powerful that four comely lasses in tandem were unable to budge the string, yet he pulled it with seeming ease. Hill adored the smooth draw and powerful cast of the English longbow, though he found it less maneuverable and more sensitive to shooting stance than the flatbow of the plains Indian. He settled on a hybrid design most like the English bow, but slightly shorter, with slightly broader limbs.

Howard Hill became the first white man on record to kill an elephant with a bow. The ponderous shafts measured over a yard, and the bow pulled 172 pounds. Hill added Cape buffalo, lion, and crocodile to a long list of lesser species. In his book *Hunting The Hard Way*, he described shooting bison from a galloping pony. Hill hunted in Wyoming, with Ned Frost, near the hills that gave Saxton Pope and Art Young their grizzly bears. Candid about his shooting, Hill admitted to missing game; he also wrote of arrowing a pronghorn on the run at 70 yards. Once, he hunted several days for elk above the Shoshone River. The last evening, he and his guide spotted a bull. They ran out of cover at 185 yards, "entirely too far for any degree of accuracy with the bow." But, after some palaver, Hill loosed a shaft. It flew high. The next struck low. The elk didn't move. Carefully, Hill shot one more arrow. "We both knew my aim had been good ... ." The broadhead struck the elk high in the chest "and buried itself to the feathers."

Hurling arrows at speeding pronghorns or launching them in five-second arcs to distant elk, any archer will miss many animals and likely cripple more than he kills. He'll burn through hunting partners, squandering chances to close on game. But we all adopt the thinking of our times. Howard Hill was not only gifted, he lived in another day; a generation earlier, Saxton Pope had shot eagles.

Budding archers brought up on Howard Hill's hunting exploits learned to shoot with Ben Pearson bows. Born a year before Hill, in Pine Bluff, Arkansas, Ben Pearson also fashioned his own longbows and used them in competition. Winning the 1927 Arkansas State Championship helped him peddle his arrows. In 1939, he added bows to the Ben Pearson catalog. His became the first U.S. company to mass-produce archery gear. By 1963, the firm was selling hundreds of bows—a day. Affordable, solid-fiberglass models came in kits, with arrows, and targets like the leopard I perforated in my backyard. Ben Pearson died March 2, 1971. Howard Hill followed February 4, 1975.

While Fred Bear's birth antedated those of Hill and Pearson by only a couple years, his interest in the bow came late, after he'd moved from his native Pennsylvania, to Michigan. At Detroit's Adams Theatre, he saw Art Young's film, *Alaskan Adventure.* Fred had found work in the auto industry, when, at age 29, he hunted deer with a bow he'd fashioned from an $8 osage stave. Six years later, he arrowed his first whitetail.

Practice at targets paid off, when Fred won State archery championships in 1934, 1937, and 1943. In 1947, he moved his nascent bow business to Grayling, gateway to Michigan's North Woods. Five years thereafter, he cataloged his first mass-produced bow, the Grizzly. By the time Fred sold controlling interest in Bear Archery, in 1968, his recurve bows were wildly popular—and his exploits had inspired a new generation of bowhunters. The film of Fred shooting a brown bear at 15 steps certainly inspired me!

Best known for his hunts on the Little Delta and other storied places in Canada, Alaska, and the Yukon, Fred Bear arrowed a tiger in India, a lion

Howard Hill used a longbow on elephants, shot for Errol Flynn in Hollywood's *The Adventures of Robin Hood.*

Wayne draws a cedar shaft. Arguably, the longbow was so named for the draw, not limb length.

in Moçambique. Twice he failed to kill a polar bear; hit with arrows, the beasts had to be stopped with a rifle. Then, in 1966, after 25 days of unseemly weather, in temperatures to 30-below, Fred killed a fine bear. It was the only one he'd seen in six weeks on the ice.

Meanwhile, another archer was making history shooting at very long distance. In fact, the sport of flight shooting rewards only distance. Bowmen launch arrows from powerful bows with the sole purpose of shooting farther than anyone else. Some of the bows are so powerful, they feature stirrups for the feet so that, from a sitting position, the archer can brace the bow with his legs and draw with both arms.

The man who all but defined modern flight shooting was Harry Drake, born in 1915. Drake not

only competed, he built the winning bows. In 1947, a Drake bow became the first to launch a shaft over 600 yards (it landed 603 yards away). For the next 29 years straight, Harry Drake's flight bows held the men's national flight records! In 1971, Harry used a bow of his design and manufacture (circa 1964) during the National Archery Association's Flight Championships at Ivanpah Dry Lake, California. The arrow flew 1,077 yards! That year he became the first person to cast an arrow over one mile—1,760 yards! Shooting his own footbow, he would later shatter that record with a shot of 2,028 yards.

Well before Fred Bear's passing, in 1988, and the motorcycle accident that put Harry Drake on his deathbed, in 1997, bowhunters began to jettison longbows and recurves in favor of compound bows. Now, traditionalists pay handsomely for longbows

BOWS OF THE MARY ROSE

Howard Hill became the first white man on record to kill an elephant with a bow. The ponderous shafts measured over a yard, and the bow pulled 172 pounds! He later added Cape buffalo, lion, and crocodile to a long list of lesser species.

Unlike the firearms that began to nudge bows off the battlefield in the sixteenth and seventeenth centuries, the English longbow had no champions to save it. Rifles and muskets found their way into collections and museums, though there are specimens, owned by royalty, that survive in almost-new condition. But bows were implements of the commoner and much more easily made than early firearms. Their value lay only in utility. Broken in battle or having lost cast over time, bows became firewood. Suddenly, it seemed, all that remained of the English longbow was its image in woodcuts and tapestries.

Then, divers discovered the *Mary Rose*. The great ship sank in the Solent, battling a French fleet, in 1545, during the reign of Henry VIII. Salvage began in the 1830s. The recovered manifest listed guns, and 250 yew longbows with arrows. It wasn't until a later effort did the bows surface in quantity. In 1979, a diver brought up a pole, black with marine accretions. Massive and "knobbly," it was nonetheless recognizably a bow, or at least the beginnings of one. Its thickness suggested a draw force of 100 pounds or more. Salvagers concluded this and other staves were unfinished. But evidence of tillering after manufacture (trimming the ends to speed limb action), and the fitting of horn nocks showed the bows ready for service. Also, in wartime, it would have made no sense to fill a ship with rough staves.

By 1981, the last bows from the *Mary Rose* had been recovered. The fine-grained yew had almost surely grown in a Mediterranean climate. Burial in silt under cold saltwater had preserved it. Cleaned, the bows revealed sapwood over a belly of heartwood. In cross-section, most limbs were D-shaped and deep, or "stacked." Unlike modern longbows, the salvaged bows lacked a central riser, that is, they were built to arc "full compass," working every inch. Tudor bowyers with access to good yew could choose staves that were straight or slightly reflexed, the limbs naturally inclining toward the back when unstrung. They heaved arrows faster than staves with deflexed limbs. Only a handful of *Mary Rose* bows showed marked deflex.

Utah bowman Aram Barsch built this osage longbow and shoots it well!

and recurves that would make Saxton Pope swoon (to say nothing of those peasant bowmen holding the ridge at Crecy). Skilled longbowmen are not a lost clan. When Hill was at his peak, some thought his shooting would never be equaled. But Bob Swinehart used a long-bow to take Africa's big five. And Byron Ferguson is a wizard with a modern long-bow, one who can thread a wedding ring at 30 feet and hit airborne tennis balls!

Like the stirrup, the longbow is simple of form; its lethality was largely lost on men brought up with early car-tridge rifles. Still, its effect on history can hardly be overstated. For thousands of years before the advent of gunpowder, arrows fed humankind and protected their dwellings. Feathered shafts have felled more adversaries than have bullets from automatic rifles. The wink of steel in steep arc once paralyzed armored troops. Hunters and soldiers now are generations removed from archers whose bodies showed the strain of daily practice with 100-pound longbows—men who, at Crecy alone, loosed *half a million arrows* to change history—and for those born after the seventeenth centu-ry, gunpowder and conical bullets would redefine the long shot.

■ ■ ■

Silent as shadow, the limbs arch, the bowman's power braking a taut string. Release! The shaft flicks forward like a fly on light line. Hiss; it's away! A bent bow calls to primal man and poet and flings the spirit high on a grey goose wing.

THE FIRST GUNS COULDN'T MATCH THE EFFECTIVE RANGE OF ARROWS. THAT WOULD CHANGE, BUT SLOWLY!

While the origins of gunpowder remain obscure, explosive "Chinese snow" appeared in fireworks a couple centuries before the English friar Roger Bacon described gunpowder, in 1249. Berthold Schwarz further investigated possibilities in gas propulsion, setting the stage for the first firearms, which appeared around the start of the fourteenth century. Guns accompanied Edward II during his 1327 invasion of Scotland.

In the U.S., a powder mill was erected at Milton, Massachusetts (near Boston), before any firearms factory appeared in the area. By the start of the Revolution, colonists had manufactured or stolen 40 tons of blackpowder! Half was wasted at Cambridge. In no time, the Continental Army had no powder. But George Washington made powder production a priority. By 1800, mills were shipping 750 tons annually!

Igniting this sulfurous fuel was easy in the open air. Setting it afire in a chamber to launch a ball challenged gun designers. The first firearms, developed in Europe a century and a half before Columbus sailed for the New World,

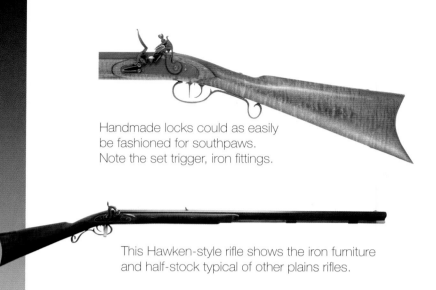

Handmade locks could as easily be fashioned for southpaws. Note the set trigger, iron fittings.

This Hawken-style rifle shows the iron furniture and half-stock typical of other plains rifles.

were heavy tubes that required two attendants. The Swiss called these weapons *culverins*. The *culveriner* steadied the tube, while the *gougat* applied a priming charge, then lit it with a smoldering stick or rope. Mechanical rests supported infantry guns; so did forks in the saddles of mounted warriors. Clumsy and inaccurate (and because they often misfired, barrels were often fitted with ax heads), *culverins* produced noise and smoke that unnerved enemies armed with pikes or even bows.

Fuses were developed for stationary cannon, whose muzzles could be aimed at a parapet or a gun emplacement. Timing mattered little, because such targets did not move. But advancing gunners couldn't wait while an assistant caught up with a burning wick, nor could they maintain aim while the fuse burned. When the enemy charged or swept by on horses, the fire in a fuse usually found the powder too late.

As guns were trimmed so one man could easily carry and aim them (and torch the charge), faster ignition became imperative. The first "lock," or firing mechanism, was a crude lever by which a smoldering wick was lowered to a touch-hole in the barrel. The wick was later replaced by a match assisted by a cord or a long wick kept smoldering atop the barrel. The shooter eased the serpentine clamp holding the match into the wick until the match caught fire. Then he moved the match to the side and lowered it to the touch-hole. Later, a spring kept the match from the touch-hole until needed; a trigger adapted from crossbows added control. Such a mechanism was called

a "matchlock," a label also applied to guns fired that way. The Spanish *arquebus* was one. *Arquebusiers* carried smoldering wicks in metal boxes on their belts.

In the sixteenth century, German inventors eliminated the unreliable wick with the "monk's gun." A spring-loaded jaw held a piece of pyrite (flint) against a serrated bar. The shooter pulled a ring at the rear of the bar, scooting it across the pyrite to produce sparks, which showered a pan containing a trail of fine gunpowder that led into the touch-hole in the barrel. A more sophisticated version called the "wheellock" appeared around 1515, in Nuremberg. It featured a spring-loaded sprocket wound with a spanner wrench and latched under tension. Pulling the trigger released the wheel to spin against a shard of pyrite held by spring tension against the wheel's teeth. Sparks flew.

In the *lock a la miquelet*, the roles of pyrite and steel were reversed. Probably a Dutch design, it was named after Spanish *miquelitos* (marauders) operating in the Pyrenees. Later, it would be modified to incorporate a spring-loaded cock that held a piece of flint and swung in an arc when released. At the end of its travel, the flint in the jaws of the cock struck a pan cover or hammer, kicking it back to expose the primed pan. Sparks landed in the pan, igniting a priming charge of powder that burned through the touch-hole in the barrel to the main charge. The cock eventually became known as the "hammer," the hammer a "frizzen." The mechanism was called a "flintlock." It was less costly than the wheellock and more reliable. By this time, guns were commonly known by the names of their firing mechanisms.

Matchlock, wheellock, and flintlock mechanisms had a common weakness: exposed priming. Wet weather could render them all useless. Producing a spark inside a barrel made no sense until early in the eighteenth century, with the discovery of fulminates (shock-sensitive salts of fulminic acid, an isomer of cyanic acid). In 1774, a physician to Louis XV wrote on the explosive nature of mercury fulminate. Englishman E.C. Howard discovered, in 1799, that adding saltpeter to fulminates produced explosives that could be set off by a jarring action, but could generally be carried safely.

"Howard's powder" may have influenced the work of Scotch clergyman Alexander John Forsythe. In 1806, Forsythe demonstrated internal ignition. Two years later, Swiss gun maker Johannes Pauly designed a breechloading percussion gun that employed a cartridge with a paper percussion cap.

A spring-loaded needle pierced the cap, detonating the fulminate.

Powder fired by a spark in the chamber marked a watershed in firearms development. New types of ammunition and the guns to fire them came pell-mell. In 1818, Englishman Joseph Manton built a gun with a spring-loaded catch that held a tiny tube of fulminate against the side of the barrel, over the touch-hole. The hammer crushed the fulminate, and breech pressure blew the tube away. The Merrill gun, 14,500 of which were bought by the British government, employed this mechanism.

In 1821, the British gun maker Westley Richards employed fulminate primers in a flintlock-style pan. The falling hammer opened the pan cover, exposing a cup containing fulminate. Two years later, American physician Dr. Samuel Guthrie found a way to produce fulminate pellets, a convenient alternative to loose fulminate and paper caps.

Flint in the hammer jaws strikes the frizzen, igniting pan powder, then the rifle's main charge.

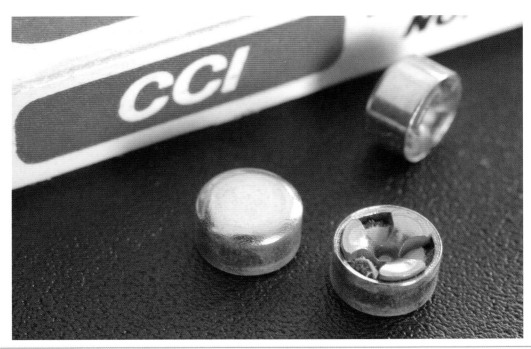

The metallic primer, credited to Joshua Shaw's work from 1814 to 1822, changed rifle design.

Many inventors claimed credit for inventing the copper percussion cap, but sea captain Joshua Shaw, of Philadelphia, evidently deserves the honor. In 1814, the British-born Shaw was denied a patent for a steel cap, because he was not yet a U.S. citizen. He persevered with a disposable pewter cap, then one of copper. Between 1812 and 1825, the U.S. Patent Office issued 72 patents for percussion caps. Only a few proved out. Some caps fragmented, spattering the shooter. Others had so little priming mix, they failed to ignite the main charge—or so much they started the ball before the burning powder built useful pressure. In 1822, Shaw patented his own lock. By that time, it was clear a percussion cap on a hollow nipple had a bright future. In 1846, Congress awarded the 70-year-old Shaw an honorarium.

Despite the obvious advantages of a closed passage to funnel sparks directly to the powder charge, percussion rifles and shotguns were slow to catch on. In the early nineteenth century, chemicals like fulminates were still widely viewed with suspicion. Also, the first caps were not consistent. Wary of new inventions, governments resisted replacing pyrite with primers. Shooters who stood by the flintlock spread rumors denigrating caplock ignition. Percussion shotguns were said to kick harder, but deliver less punch. Even Britain's Colonel Hawker, a firearms authority, embraced the fiction:

For killing single shots at wildfowl rapidly flying ... there is not a question in favour of the detonating system, as its trifling inferiority to the flint gun is tenfold repaid by the wonderful accuracy it gives in so readily obeying the eye. But in firing a heavy charge among a large flock of birds the flint has the decided advantage.

Eventually, the convenient, weatherproof percussion cap would win out.

Meanwhile, firearms were becoming shorter and slimmer, with smaller bores and more sensitive triggers. The cumbersome firearms that had come from Europe with the Pilgrims in the early

The Kentucky rifle proved superior to the Brown Bess musket of the British troops. Our Colonists trounced other troops who had to load their rifles with tight-fitting balls.

seventeenth century were typically .75-caliber smooth-bore flintlocks six feet long. Though rifled barrels had shown a decided edge in accuracy and reach (dating to matches in Leipzig, as early as 1498, and Zurich, in 1504), rifles were costly to make and slow to load. Firearms of that day were judged mainly on their military merits. Warfare did not require fine accuracy; more important was prompt reloading by green recruits.

The New World presented different challenges, even in battle. The enemy did not fight in close ranks, rather, he was a lone wraith, partly hidden behind vegetation. Accuracy mattered there and on the hunt. Long, careful shots were often pivotal. Americans favored the French-style flintlock popular in Europe early in the eighteenth century. The *jaeger* (hunter) rifle that evolved from it on the Ohio frontier had a 24- to 30-inch barrel of .65- to .70-caliber, with seven to nine deep, slow-twist grooves. Most *jaegers* had a rectangular patch-box and a wide, flat buttplate. Double set triggers were common. To conserve lead, rifle makers built jaegers with .50-, .45-, even .40-caliber bores; a pound of lead yields 70 .40-caliber balls, but only 15 of .70-inch diameter. At the same time, the makers lengthened the barrel, replaced the sliding patch-box cover with a hinged lid, and installed a crescent butt to fit the shooter's upper arm. These changes were wrought in Pennsylvania by German gunsmiths, but the redesigned jaeger became known as the Kentucky rifle.

In guerilla conflict, this accurate, distinctively American rifle proved superior to the Brown Bess musket issued to British troops. Militiamen in the ragtag Revolutionary Army had found that pounding home full-diameter balls against the rifling in a reload was slow and difficult and made noise that divulged the shooter's position. So they cast undersized balls and swathed them in greased linen patches that engaged the rifling. The Colonists trounced other troops—even crack mercenaries—who loaded their rifles with tight-fitting balls. The patched ball also cleaned the bore and softened fouling. It quickly gained favor with hunters. Animal fat was commonly used to grease the patch but, in a pinch, a shooter could use saliva.

By the close of the eighteenth century, hunters on the American frontier had, arguably, the best rifles in the world, renowned for their accuracy and reach.

Still, building a rifle was an individual project. For rifles (and repairs), pioneers threading the Alleghenies depended on the resourcefulness of backwoods gunsmiths. It would be decades before Eli Whitney and others successfully employed mass production.

Beyond the forests of the East, hunters found smallbore Kentucky rifles inadequate for grizzlies and bison. The Kentucky's long barrel proved awkward to carry on horseback, and its slender stock often failed to survive the rigors of life in the saddle. Even before the plains rifle achieved iconic status, flintlocks of late eighteenth-century settlers and frontiersmen were changing. Iron hardware replaced brass, beefier stocks cradled shorter barrels with bigger bores. The "mountain" or "Tennessee" rifle resulted.

In the early nineteenth century, there could have been 60 million bison afoot on the prairies of North America. Or not. Nobody counted until the beasts had been shot to near-extinction. But astute visitors saw the numbers slipping. In 1843, John James Audubon observed that "There is a perceptible difference in the

Patched balls eased loading, kept fouling at bay. Rifling spun the patch that gripped the ball.

Reproductions like this T/C caplock "Hawken" are affordable, accurate, and quite authentic.

size of the herds, and before many years the Buffalo, like the Great Auk, will have disappeared … ."

During the summer of 1846, Francis Parkman traveled throughout the West. He was 23 and had just graduated from Harvard Law School. "With the stream of emigration to Oregon and California," he observed, "The buffalo will dwindle away, and the large wandering [Indian] communities who depend on them for support must be broken and scattered."

Parkman was fascinated by plains tribes and their ties to the great herds. In his 1849 book, *The California and Oregon Trail*, he described the "running" of buffalo:

[The hunter] dashes forward in utter reckless-ness and self-abandonment … . In the midst of the flying herd, where the uproar and the dust are thickest, it never wavers for a moment; he drops the rein and abandons his horse to his furious career; he levels his gun, the report sounds faint amid the thunder of the buffalo; and when his wounded en-

emy leaps in vain fury upon him, his heart thrills with a feeling like the fierce delight of the battlefield … .

Permitting Parkman some license for hyperbole, historians find his observations ring true. Those stir-ring words, like Frederic Remington's oils, resonated with readers who'd not experienced firsthand the perils and grinding deprivations of the frontier, who saw in it more romance than hardship. Novels soon made legends of misfits. Manifest Destiny became at once a national mission and an excuse.

Parkman was also analytical. In his 1849 book he wrote:

The chief difficulty in running buffalo, it seems to me is that of loading the gun or pistol at full gal-lop. Many hunters for convenience's sake carry three or four bullets in the mouth; the powder is poured down the muzzle … the bullet dropped in after it, the stock struck hard upon the pommel of the saddle, and the work is done. [However], should the blow on the pommel fail to send the bullet home, or should the latter, in the act of aiming, start from its place and roll toward the muzzle, the gun would probably burst in discharging … . [To securely seat their bullets], some hunters make use of a ramrod, usually hung by a string from the neck, but this materially increases the difficulty of loading.

Not long after Lewis and Clark completed their epic journey, in 1805, General W.H. Ashley, of the Rocky Mountain Fur Company, promoted the Rendezvous as a way to gather furs from trappers probing far-flung places. Subsequently, tons of pelts funneled from frontier outposts to St. Louis, which became a gateway to the West, as well as its supply hub. Easterners of various trades relocated there. Among them was gun maker Jacob Hawkins. Born in 1786, he moved to Missouri as a young man and, in 1818, entered into partnership with local gunsmith James Lakenan. In 1821, Jake's father died. Shortly thereafter, his younger brother Samuel (born 1792) lost his wife and closed his gun shop in Xenia, Ohio, to join Jake. Following James Lakenan's death, in 1825, the Hawkins brothers became partners and changed their surname to the original Dutch "Hawken," a name that would come to define the rifle for their times.

Building their first rifles, the Hawkens borrowed heavily from the design of a North Carolinian named Youmans, a preeminent maker of Tennessee rifles. These muscular but beautiful firearms were still fashioned one at a time, and so varied widely in detail. The Hawken brothers added refinements of their own. A typical Hawken rifle featured a relatively short, stiff barrel and weighed about 10 pounds. Its half-stock, secured by two keys, was generally of maple (in 1845, rough-cut sugar maple cost $2 per hundred board feet). The patch-boxes of Kentucky and Tennessee rifles seldom appeared on Hawkens. Flint was the standard type of ignition, until about 1840. The Hawken brothers used Ashmore locks, as well as their own. Many Hawken ri-

> Hawken rifles delivered great precision at distance. Francis Parkman told of killing a pronghorn at 204 paces and watching another hunter drop a bison at nearly 300!

fles boasted double set triggers. During the brief era of the Rendezvous—perhaps two decades—the Hawken established itself as the quintessential plains rifle (though Henry Lehman and James Henry and George Tryon built similar, equally serviceable firearms).

Demand for Hawken rifles grew with their reputation for accuracy and reach. While other rifles in skilled hands might match the performance of a Hawken, men with their lives on the line learned by word of mouth to trust the Hawken name.

Such faith rested on more than myth and fireside tale. A Hawken's octagonal barrel, typically of .50-caliber and 38 inches long, was made of soft iron and had a slow rifling twist to stabilize the patched round ball still in common use. The iron barrel was easier to load, too, and proved less susceptible to fouling than the quick-twist, hard-steel bores of contemporary English rifles built only for conical bullets. (The soft barrel better retained traces of bullet lube.)

Hawken rifles delivered great precision at distance. Francis Parkman told of killing a pronghorn at 204 paces and of watching another hunter drop a bison at nearly 300! While charge weights for big game typically ran 150 to 215 grains of powder, Hawken rifles were known for their ability to handle a wide range of loads. Bore size increased as lead became easier to get and buffalo more valuable at market. In an article for the *Saturday Evening Post* (February 21, 1920 as cited by Hanson in *The Plains Rifle*), Horace Kephart wrote of one new Hawken rifle:

It would shoot straight with any powder charge [and] equal weights of powder and ball. With a round ball of pure lead weighing 217 grains, patched with fine linen so that it fitted tight, and 205 grains of powder, it gave very flat trajectory … and yet the recoil was no more severe than that of a .45 caliber breech loader charged with seventy grains of powder and a 500-grain service bullet … .

Wayne killed this Utah buck at 90 yards, with an iron-sighted blackpowder rifle firing a Maxi-Ball.

The growing popularity of Hawken rifles on the frontier kept Sam and Jake busy building them. But the brothers repaired firearms, too. On December 26, 1825, the Hawkens billed the Indian Department, through its agent Richard Graham, $1.25 for "Cutting Barrel & new birch" and 50 cents for "Repairing Rifle." For "Repairing Lock, bullet molds, ram rod, & hind sight" a bill totaled $2. The Hawkens charged 50 cents for shoeing a horse and 18 cents for fixing spurs. They made iron hatchets, and even arrowheads.

When California's gold fields drew hordes of fortune-seekers, in 1849, a basic Hawken rifle cost $22.50—a substantial price, but one willingly paid by men whose future might hang on one accurate shot. That year, Jake Hawken died of cholera. Sam kept the business alive, turning it over to his son, William, who had earlier ridden with Kit Carson's mounted rifles. (On September 23, 1847, during the Battle of Monterey, William and a group of 42 frontiersmen fought to secure a bridge over San Juan Creek. Vastly out-numbered, the Americans emerged with only nine ambulatory men. William was among the injured.) In 1855, William partnered at the St. Louis shop with Tristam Campbell. This alliance soon failed, though, leaving William in charge. In 1859, Samuel Hawken made his first pilgrimage to the Rocky Mountains, where fron-

Jim Bridger was typical of mountain men at General Ashley's Rendezvous, circa 1820s.

Frontier Scout Kit Carson lived in the days of Hawken rifles, which were birthed in St. Louis, in 1825.

tiersmen had carried Hawken rifles. Sam worked in Colorado mines a week, then headed home. Upon his return, he declared, "And here I am once more at my old trade, putting guns and pistols in order ... ."

William Hawken's tenure at the shop introduced him to other men who had endured the rigors of the American West, and who appreciated accurate rifles. He received this note dated November 27, 1858:

Mr. Wm. Hawkins

Sir, I have waited with patience for my gun, I am in almost in a hurry 2 weeks was out last Monday. I will wait a short time for it and if it don't come I will either go or send. If you are still waiting to make me a good one it is all right. Please send as soon as possible. Game is plenty and I have no gun.

Yours a friend.
Daniel W. Boon

William traveled west again, after his father relieved him in St. Louis. Then he disappeared. Some years later, a .56-caliber muzzleloader bearing William's name was found under a pile of rocks in Querino Canyon, Arizona. The man's fate remains a mystery.

As civil war shook the Union, Sam Hawken hired a helper. Immigrant J.P. Gemmer had arrived in the U.S., from Germany, in 1838. He proved capable and industrious. In 1862, he bought the Hawken business. Gemmer may have used the "S. Hawken" stamp on some rifles, but marked most "J.P. Gemmer, St. Louis." As cartridge rifles (the Sharps 1874 and the Remington Rolling Block) sealed the bison's demise, Gemmer offered smaller bores and target options in Hawken rifles.

Sam Hawken continued to visit the shop in retirement. He outlived Jim Bridger, Kit Carson, and other mountain men who had depended on Hawken rifles. When Sam died on May 9, 1884, at age 92, the establishment was still open for business. It had changed locations within St. Louis in 1870, 1876, and 1880. A final move followed, in 1912, but the doors closed in 1915. J.P. Gemmer died four years later. The Hawken rifle faded, as settlers with cartridge repeaters funneled west on trails blazed by mountain men.

A FRONTIER RIFLE OF NOTE

When it had cooled, Eliphalet Remington II would have checked his barrel for straightness and hammered out irregularities. He'd grind and file eight flats to make the tube octagonal, then travel to Utica to pay a gunsmith the equivalent of a dollar to cut the rifling.

America's oldest gun maker, Remington, got its start, in 1816, when Eliphalet "Lite" Remington II put his hand to his father's forge in Litchfield, four miles from New York's Mohawk River. Lite was 22, living with his wife, Abigail, in his father's stone house on Staley (or Steele) Creek. Having learned from his father how to work iron, Lite would have made the barrel by pumping bellows to heat an iron rod or flat skelp cherry-red. This iron would have been wound about a mandrel slightly smaller than the finished bore. Heating the tube white-hot, Lite might have sprinkled it with Borax and sand, held one end in his tongs, then pounded the other on the forge's stone floor to seat the coils. He may also have used a hammer or water-powered trip-hammer to pound heated sections of the tube into a solid tube. When it had cooled, Lite would have checked his barrel for straightness and hammered out irregularities. He'd grind and file eight flats to make the tube octagonal, then travel to Utica to pay a gunsmith the equivalent of a dollar to cut the rifling.

Accounts vary as to whether Remington finished the rifle himself. Making lock and stock both required skills probably rare among young frontier lads. But both would have been handmade and finished with files. He may well have used uric acid and iron oxide to finish the steel a hazel brown, then smoothed the wood with sandstone, sealing it with beeswax. Hand-wrought screws and pins fastened the parts. Legend has it that Lite christened his rifle at a local shooting match, placing second and prompting the winner to order a rifle just like it! Remington is said to have charged $10 and finished the rifle in 10 days!

WITH METALLIC CARTRIDGES, HUNTERS, SETTLERS, AND SOLDIERS BOOSTED BOTH THEIR REACH AND FIREPOWER.

Loading from the breech had been a dream long before the advent of the percussion cap. Guns with a hinged breech date to at least 1537! A seventeenth-century French musket had a cylindrical breech plug that dropped when the guard was rotated. A rifle developed in 1776 by British Major Patrick Ferguson featured a threaded breech plug, retracted by rotating the threaded guard. Alas, raising the block back into battery sometimes pinched the powder and caused premature firing.

At the close of the eighteenth century, Americans Eli Whitney and Simeon North, working independently, came up with machines that manufactured uniform parts. They each won a government contract for firearms. Sixteen years later, in 1813, North got the first contract for guns with *interchangeable* components. However, a rifle needed more than close-fitting parts to function as a breechloader. Captain John H. Hall, of Maine, designed one of the first successful breechloaders in the U.S. This crude flintlock was issued in limited numbers to U.S. soldiers in 1817, six years after its debut. It earned little praise.

Breechloading was a lot more feasible with cartridges than with loose powder and ball. The first cartridges (assembled in 1586!) were of paper and loaded from the muzzle. Biting or ripping off the base of the husk exposed the powder. The husk burned to ashes upon firing. Replacing pyrite with a percussion cap did away with the biting and tearing, because the cap's more powerful spark penetrated the thin paper.

Across the Atlantic, Johann Nikolaus von Dreyse was among the first inventors to install a primer in a cartridge. His paper hull clasped a bullet with a pellet of fulminate at its base. A long striker punched through paper and powder to smash the pellet. Roughly 300,000 von Dreyse "needle guns" were built for the Prussian army, between 1835 and 1865. Incidentally, the needle gun referenced by post-Civil War writers was not the European Dreyse, but rather the .50-70 Springfield that sired, in 1873, the .45-70 trap-door rifle used in the last Indian wars. Its long breech block required a long firing pin.

Stateside, Stephen Taylor patented a hollow-based bullet with an internal powder charge held in place by a perforated heel cap that admitted sparks from an external primer. A year later, in 1848, New York inventor Walter Hunt devised a similar bullet. This one had a cork cap covered with paper. Primer sparks shot through the paper. To fire this "rocket ball," Hunt developed a repeating rifle with a pillbox mechanism to advance metallic primers. Its tubular magazine was a brilliant feature, but the lever-action was prone to malfunction. Lacking the money to refine or promote his "Volitional" rifle, Hunt sold patent rights to fellow

New Yorker George Arrowsmith. Lewis Jennings, a gifted engineer in Arrowsmith's shop, improved the Hunt repeater. After receiving patents for Jennings' work, Arrowsmith sold the Hunt rifle for $100,000 to railroad magnate and New York hardware merchant Courtland Palmer.

Meanwhile, Palmer's financial backing helped gun designers Horace Smith and Daniel Wesson develop a metallic cartridge like that patented, in 1846 and 1849, by the Frenchman Flobert. Smith and Wesson modified a rocket ball to include a copper base that held fulminate priming. In 1854, Courtland Palmer joined his designers in a limited partnership, putting up $10,000 for tooling in a firm to become known as "Smith and Wesson." A year later, a group of 40 New York and New Haven investors bought out Smith, Wesson, and Palmer to establish the Volcanic Repeating Arms Company. The investors chose as company director Oliver F. Winchester, a shirt merchant. Winchester moved the company from Norwich to New Haven. Slow sales of Volcanic guns sent it into receivership, in 1857, but Winchester reorganized, after buying all assets for $40,000.

The New Haven Arms Company hired Benjamin Tyler Henry to fix the Hunt design. In 1860, Henry received a patent for a 15-shot repeating rifle chambered for .44 rimfire cartridges. The Henry lacked the reach and punch of front-loaders like the Hawken. Nonetheless, it was coveted by soldiers, because it could be recharged from the shoulder with a flick of the hand.

Montana-based Shiloh Sharps makes beautiful rifles faithful to the legendary 1874 Sharps. This one has more embellishment than buffalo hunters would have ordered!

As legions of mechanics struggled with this and other repeating actions, Christian Sharps built a stronger breechloading *single-shot*. The New Jersey native had apprenticed under John Hall at Harpers Ferry Arsenal. In 1848, he received his first patent, for a sliding breech block. The tight breeching held promise for hunters, because it could handle cartridges that would hit hard at long range.

SHARPS: BUFFALO RIFLE!

Sharps rifles played a signal role in the act of clearing the plains of large animals. It was a period of shameless killing and insatiable appetites. The U.S. Army turned a blind eye to the slaughter, as it advanced its own aim to bring recalcitrant plains Indians to heel. Starving tribes capitulated.

In a 1930 edition of the *Kansas City Star*, hunter George Reighard explained how he shot bison:

In 1872 I organized my own outfit and went south from Fort Dodge to shoot buffaloes for their hides. I furnished the team and wagon and did the killing. [My partners] furnished the supplies and the skinning, stretching and cooking. They got half the hides… . I had two big .50 Sharps rifles … .

Usually I went to the top of some rise to spy out the herd, [then I'd] sneak up to within good ranges. Between 200 and 350 yards was all right … . I carried a gun rest made from a tree crotch … .

The time I made my biggest kill I lay on a slight ridge behind a tuft of weeds l00 yards from a bunch of 1,000 buffaloes … . After I had killed about 25

my gun barrel became hot and began to expand. A bullet from an overheated gun does not go straight, it wobbles, so I put that gun aside and took the other. By the time that became hot the other had cooled, but then the powder smoke in front of me was so thick I could not see through it; there was not a breath of wind to carry it away, and I had to crawl backward, dragging my two guns, and work around to another position on the ridge, from which I killed 54 more. In 1½ hours I had fired 91 shots, as a count of the empty shells showed afterwards, and had killed 79 buffaloes, and we figured that they all lay within an area of about 2 acres of ground. My right hand and arm were so sore from working the gun that I was not sorry to see the remaining buffaloes start off on a brisk run … .

That expedition yielded "a few more than 1,000 buffaloes in one month."

The last half of the nineteenth century was the most productive period in firearms history, albeit progress came in fits and starts. Christian Sharps fielded several forgettable rifles before his company came up with its powerful, long-range "buffalo rifles." The first patent model Sharps was an 1841 Mississippi rifle with a new breech that featured a vertical sliding block operated by a guard-bow finger lever. A Sharps rifle operated as easily as a Hall, but sealed the barrel more effectively.

Like many inventors, Christian Sharps knew little about marketing. He did know he wanted an Army contract. He was almost broke when, in February 1849, he met Pennsylvania gunsmith Albert S. Nippes.

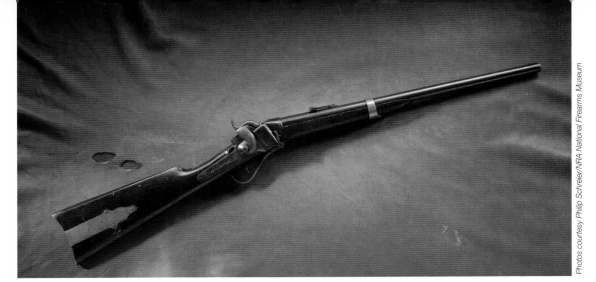

A vintage Civil War-era Sharps rifle, such as might have been used by a sniper of the time.

The two men committed to building rifles, sharing labor and tooling costs. Though Sharps spent more of his time designing new mechanisms than he did helping Nippes, the pair soon cofounded another gun-making enterprise.

Chasing his dream of a government contract, Christian Sharps formed his own company shortly after his 1849 contract with Nippes expired. Early in 1851, entrepreneur George H. Penfield hired Christian Sharps for "making models and making improvements," if Sharps would grant him nine-sixteenths of the patent rights. Clearing interests by Nippes and Maynard (Sharps' partner, briefly), Penfield bought up remaining Sharps stock. All told, he paid $22,853 for the rights to Sharps rifles. Penfield contracted with Robbins & Lawrence for 5,000 Sharps rifles, then spent $100,000 to capitalize the Sharps Rifle Manufacturing Company, incorporating it October 8, 1851. Robbins & Lawrence folded

in 1856, the Sharps corporation foreclosing on its mortgage.

To this time, six rifles had been produced under the Sharps name: Models 1849, 1850, 185l, 1852, 1853, and 1855. The last four were "slant-breech" rifles, the breechblock operating at a 112-degree angle to the bore. Some military versions had a "coffee mill" in the buttstock (most soldiers of the day used it to grind grain). During the late '50s, Sharps rifles were shipped by abolitionists to Kansas "Free Staters," to get votes against slavery. A shipment of 200 carbines got to John Brown. In the West, the Sharps rifle became known as "Beecher's Bible," after a news item described abolitionist Henry Ward Beecher's observation that, "You might as well read the Bible to buffaloes as to those fellows who follow Atchison and Stringfellow; but they have a supreme respect for the logic [of] Sharps rifles." When the Civil War broke, the Sharps enterprise was producing 30,000 guns annually in a factory driven by a 250-horsepower, single-cylinder Corliss steam engine.

The Model 1859 was followed by New Models 1859, 1863, and 1865. The strength, accuracy, and potent chamberings of Sharps rifles would endear them to hunters. The Civil War put them into the hands of Colonel Hiram Berdan's Sharpshooters. Initially, these troops were equipped with muzzleloaders, and Berdan's request for breechloaders brought only surplus Colt's revolving rifles. These he refused, and his men threatened mutiny! They finally got Sharps, though these lacked the double set triggers Berdan had ordered. At Gettysburg, 100 Sharpshooters and 200 Maine regulars held Little Round Top against 30,000 Confederates. They fired nearly 10,000 rounds in 20 minutes!

As government contracts dried up after the war, the Sharps Rifle Manufacturing Company shifted its focus to sportsmen. The New Model 1869 was the first cartridge Sharps with no provision for outside priming. It came in .40-50, .40-70, .44-77, .45-70, and .50-70. Only 650 were produced before the Model 1874, announced in 1870, replaced it. The 1874 in myriad forms would remain popular for 12 years. Christian Sharps died of tuberculosis, in 1874, but the Sharps Rifle Manufacturing Company, built on patents Sharps had bargained away to Penfield, chugged along.

The Model 1875 Sharps rifle incorporated patents by Rollin White and Nelson King. A Long-Range version shown at the Philadelphia Exposition was bought there for $300 by Colonel John Bodine. It remains the only surviving specimen, as no other 1875s were made. But Charles Overbaugh and A.O. Zischang, who had helped design the rifle, delivered a replacement. The Model 1877 had a leaner, rounder action. Locks and barrel blanks came from Webley, of England. Like the Model 1874 Creedmoor that would hand Americans their victory over the Irish in the first Creedmoor match, it excelled at

distance. Fewer than 300 Model 1877s were built, in three grades priced at $75, $100, and $125. Overbaugh made 73 into scheutzen rifles. Denver dealer J.P. Lower sold 75 as "special Model 1874s." These became known as "Lower Sharps" rifles.

Hugo Borchardt joined Sharps soon after the Model 1875's debut. Like Nelson King of Winchester fame, who became plant superintendent at Sharps, Hugo Borchardt turned his hand to rifle design at the firm. He earned $1,855 for his first rifle, the Sharps Model 1878. The first 300 Borchardt rifles went to the Chinese government, in 1877. Its action also showed up in hunting and target guns priced as low as $18. In May 1879, Hugo Borchardt sailed to Europe seeking military contracts. He got none. Sharps' efforts to field a repeating rifle came to naught, and the company scrambled. Retailers were given huge markdowns on re-barreled Sharps rifles. Carlos Grove & Son, of Denver, took 270 Model 1874s at $15 to $17 each! It was the beginning of the end. The Sharps Rifle Manufacturing Company vanished from Connecticut records, in 1905.

The Sharps rifle most celebrated is the 1874, which, if you'd bought one with double set triggers in 1878, would have cost $44. *Replicas* can bring a hundred times as much now. The movie *Quigley Down Under* introduced the Sharps to people who'd never heard the name. Following the film, in which its star, Tom Selleck, drills a bucket far away, the Quigley Match emerged, in Forsyth, Montana. A bucket-shaped target, 44 inches wide at the top, is 1,000 yards off—a long shot for a scoped bolt rifle. For a blackpowder Sharps, iron sights, and round-nose bullets at 1,400 fps, it is indeed a challenge! Still, many shooters hit that bucket regularly!

Surely the best known—and most debated—of Sharps feats occurred at the frontier town of Adobe Walls, in the north Texas panhandle. Buffalo hunter Billy Dixon was one of just 28 men sleeping in the tiny

The Sharps rifle most celebrated is the Model 1874, which, if you'd bought one with double set triggers in 1878, would have cost you $44. Today's very fine replicas can bring a hundred times that much.

Prairies where bison fell to blackpowder and ball now yield mule deer to scoped bolt rifles.

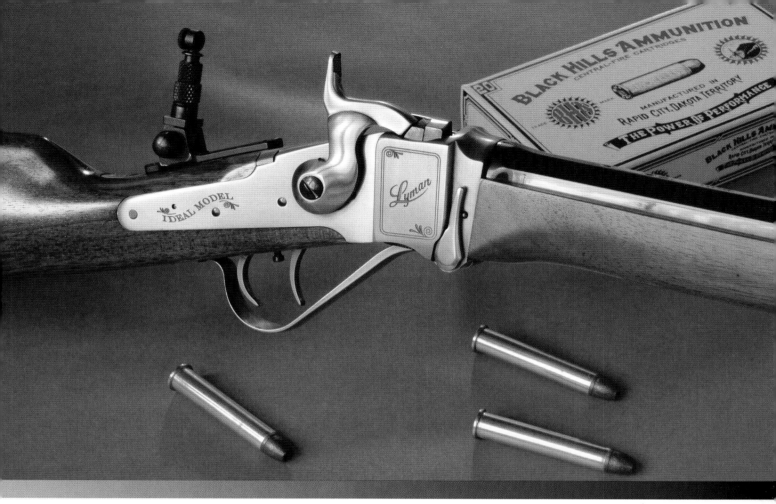

This lovely Italian Sharps reproduction for Lyman shoots mild Black Hills ammo well!

settlement on June 26, 1874. At dawn, a swarm of Comanche warriors thundered in at full gallop. The 700 braves, led by chief Quanah Parker, killed three whites before the remaining defenders barricaded themselves in buildings. Most were hunters, well armed. They repulsed the charge with withering rifle fire, but they were badly outnumbered, and many of the Comanches had repeating rifles. The battle wasn't over.

Two days later, some warriors still lurked, like circling wolves, on the perimeter of Adobe Walls. As legend has it, about 15 appeared on a bluff nearly a mile off. Billy Dixon, renowned for his marksmanship, was urged to take a shot with the local saloon owner's .50-bore 1874 Sharps. Dixon had used this rifle during the initial attack, so, when he took aim, there was more than hope at play. Still, onlookers were astonished, when, seconds after the blast, one of the Indians fell off his horse. The distance was later surveyed at 1,538 yards. Possible? Yes. Probable? Certainly not. Wind drift aside, that bullet would have

been descending so sharply that a range estimation error of just 50 yards would have caused a miss. Whether or not you believe Billy Dixon hit a Comanche at more than 1,500 yards with a blackpowder Sharps, you'll have plenty of company!

The Sharps 1874 has come to rival the Winchester 1873 as a signature rifle of the post-Civil War West. Shiloh Sharps, a Montana company that now builds Sharps rifles after their original design, put an 1877 Sharps on its list, in 2013. Given the quality and attention to detail lavished on its 1874s, from Old Faithful hunting rifles to Creedmoor target versions— and the strong demand for them—the 1877 likely will build a list of backorders. Mike Venturino, in his book *Shooting Buffalo Rifles of the Old West*, confirms you don't have to kill buffalo to appreciate a Sharps:

Some of my most enjoyable long-range shooting has been done with a Shiloh Model 1874 Quigley in .45-110 [and using a tang sight on] a life-size metal silhouette of a buffalo at a surveyed 956 yards.

THE ROLLING BLOCK

Among the few rifles that gave the Sharps 1874 serious competition, Remington's Rolling Block distinguished itself both on the prairie and at long-range matches. It came by that versatility naturally. The first rifle with that name, hand-built in 1816 by Eliphalet ("Lite") Remington, performed so well at a local shooting match, it drew an order for a duplicate from the match winner! During the summer of 1817, Lite, his wife, Abigail, and young son, Philo, shared a new home with rifle customers. The gun maker scoured the countryside for plowshares, horseshoes—anything that could be smelted down. During his fourth year in business, Lite sold more than 200 barrels and rifles. Iron barrels cost $3, steel barrels $6.

Completion of the Erie Canal, on October 26, 1825, cut the cost of shipping a ton of goods from New York to Buffalo from $100 to $12. For family reasons, Lite delayed a move until January 1828, when he bought 100 acres on the Mohawk River, for $28 an acre. Remington Arms still occupies this land, in Ilion.

Remington's first foundry and factory ran seasonally, until winter ice stopped water-powered equipment. Then, workers assembled guns full time, wrapped them in bundles and, as long as the Canal stayed open, carted them to a bridge. There the bundles were tossed atop the cabins of passing freighters! Lite traveled to seek new markets, logging many miles along the Canal. Pulled by relays of horses, Canal packets took passengers from Buffalo to Albany, a 300-mile trip, for $14.33, meals included.

With progress came tragedy. On June 22, 1828, Lite's father was hauling timber from where he'd once surveyed land on Staley Creek, when he was thrown from a loaded wagon on a steep grade. An iron wheel crushed his chest. Five days later he died. Then, on August 12, 1841, Abigail and her daughter Maria hitched a spirited horse to her carriage for a drive to their old house. On the road that had claimed Lite's father, Maria opened her parasol. It popped like a pistol shot. The startled horse lunged across a stream, smashing the carriage to pieces against a great oak. Abigail died instantly.

The accident devastated Lite Remington; still, his company prospered. Philo joined it and added his ideas. Instead of straightening barrels with the traditional plumb line, he used the shadow of a window bar in the bore—a superior method—and he put steel facings on trip hammers to trim tolerances. Remington bought the N.P. Ames Company, with the services of Welsh designer William Jenks, who'd fashioned a breechloading carbine. Submitting his carbine for military trials, Jenks had become disheartened when, in one 1,500-round test, a nipple broke after 1,400 shots. Jenks turned to France and England, where his designs earned praise. When, at last, the U.S. government came to its senses, Jenks returned at its bequest, offering a new carbine, in 1858. It reliably fed cardboard cartridges coated with tallow and beeswax.

A year later, William Jenks fell from a hay wagon on his farm. He did not survive his injuries.

Lite Remington died during the Civil War. After the funeral, the Remington factory resumed full-throttle production under Philo, Samuel, and Eliphalet III. Then, suddenly, the war—and demand for rifles—came to a halt. In April 1865, employees at Ilion watched parades, as their heavily mortgaged machines sat silent.

Remington mitigated the effect of cancelled military contracts with a breechloading rifle. But Joseph Rider's improvements on Leonard Geiger's split-breech mechanism had been rushed, and the rifle fared poorly in Army trials against the Henry, Peabody, and Sharps. By early 1866, Rider had corrected the flaws, and Remington trotted out its new Rolling Block Rifle.

Strong and simple, the Rolling Block had a hinged breech block. To load, you drew the ham-

The Farquharson, designed by a Scot in 1872, was, like John Browning's single-shot, a defining rifle of its time.

mer to full cock, then rolled back the breech block by thumbing its right-hand tab. After inserting a round, you pushed the breech block forward, aimed, and fired. Breech block and hammer were of high-tensile steel and interlocked upon firing. The mechanism was so quick to load, a practiced shooter could fire 20 rounds a minute! It was strong, too. In one test, a Rolling Block .50 was loaded with *40 balls and 750 grains of powder*, the charge filling 36 inches of a 40-inch barrel! Firing the rifle produced no untoward results.

Designed, as were most rifles then, with an eye to military service, as well as to sport and market hunting, the Rolling Block got a baptism of fire, in 1866. A band of 30 cowboys, led by Nelson Story, were herding 3,000 cattle through Wyoming, when Indians attacked them near Fort Laramie. They repulsed the hostiles with Rolling Blocks they'd just bought. Forbidden to proceed beyond Fort Kearney, Story waited two weeks, then lost patience and moved his herd north on October 22. Sioux warriors led by Red Cloud and Crazy Horse swooped from the hills upon the drive. The barrels of their Rolling Blocks became so hot, the cowboys cooled them with water from their canteens. The Indians expected

a pause in the deadly fire, but none came. Retreating, they paused to look back, and promptly found those Remingtons had extraordinary reach! Story's cowboys twice more blunted Indian attacks during that drive, but, in sum, they lost just one man.

That year, Samuel Remington replaced Philo as company president. Sam sold the Rolling Block rifle to several European heads of state who enjoyed hunting. In Prussia, alas, amid great pomp, the man who would soon become Kaiser Wilhelm I of Germany pulled the trigger on a dud cartridge. Angrily he rode off. But such failures didn't stem demand. By 1870, Remington Arms occupied 15 acres of floor space and its monthly payroll totaled $140,000—this when dinner at a good restaurant cost 25 cents. Fulfilling a French contract, production peaked at 1,530 rifles a day.

Though Remington cataloged several sporting rifles at this time (one for $8!), the Rolling Block dominated sales. It met a different need than did the popular Winchester Model 1873 lever-action, which, in .44-40, offered more power than its predecessor, the 1866. But the 1873 couldn't fire truly potent rounds like the .45-70. The Rolling Block did, and with greater accuracy. Following a hunting expedition, in 1873, George Armstrong Custer enthused, "With your rifle I killed far more game than any other … at longer range." Ironically, on the Little Big Horn, in 1876, Custer's troops carried converted Springfields, while attacking Sioux used rifles by Sharps, Winchester, and Remington.

The reach and accuracy of Rolling Block rifles led to their use as long-range target guns. In 1874, Remington engineer L.L. Hepburn began work on a match rifle like those used by the Irish in their recent victory at Wimbledon. The Irish had subsequently challenged the Americans to a long-range team event. Each team would comprise six men, firing at three distances—800, 900, and 1,000 yards—15 shots each. A newly formed National Rifle Association and the cities of New York and Brooklyn put up $5,000 apiece to build a range for the match on Long Island's Creed's Farm, provided by the State of New York.

In March 1874, Remington unveiled a new target rifle, a .44-90 hurling 550-grain conical bullets. In September, a favored Irish team firing muzzleloaders bowed to the Americans and their Remington and Sharps breechloaders. The score was 934 to 931, with one Irish crossfire. Matches held in 1875 and 1876 were won decisively by the U.S. team, with Remington's "Creedmoor" rifles posting the highest scores.

Meanwhile, on the prairies, buffalo hunters cashed in with their Rolling Blocks. During the 1870s and early 1880s, buffalo hides brought up to $50; skilled hunters could earn $10,000 a year. Brazos Bob McRae once killed 54 buffalo with as many shots at a single stand, using a scoped .44-90-400 Remington.

The Rolling Block also appeared in military form, with banded full-length stock and bayonet. Off-shore military sales began to absorb most Rolling Block production. Thousands of rifles were barreled to .43 Egyptian and .43 Spanish. The U.S. Army stuck with the 1873 Springfield.

In 1878, military Rolling Blocks listed for $16.50, a standard Sporting version for $30. You could order rifles "as light as 8½ pounds and as heavy as 15," says Mike Venturino. "Standard barrel length was 26 inches, but you could specify any length to 34 inches, for 50 cents an inch. The single set trigger cost $2.50."

Rifles built for competitive shooting, with heavy barrel, tang sight, set trigger, and checkered stock, were expensive; 130 years ago, Creedmoor-type Rolling Block rifles started at $100!

WINCHESTER'S 1885 HIGHWALL

While Remington's Rolling Block made the transition to smokeless powder and the Sharps Rifle Manufacturing Company struggled to keep its rifles relevant, a young inventor on the hem of the Great Salt Lake was designing his own single-shot. John Moses Browning was born in frontier Utah, but his family hailed from Brushy Fork, Sumner County, Tennessee. There, 13-year-old Jonathan Browning was given a broken flintlock rifle as payment for labor on a nearby homestead. A blacksmith helped him fix it. Jonathan sold the rifle for $4—to its original owner!

In November 1826, Jonathan turned 21 and married Elizabeth Stalcup. Eight years later, after his father died, Jonathan moved his family 400 miles to Quincy, Illinois. By age 35, he'd turned his hand to gun design. Recent invention of the percussion cap had spawned the revolving cylinder. But boring and indexing cylinders was expensive, so Jonathan adopted a simpler mechanism. His "slide gun" featured a rectangular bar that moved side to side through a slot. The bar had five chambers, indexed and sealed by a thumb lever. The guard doubled as a mainspring. The hammer lay underneath and swung *up*.

In 1842, the Brownings moved to Nauvoo, founded three years earlier by Mormons under Joseph Smith. Jonathan joined them and set up a gun shop. Then, on June 25, 1844, a mob killed Joseph Smith and his brother Hyrum, in Carthage. The same pressure forced Brigham Young and his band of Mormons on a hard exodus across river ice, in February 1846. Asked by Young to supply rifles to other refugees on the trail, Jonathan Browning opened shop in what is now Council Bluffs, Iowa. Slide guns that held up to 25 shots were ponderous, but deadly against Indians who drew fire, then attacked while settlers reloaded.

Thinned by time and hardship to 143 people, Brigham Young's band reached Salt Lake City, July 24, 1847. Five years later, Jonathan Browning brought

John Moses Browning, here with a .22 auto-loader, developed what would become Winchester's Model 1885 single-shot.

his family to Ogden (named for Hudson's Bay Company explorer Peter Skene Ogden). With $600 hidden in the floor of one of his six wagons, he built a house. Jonathan had 11 children. He'd take a second wife and father 11 more, one of them John Moses.

In 1862, John was seven years old and riding the horse that plodded in circles to run machinery in his father's tannery. His mother insisted he attend school. John did, until age 15. The schoolmaster then told him forthrightly, "No sense continuing. You know as much as I do."

Intellectually gifted, John had an uncommon knack with things mechanical. As a 10-year-old, he built his first gun, a flintlock made from a scrapped musket barrel and a board shaped with a hatchet. John fashioned a crude pan and screwed it to the board, which he wired to the barrel. He stuffed the barrel with powder and rough shot, then heated a batch of coke on the forge. He dumped it into a perforated can and gave that to young brother Matt, who swung the can on a string to pump air to the coke. On a sage flat, the boys found dusting prairie chickens. John aimed as Matt stuck a glowing splinter through the touch-hole. The blast put John on the ground. It also claimed two birds.

Jonathan Browning listened to the tale. "Can't you make a better gun than that?" he chided.

He could. And he did. Growing up at one of the great crossroads of the West, John M. Browning was perfectly placed to design firearms. In 1869, two railways were joined at Promontory Point, only 50 miles from Ogden. Nine years later, when John turned 23, he built a single-shot action, hand-forging the parts. A foot lathe Jonathan had brought by ox-cart from Missouri helped. John filed for his first patent May 12, 1879.

As he awaited action on the filing, Jonathan Browning died. Now head of two households, John needed to build *and* sell guns. Brothers Matt, Ed, Sam, and George assisted, with a 25x50 shop on a 30-foot lot at the edge of Ogden's business district. To turn it into a factory, the Brownings ordered power equipment. By great good luck, Frank Rushton, an English gun maker on a tour of the West, wandered in to help install it and instruct the lads on its use. Ed ran the mill, Sam and George rough-filed receivers, John finished the filing, and Matt made stocks.

John Browning priced his single-shot rifle at $25. Just a week after opening a retail counter at the shop, the young men had sold all the rifles they'd finished in three months! Buoyed by this success, John ordered materials for more rifles. Alas, the factory and Matt's newly stocked retail counter were promptly burglarized. Everything of value vanished—including the prototype of John's rifle.

Shortly, John made Matt a partner. While the other Brownings repaired guns and built as many as three rifles a day, John designed new models. Even before he'd received a patent for his first single-shot, he had came up with another dropping-block action. By 1882, he'd sketched and built a repeater, then tackled another, completing it the same year, all while managing a factory and earning patents for his designs!

In 1883, Winchester salesman Andrew McAusland came across a used Browning single-shot rifle and delivered it to Winchester president Thomas G. Bennett. At that time, Winchester had a stranglehold on the lever-rifle market, but its lever-actions wouldn't handle the powerful, popular .45-70 round. This Browning would. Bennett had never heard of John Browning, but he lost no time traveling to Ogden and what was billed as "the biggest gun store between Omaha and the Pacific." He found half a dozen striplings, barely out of their teens, tinkering in a shop smaller than a livery. But Bennett was no fool. He found John and came straight to the point.

"How much for your rifle?"

One rifle?

No, *the* rifle. All rights.

"Ten thousand dollars," replied John, as if pawning a saddle.

In 1883, that was a fortune! Bennett bought the rifle for $8,000 and paid $1,000 up front. Hours later, he was aboard a train for the six-day ride back to New Haven. When, later, the promised $7,000 arrived, Bennett had to remind Browning his rifle was now a Winchester product. Red-faced, John stopped building it.

The rifle appeared in Winchester's 1885 catalog and was named for that year. A "high-wall" version, after the original Browning design, had the strength for long-range cartridges. A trim "low-wall" offered easier loading access for smaller rounds. Like the Sharps 1874 and Remington's Rolling Block, the

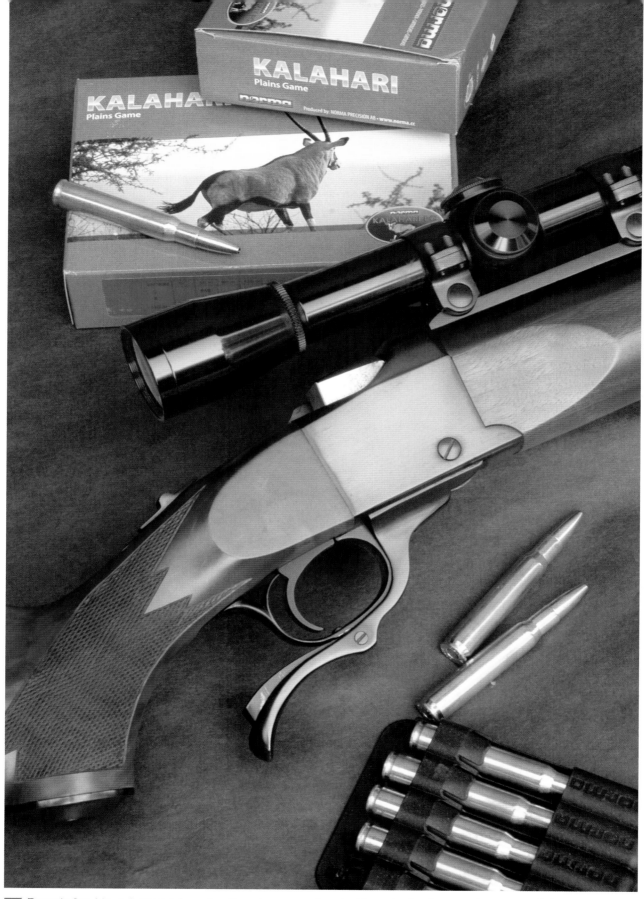

Ruger's fine No. 1 borrows from the Farquharson action, but has sleeker lines and costs much less!

Winchester 1885 High Wall was equipped with folding tang sights for precise aim at distant targets.

During the last two decades of the nineteenth century, John Browning worked almost without pause in his Utah shop, designing 40 firearms for Winchester. Bennett bought them all, to ensure Browning would sell nothing to the competition, and Winchester built a lever-action dynasty on the Models 1886, 1892, and 1894, while its Model 1890 .22 rifle and 1897 shotgun laid the foundation for the slide-action firearms to follow.

Because Browning's rifles were strong, the change from black- to smokeless powder was often as easy as switching to barrels of high-tensile steel. The famous Model 1894, originally bored to .32-40 and .38-55, accommodated the "high-velocity" smokeless .30-30 with no redesign. As bullets went faster and flatter and hunters turned to optical sights, Browning rifles kept up with the trend to longer shots.

By November 1890, John Browning had filed for a patent on an "Automatic Machine Gun." He asked Colt's to consider it, as Colt's had built all U.S. Gatling guns since 1866. The hardware John and Matt unwrapped in Colt's Hartford shooting range was homely, but, when John pressed the trigger, 200 bullets sped away in seconds. A Gatling could be fired faster, but Browning's machine gun needed only one pull of the trigger, not continuous cranking. At 40 pounds, it also weighed half as much as the Gatling. In an 1,800-round test (canvas cartridge loops all hand-stitched), the Browning spewed a burst that heated the barrel red. The last bullets melted in passage, but the gun cycled seamlessly.

John Browning was the toast of Hartford. By 1910, he had designed a water-cooled machine gun. America's entry into the war hurried testing. After 20,000 rounds, John rattled off 20,000 more! Not one hiccup. The audience stood spellbound, as he loaded a second gun to prove the first had no special tuning. Browning held the trigger for 48 minutes and 12 seconds, while his invention roared nonstop!

The Browning Automatic Rifle (BAR) came next, providing "walking fire" for infantry. Its cyclic rate of 480 .30-06 rounds per minute emptied its 20-shot magazine in three seconds. John got $750,000 from the U.S. government for manufacturing rights to his machine gun, the BAR, and a pistol he designed for Colt's—the 1911. He could have sold them privately for $12 million.

From 1914 through the Korean War ending in 1952, every U.S. machine gun would borrow from a Browning patent. The .50 Browning Machine Gun round that dismayed the Luftwaffe now serves U.S. snipers and long-range competitive shooters.

John Moses Browning died, in 1926, at age 71, while checking production of his firearms on his sixty-first visit to Belgium's FN plant. During a half-century of designing firearms, John had garnered 128 patents. No one in the shooting industry has yet matched his genius. As prolific and practical as he was brilliant, John M. Browning extended the reach and increased the effectiveness of the American rifleman.

MISS ANNIE OAKLEY,
(LITTLE SURE SHOT.)
BUFFALO BILL'S WILD WEST.

Born poor in Ohio, in 1860, on the eve of cartridge rifles, Annie Oakley excelled with them!

CHAPTER FOUR
—PIONEERING THE LONG POKE

WITH HIGH-OCTANE CARTRIDGES, ACCURATE RIFLES, AND PROGRAMMED SIGHTS, THESE PIONEERS HELP YOU HIT!

CHARLES NEWTON

Like many rifle makers of his day, Charles Newton hailed from the nineteenth century, but embraced the perquisites and promises of the twentieth. Born in Delavan, New York, January 8, 1870, Charles worked on his father's farm, until finishing school at age 16. He taught school for two years, then applied his quick mind to the study of law and was admitted to the state bar. But his heart was not in courtrooms. After a six-year stint in the New York National Guard, Newton devoted his life to firearms and to frisky cartridges using then-new smokeless powders. Early association with Fred Adolph fed this addiction.

An accomplished German riflesmith, Adolph immigrated to the U.S., in 1908, and established a gun shop in Genoa, New York. By 1914, he had published a catalog of rifles, shotguns, and combination guns. Some were imported, others he built. Adolph distinguished his business by chambering powerful, high-velocity cartridges, among them at least 10 designed by Charles Newton. The smallest, but perhaps best known, was the .22 High-Power. A 1905

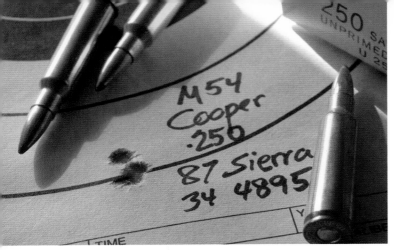

Charles Newton developed the .250-3000 for Savage. Wayne fired this group with a Cooper M54.

development on the .25-35 case, it pushed 70-grain .228 bullets at 2,800 fps. The "Imp" built a bigger-than-life reputation on game as formidable as tigers. More realistically, it proved a stellar match for whitetail deer. It inspired shooters to think of reaching beyond the traditional ranges imposed by iron sights and flat-nosed bullets.

In 1912, the talented Newton necked the .30-06 down to .257. He called it the .25 Newton Special. Another of his cartridges, the 7mm Special, foreshadowed the .280 Remington by half a century (as did the 7x64 Brenneke, developed across the Atlantic about the same time). Also in 1912, Newton delivered to Savage the short, rimless, .250-3000. It followed the .22 High-Power as a new chambering for the Model 99 lever rifle. Savage noted in ads that it launched an 87-grain bullet at 3,000 fps—a rocket in those days.

Newton came up with a .22 Long Range pistol cartridge by shortening and necking down the .28-30 Stevens. The bullet was the same .228 jacketed spitzer loaded in the .22 High-Power. He fashioned his .22 Newton from the 7x57 hull, driving a 90-grain bullet at 3,100 fps from a barrel with fast 1:8 twist. The .22 Special, on .30-40 Krag brass, launched a 68-grain bullet at nearly 3,300.

Feeding a passion for single-shot rifles, Charles Newton experimented with big, rimmed cases like the .405 Winchester, necking it to 7mm, even .25-caliber. He designed .30, 8mm, and .35 Express rounds from the 3¼-inch Sharps. His rimless .30 Newton had the profile of modern belted short magnums. It delivered more punch than hunters of the day considered necessary for most North American game. The .35 Newton and other rimless and rebated cartridges inspired by the .404 Jeffery appeared around 1910.

Significant among Newton's early efforts was the .256 Newton. Ballistically similar to the .257 Roberts Improved, it fired a .264 bullet, not a .257. Charles preferred it to the .25-06 for two reasons. First, .25-06 chambers of that time varied in dimensions. Tight chambers hike pressures, and Newton did not want to be linked to rifles that fell apart. Second, though no U.S. ammunition then featured 6.5mm bullets, Mauser produced 6.5mm barrels.

Early in his cartridge-designing days, Newton dreamed of producing his own rifles. In 1914, he formed the Newton Arms Company, in Buffalo, New York. With a factory under construction there, he traveled to Germany, to seek a supply of rifles from Mauser and J.P. Sauer & Sohn, intending to restock them and rebarrel to .256 Newton and .30 Adolph Express. A flier advertised .256 Newton barrels "of the best Krupp steel," with raised, matted ribs and sight slots—for $17. In March 1915, the first Newton

Charles Newton may have wildcatted the .25-06 (gone commercial in 1969), before anyone else.

rifles appeared in a catalog. Their 98 Mauser actions were barreled to .256, .30, and .35 Newton. Hunting-style stocks by Fred Adolph and California gunsmith Ludwig Wundhammer (namesake of the "Wundhammer swell" on grips), gave them a sporting look. They came in three grades, priced from $42.50 to $80.

The rifles had a lot going for them, but Charles Newton's timing could hardly have been worse! The first two-dozen Mauser rifles were to arrive August 15, 1914. Germany had gone to war the day before.

When the Great War choked off his promised supply of Mauser rifles, Charles Newton turned to the Marlin Firearms Company for barrels in .256 Newton and threaded for 1903 Springfields. He planned to sell them for $12.50 as replacements to hunters who wanted something other than a .30-06. He would fit them with Springfield sporter stocks. But rifles and components were in short supply during the war, and all plants capable of rifle production were up to their chins in lucrative government contracts.

Though Charles Newton had to sit on his hands, he hadn't stopped thinking. By 1916, he'd incorporated desirable features of the Mauser and Springfield designs into a rifle whose only non-original part was the mainspring. He hired legendary barrel maker Harry Pope to oversee barrel production and claimed that Pope had helped him develop segmented rifling in Newton barrels.

The first of Newton's new rifles went on sale January 1, 1917. They got favorable press. But, once again, the timing was wrong. The U.S. entered the war on April 6, and the government took control of all ammunition production. Though Newton loaded his own cartridges, he depended on Remington for cases. Early in 1918, ammo was coming off the line, but the banks supporting the firm sent it into receivership. By year's end, the Newton Arms Company was no more. About 2,400 rifles had been built. Another 1,600 were completed by Bert Holmes, who acquired all assets. Holmes sold more than 1,000 rifles for $5 each, before giving up trying to run the plant himself.

In April 1919, New York machinery dealers Lamberg, Schwartz and Land formed the Newton Arms Corporation. Their plan was to market as genuine Newtons several bin-loads of poor-quality rifles they had bought from Bert Holmes. Charles Newton

An attorney by training, Newton gained fame designing rifles and flat-shooting cartridges.

filed suit and won a delayed settlement. Marshaling assets, he launched the Chas. Newton Rifle Corporation on April 19, 1919, planning to equip a new factory with surplus tooling from Eddystone Arsenal.

Nothing came of the Eddystone deal. The only rifles sold by the Chas. Newton Rifle Corporation were commercial Mausers. They had butter-knife bolt handles, double set triggers, triple leaf sights. Some had parabolic rifling, some a cloverleaf of muzzle grooves to vent gas evenly and prevent bullet tipping. Newton stocks added appeal. About 1,000 orders came in.

Alas, Germany's overheated post-war economy could not supply that many rifles under the terms of the contract. About 100 arrived in the States. Ever optimistic, Charles Newton began anew, in 1923, with Arthur Dayton and Dayton Evans, who had helped him bankroll his 1919 venture. The Buffalo Newton Rifle Corporation, established in Buffalo, moved to New Haven, Connecticut, where the first "Buffalo Newton" rifles shipped, in 1924. They had

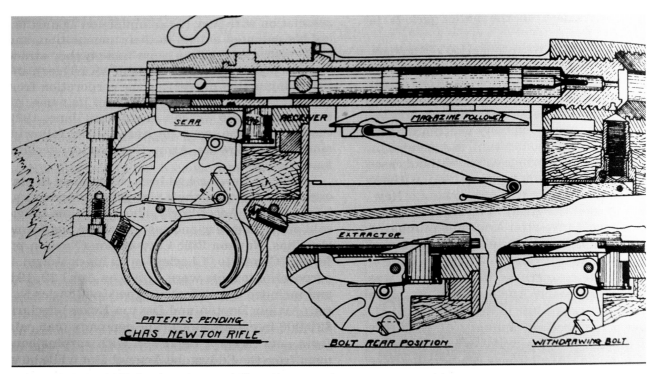

Newton (1870-1932) developed several rifles. Alas, none became commercial successes.

four-groove nickel-steel barrels in .30-06 and four Newton chamberings, .256, .280, .30, and .35. Interrupted-thread locking lugs were distinctive. Walnut stocks featured a crossbolt behind the magazine well—but lacked a receiver lug to absorb recoil! Many stocks split. Western Cartridge Company, which had begun supplying Newton rounds in 1921, listed Buffalo Newton ammunition.

Money had again become scarce for Charles Newton. After borrowing on his life insurance, he pleaded with Marlin to build his rifles under contract. Marlin's Frank Kenna demurred, despite Newton's insistence that his company was on the brink of success and that, at a rate of 1,000 rifles a month, it could build rifles for $8 each. Buffalo Newtons then retailed for $60.

The Buffalo Newton Rifle Corporation folded, in 1929, after producing around 1,500 rifles. With characteristic zeal, Charles Newton applied himself to another action design and came up with the New Newton Straight Pull Rifle. Its two-lug bolt and Springfield cocking piece suggested bolt-rifle ancestry, but Newton had also borrowed from the straight-pull Lee Navy and Winchester lever-action designs. In fact, Newton renamed the rifle the "Le-

verbolt." Again he approached Frank Kenna. If Marlin produced the rifle, said Newton, he'd split profits down the middle. The shrewd Kenna required proof of demand, so Newton published a flyer soliciting a $25 down-payment for each Leverbolt rifle. The remaining $35 would be due when the rifle was delivered. Sadly, even this offer failed to bring the necessary 500 orders.

The .270 (here in a modern Sako with an impala), came a decade after Newton's speedy .250.

In October, Wall Street collapsed, dashing Newton's dreams. Even his irrepressible spirit could not surmount the Depression. He died at home, in New Haven, March 9, 1932, at age 62.

Charles Newton's work with high-performance cartridges set the stage for the post-WWII debut of short belted magnums. While the .25-06 is generally credited to Neidner, it may well have appeared on Newton's bench first. A generation before Roy Weatherby, Newton had game bullets clocking over 3,000 fps. He developed bolt rifles able to bottle pressures from potent, long-range cartridges. His interrupted-thread locking lugs predated the Weatherby Mark V bolt by 30 years. His three-position safety appeared 20 years before Winchester's. This lawyer-turned-inventor also fashioned a partition-style bullet, in 1915.

Alas, Charles Newton's brilliance as an architect of rifles and cartridges, and his perseverance in bringing them to riflemen, earned him few rewards. Luck does not always favor the most deserving.

ROY WEATHERBY

Good fortune, and much better timing, smiled on Roy Weatherby. The Kansas farm boy was 15, in 1925, when the .270 Winchester and .300 Holland & Holland Magnum appeared. Thanks largely to Jack O'Connor's high praise, the .270 would become a quick and enduring success. The .300 H&H got nowhere near the plaudits, in part because its long, tapered hull and belted base required a leggy action and a more open bolt face. Winchester's Model 54 adopted the .270 right away. Not until the Model 70 appeared, 12 years later, would a commercial U.S. rifle be offered in .300 H&H. Besides, hunters of that day were still in awe of the tremendous blow delivered by the .30-06. It had more than enough punch for any North American game. They didn't need a magnum that whacked clavicles.

Twenty years later, however, hunters began to reconsider. Some became persuaded that bullets faster than the '06's and heavier than the .270's made sense. The prophet to preach that gospel and sell long-range rifles as a path to redemption afield was California insurance salesman Roy Weatherby.

Since his boyhood days trapping 'possums, Roy had indulged an interest in the outdoors. But his prospects for success in the shooting industry no

Radiused shoulders mark Weatherby cartridges, here a .257 Magnum. Norma loads Weatherby ammo.

doubt seemed bleak early on. One of 10 children, he'd later recall walking behind an aging plow horse, watching enviously as a neighbor pulled five bottoms three times as fast with a Fordson tractor. Roy's family had no automobile, no electrical service or indoor plumbing. In 1923, his father, George, opened a one-pump filling station, in Salina. A move to Florida put "nine of us in a four-passenger Dodge, camping in a tent along the way." George laid bricks, while Roy hauled mortar. Growing up, Roy would clerk in a music store, sell washing machines, and drive a bread truck. Enrolled at the University of Wichita, he met Camilla Jackson. They married, in 1936, and Roy got work at Southwestern Bell Telephone. Then the couple headed west, settling in San Diego. Employed by a local utility, then the Automobile Club of Southern California, Roy was soon earning $200 a month.

While insurance sales paid the bills, Weatherby moonlighted in his basement shop, building rifles on surplus military actions. His shop birthed a series of wildcat rounds based on the .300 H&H Magnum. He reduced its body taper and gave it a "double-radius" shoulder. The full-length version became the .300 Weatherby, but his first magnums were necked to .257, .277, and .284, the hulls trimmed to 2½ inches so loaded cartridges would fit .30-06-length magazines.

While there's no question the subsequent success of Weatherby rifles and cartridges resulted mainly from Roy's hard work and brilliant sales-

Accurate, flat-shooting rifles have made the Weatherby name popular with sheep hunters.

Wayne examines an early Weatherby. Roy commonly used Mauser actions like this one.

manship, his early magnums owe much to fellow Californian and wildcatter R.W. Miller. In 1940, Miller was loading the .300 Hoffman, dropped from the Western Cartridge Company line seven years earlier. Western claimed the steep Hoffman shoulder hiked pressures and, loaded to acceptable pressures, wouldn't exceed the velocity of the .300 Holland from which it derived. Miller reasoned that, if he replaced the angular juncture at case neck and shoulder with one that was rounded or radiused, he'd enable powder gas to flow more smoothly, directing more of its energy at the bullet base. This done, he lengthened the barrel's throat to reduce pressures as the bullet accelerated from the case.

After he wrote letters to *The American Rifleman* about his work, the magazine sent out authority E. Baden Powell to take a look. Powell advised Miller to straighten the case body, further throttling bolt thrust and preventing premature escape of powder gas. The new cartridge was called the PMVF—Powell Miller Venturi Freebore. In 1944, the two men went into business under the name of Vard, Inc. But money ran short and, in 1945, they sold to Hollywood Tool and Die, which renamed the cartridge CCC: Controlled Combustion Chamberage.

About this time, Roy Weatherby was designing his own wildcats. He carried a .270 PMVF on a deer hunt and liked it. Weatherby asked Miller to help incorporate the radiused shoulder on his rounds. But Miller demurred. Roy went next to George Fuller, a machinist friend who had fashioned the reamer for Weatherby's .220 Rocket. Fuller argued that a radius at the bottom of the shoulder would be hard to tool for, but, finally, he capitulated. Roy Weatherby followed with a marketing package that would bring his venture lasting success.

Roy's first store opened in 1945, on Long Beach Boulevard, in Los Angeles. In 1946, he pledged "everything I owned" to get a $5,000 business loan from the Bank of America. It was a start. Bankruptcy would remain a threat during those early years, as Roy, committing to the rifle business full time, pushed ahead.

One day, behind the counter at his retail shop, he watched Gary Cooper walk in the door. It was a pivotal moment. Post-war prosperity had put Hollywood in America's spotlight. Weatherby took note and recruited celebrities to carry his message. He put himself in photos with actors like Roy Rogers, world-traveled hunters like Elgin Gates, and foreign dignitaries like the Shah of Iran. He shared the lens with Elmer Keith and Jack O'Connor, with Jimmy Doolittle and Joe Foss. Roy's magazine article, "Overgunned and Undergunned," reached Sheldon Coleman, who became a customer. Phil Sharpe put Weatherby rifles and cartridges in his *Complete Guide To Handloading*. Roy's ads drummed the message that a Weatherby Magnum stretches your reach and puts you in elite company. A subliminal footnote: "Weatherby helps you become more than you are."

An auto accident late in 1946 put Roy on crutches—but that month, the cover of *The American Rifleman* featured a Weatherby rifle!

His storefront business moved shortly after Weatherby's (later Weatherby), Inc. was founded in May, 1949. Texas oilman and big-game hunter Herb Klein, who already used Weatherby rifles, bought $10,000 in stock. He and Phil Sharpe became vice presidents. The new Firestone Boulevard address, in Southgate, would be Weatherby's headquarters and retail outlet for more than 40 years.

Roy worked tirelessly, always looking for new ways to market rifles. In 1950, he boldly painted a new Ford van with the Weatherby logo and the image of a rifle, for travel to dealers. He outfitted a Buick wagon with a built-in walnut gun vault. Roy cultivated

This Alaskan black bear fell to a hunter's .340 Weatherby Magnum. The round appeared in 1962.

The big, nine-lug Mark V action, by Roy Weatherby and Fred Jennie, appeared in 1957.

an active, mobile sales force. A super salesman, he valued personal contacts. For years after rising postage costs might have stopped him, Roy sent Christmas cards to every Weatherby customer. He also used television to reach the masses of hunters who'd not yet fired a Weatherby rifle. To demonstrate the power of his .300 (whose bullets clocked 300 fps faster than those from a .300 H&H), Roy severed a thick tree limb, on camera, with a single shot and a straight face.

Herb Klein played a big role early on. "He was crucial to our success," recalls Dean Rumbaugh, who, at this writing, has worked at Weatherby for 50 years. "But he and Roy didn't always see eye to eye." After the inevitable split, Roy engaged J.P. Sauer and its owner, Dynamit-Nobel, as partners. That union lasted four years. In 1966, it sold their interests to Roy's friend Leo Roethe for $500,000 ($187,000 less than they'd paid for it!).

Beginning in 1954, Roy Weatherby marketed Imperial scopes to complement his rifles. Built by Hertel & Reuss of Germany, the stable comprised 2¾x, 4x, and 6x models, plus 2-7x and 2¾-10x

Wayne killed this Montana elk with his .270 Weatherby, at 300 yards. "A top pick for long shots!"

variables. In the early 1960s, constantly centered reticles in the second focal plane appeared. The Hertel & Reuss design didn't lend itself to other changes, so, in 1972, Roy asked Asia Optical, a Japanese firm, to build a new Premier scope. In 1984, that was replaced by the Supreme series, also from Asia Optical. Soon thereafter, Weatherby stopped listing scopes.

Roy Weatherby died in 1988, 14 years after his friend Herb Klein. Son Ed brought the company north, to Atascadero. A later move landed Weatherby headquarters at its current location, in Paso Robles.

The first Weatherby rifles were built on the most available actions: Mauser, Springfield, Enfield. Roy also used Model 70 Winchesters and other customer-supplied mechanisms. Neither the .220 Rocket, a blown-out Swift, nor the .228 Weatherby Magnum got commercial traction. But the .270 Magnum that followed has endured. It's one of my favorites, shooting chalk-line flat and hitting hard without beating me blue. With the .257 and 7mm Weatherby Magnums (same case, different necks) that appeared about the same time, it became a model for the short magnums that appeared under different labels in the 1950s and '60s. Roy's sales pitch earned him the moniker "High Priest of High Velocity." Lightweight bullets driven fast, he said,

Weatherby's Vanguard, on the Howa action, has earned a reputation for fine accuracy.

The Mark V Magnum uses interrupted-thread breeching, nine lugs in three rows of three.

delivered an effect all out of proportion to their size. Flat flight meant easier hits.

Weatherby once sold barrels and loading equipment, as well as rifles, from retail outlets. Post-war calls on ammunition firms added cartridges to the Long Beach store inventory, in 1948. Norma has loaded Weatherby-brand ammo since the early 1950s.

Roy deep-hole-drilled and contoured his own barrels. He fashioned his own stocks. He installed Jaeger triggers, Buehler safeties and scope mounts. "Roy and Maynard Buehler were friends," says Dean Rumbaugh. In 1957, Roy and engineer Fred Jennie developed the Mark V action to replace the Danish Shultz & Larsen, one of few big enough for Weatherby's .378 Magnum, introduced in 1953. The .378 would later spawn the .460 and .416 Weatherby Magnums. The Mark V rifle, with its nine-lug breeching and rakish Claro stocks, became *the* Weatherby. According to Dean Rumbaugh, the first Weatherby Mark V receivers were manufactured by Pacific Foundry International, in California, from sand castings. But too many failed, so Roy went to forged receivers from J.P. Sauer. You won't find Mark Vs with single-digit serial numbers. PFIs were numbered from 15,000 into the 16,000s. Sauer-built actions began at 20,000.

By the late 1970s, Weatherby had a close working relationship with Calico, a California walnut supplier that still furnishes most Mark V wood. In 1977, Mark V manufacture moved from Germany to Japan, a cost-saving measure that did not affect rifle quality. During the 1980s, Weatherby announced its Vanguard rifle, a popularly priced alternative to the flagship Mark V. Built on a Howa action in chrome-moly or stainless steel, it was reintroduced in 1994, then upgraded. Initially bored for standard rounds like the .30-06, the Vanguard list came to include the .257 and .300 Weatherby with other magnums.

During the 1990s, a six-lug Mark V appeared. This scaled-down action weighed 26 ounces, about 28-percent less than the Mark V Magnum's. Teamed with slender, fluted barrels, this receiver better fitted .30-06-size cartridges and enabled Weatherby to build hunting rifles as light as 5¾ pounds. For its Ultra Lightweights, Weatherby was smart not to compromise bullet speed by chopping barrels. It left barrels for the Weatherby Magnum rounds at 26 inches, those for standard cartridges and the 7mm Remington and .300 Winchester Magnum at 24. Button rifled Criterion barrels from John Krieger were cryogenically treated (the barrel temperature is lowered to -300 degrees F to relieve stresses imparted during manufacturing).

Weatherby brought its Mark V back to the U.S., in 1996, contracting with Saco Defense, in Maine, to build the Magnum version. Assembly of six-lug rifles went to Acrometal, in Brainerd, Minnesota. Rifles produced there wore button rifled Krieger Criterion barrels, hand-laid synthetic Bell & Carlson stocks, and adjustable triggers with .012 to .015 sear engagement. Barrels for Super Varmint Master rifles were hand-lapped. Superior results at Brainerd, and an ownership change at Saco, shifted all Mark V production to Acrometal, in 2001. By this time, the Buehler scope mounts, once standard on Weatherby rifles, had been replaced by those from Talley, later run by Dave Talley's son Gary Turner.

Interest in long-range shooting prompted Weatherby to design its TRR (Threat Response Rifle) series. These Custom Shop rifles featured adjustable target-style stocks with optional Picatinny rails. A compact version in .223 or .308 had a 22-inch barrel miking .839 at the muzzle. A TRR Desert Magnum, in more potent chamberings, boasted the Mark V Magnum action and a stiff 28-inch barrel.

Weatherby's cartridge line continued to grow. In 1962 came the .340, a necked-up .300. In 1968, Weatherby announced the .240, a belted 6mm on a .30-06-size hull. The .30-378 arrived in 1998. It was

an unlikely hit—an *uber*-magnum that upstaged even the .300 Weatherby. According to Ed, it still tops sales charts in the Mark V. The .338-378 carries even more smash, packing 2,500 ft-lbs—*at 500 yards!* But recoil is significant. Once, after firing a two-inch group with a .338-378 at 300 yards, I removed the brake. A couple of rounds with *that* mule was enough; I re-installed the brake. Weatherby has since resurrected its .375 Magnum, a necked-up .300 Weatherby. It handily trumps the .375 H&H and seems to me to be one of Weatherby's most practical rounds for truly big game.

Mark Vs and Vanguards now earn Weatherby's "Range Certified" 1-MOA guarantee.

Vanguards are fitted with walnut or synthetic stocks of signature Weatherby profile.

ROCKY GIBBS

During a March snowstorm, in 1955, rifle maker and wildcat cartridge enthusiast Rocky Gibbs moved from Richmond, California, to Viola, Idaho, eight miles north of Moscow. He'd purchased a 35-acre tract laid out to accommodate a 500-yard rifle range. In his shop, Rocky reestablished his business, Gibbs Rifle Products. Until his death from leukemia, at age 58, in 1973, Rocky hawked his high-velocity cartridges based on the .30-06 case. He left no hard evidence of how he achieved the bullet speeds some hand-loaders have questioned—following his instructions, his family burned all the records! Gibbs had a flair for the dramatic and was openly concerned about other wildcatters pirating his know-how.

Rocky wasn't born "Rocky." Christened Manolis Aamoen Gibbs for no apparent reason, he grew up with only one functional eye, having lost the sight in his right during a childhood battle with typhus. Soon after graduating high school in Gainesville, Texas, he boarded a train for California. As the story goes, he had it in his head to be widely remembered and decided another name would be a first step. He asked the train conductor about the mountains looming in the distance. The Rockies, he was told. There in the coach, he assumed the name Rocky Edward Gibbs.

His California sojourn brought Rocky in contact with other rifle enthusiasts working to better the performance of commercial ammunition. A match at the local Richmond shooting club fueled his search for a cartridge with exceptional reach and violin-string trajectory. Each year, the match winner would earn his crown by shooting groups at 100, 200, 300, and 400 yards. But group size wasn't all that mattered. Part of the score derived from bullet drop measurements at 400 yards. Flat-shooting rifles had a decided edge. Now, Rocky's Model 721 Remington in .270 carried plenty of sauce to kill deer as far away as he cared to shoot them. But in the rarified company of wildcatters, it seemed plain. Rocky followed his gunsmith's advice and re-chambered to .270 Ackley Improved. Extraction problems prompted him to sell the Remington and buy a Winchester Model 70 in .270. With that rifle, he at last shot a winning score. Still, his quest for fast, flat-shooting cartridges had just begun.

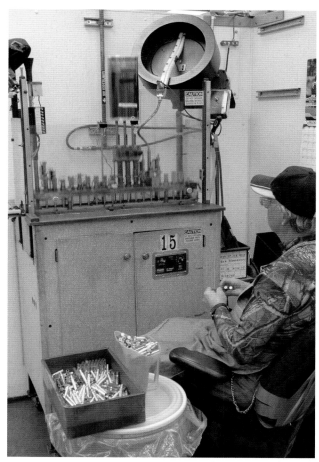

Rocky Gibbs would have coveted an ammo-loading machine like this one at Black Hills.

Hot-rodding his .270, Rocky dismissed Ackley's 40-degree shoulder, a suspect in the sticky extraction. He ordered a reamer that cut a long body with a 35-degree shoulder from Keith Francis, in Talent, Oregon. Rocky called the cartridge the .270 Gibbs. Unlike the Ackleys, this wasn't an Improved round. The neck measured only .250 in length, so you couldn't headspace a standard .270 in a Gibbs chamber. It had to be formed in a die or fire-formed in steps. The pay-off was greater case capacity. Reportedly, Rocky Gibbs set a record with his new cartridge at the next Richmond match. That was in 1953. A year later, Rocky had put six more cartridges in a proprietary stable that would change little over the years. He stuck with the .30-06 as the parent case, largely because, in the 1950s, there was still a surfeit of military '06 brass.

By the time he migrated to northern Idaho, Rocky had something of a reputation as a gunsmith

Accurate, flat-shooting rifles appealed to 1950s Idaho wildcatter Rocky Gibbs.

and cartridge designer. He published a booklet entitled *Front Ignition Loading Technique*, which treated the subject of duplex charges developed by Charlie O'Neil, Elmer Keith, and Don Hopkins of OKH fame. Alas, just three years after Rocky had set up shop in Viola, a fire demolished the family's home and with it all the booklets not distributed. Gibbs never reprinted the treatise. But his family of cartridges and his enthusiasm for wildcatting survived the blaze.

The .240 Gibbs, most easily formed from .25-06 brass, is among the most enduring of the Gibbs wildcats (though Rocky made relatively few rifles so chambered). He recorded over 3,600 fps with 75-grain bullets, 3,500 with 85-grain bullets, and 3,250 with 105-grain Speers. Rocky described the .25 Gibbs as the only wildcat that shot flatter than his .240 and compared it with the .257 Weatherby. His records showed 3,900 fps from 75-grain bullets and nearly 3,550 with 100-grain spitzers. Rocky clocked 3,330 fps with 117-grain bullets. The .25 Gibbs became quite popular, outselling the more versatile 6.5 Gibbs.

Rocky claimed his .270 Gibbs was "the best all-around cartridge for a handloader." Even Jack O'Connor acknowledged its merits in *Outdoor Life*: "As far as I can tell, Brother Gibbs doesn't do it with mirrors." Launching a 130-grain bullet at 3,400 fps placed the Gibbs in league with the .270 Weatherby Magnum and a tall rung above the .270 Winchester. While Rocky also championed his 7mm and claimed 3,300 fps with a 139-grain bullet, that wildcat never sold particularly well.

The .30 Gibbs earned some notoriety as a poor man's magnum. Francis Sell wrote about it in his excellent book on deer hunting. Rocky massaged 3,000 fps from that .30 with 180-grain bullets, a match for the modern .300 Winchester Magnum and .300 WSM. Certainly the .30 was much more popular than the 8mm Gibbs, which Rocky thought was a good way to salvage 8x57 Mausers that made their way Stateside on the heels of the second World War. Driving 170-grain bullets at 3,200 fps and 220s at 2,800, the 8mm Gibbs surely qualified as a killer of moose, elk, and big bears. But, like the 6.5, it suffered from the curious American aversion to most metric numbers.

The .338 Gibbs joined Rocky's line sometime after 1958. By then, the appeal of surplus rifles and ammo had worn thin, largely because supplies of both were drying up. The .338 Winchester Magnum had just appeared, and the .340 Weatherby was still a few years off, so .33-caliber barrels were special-order. An entrepreneur who could see the sunny side of any situation, Rocky might have thought the .338 would elicit more press from O'Connor and Bob Hutton, and perhaps fellow Idahoan and big-bore advocate Elmer Keith. But he could hardly predict brisk demand. After all, he'd advertised the 6.5 Gibbs as "a vicious big-game rifle, fit for gophers to grizzlies." Why choose a hard-kicking .338? The popularity and versatility of the .30 Gibbs cast a long shadow, too, and Rocky himself preferred 250-grain bullets in .338s. These were a tight fit in .30-06-length magazines. While he claimed 3,050 fps with 200-grain bullets and 2,700 with 250s, Rocky had little luck at market with the .338 Gibbs. He dropped it after two years.

Rocky and his data have drawn barbs from many shooters, who say the bullet speeds he claimed are unlikely, at least given sane pressures. Like other wildcatters who've recruited disciples among the great unwashed, he may have embellished the numbers when describing what his cartridges could do. He evidently measured pressures, probably in copper units, but he appeared little concerned with keeping them below what are now considered reasonable thresholds. Velocity readings were taken from barrels that may have been a couple of inches longer than his stated measure, as

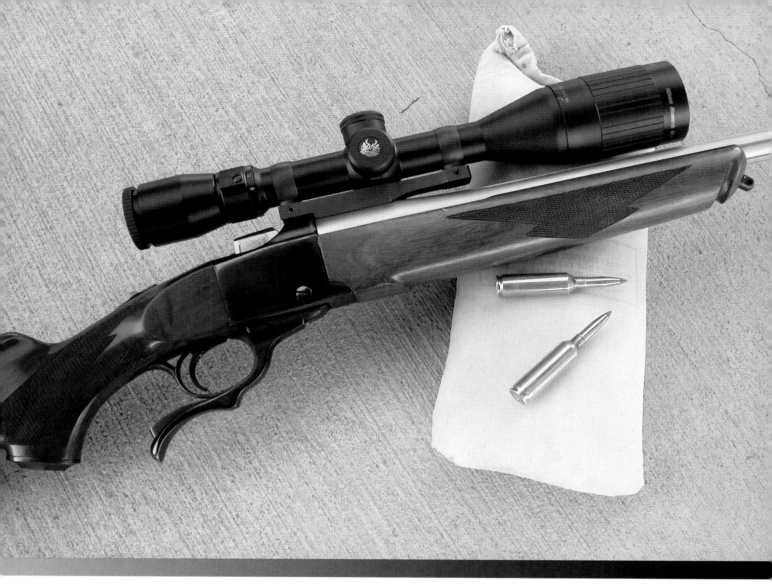

This 6.5 WSM, wildcatted by Ken Nagel, would have appealed to Rocky Gibbs!

he considered only the bore, not the chamber, in that length. Finally, like many handloaders, he remembered and repeated bullet speeds at the top of the range. Averages didn't impress prospective buyers as much as did top velocity readings.

On the other hand, Rocky Gibbs brought high-performance cartridges to many shooters before the .264 Winchester and 7mm Remington Magnum were duking it out, before the .300 Winchester appeared. From a surplus Mauser or Springfield, a second-hand Remington 721 or Winchester 70, you could build a rifle with greater reach and feed it with cartridges fashioned from GI hulls. Manolis Aamoen Gibbs got shooters to think beyond traditional limits and test their bullets and skills farther along the arc. His work furthered the development of long-range rifles and cartridges.

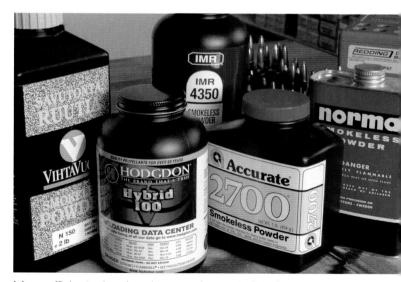

Many efficient, slow-burning powders antedated Gibbs, who claimed dizzying velocities.

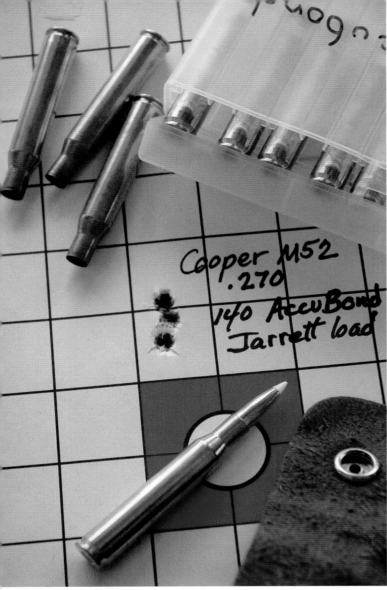

Handwritten on target: Cooper M52 .270 140 AccuBond Jarrett load

Kenny Jarrett's care in rifle building carried over to his high-velocity ammunition.

KENNY JARRETT

An accurate rifle identifies itself only when you fire it, and often not then. Unless you hold in the same place for each shot, support the rifle exactly the same way, and crush the trigger without disturbing the sight picture, you'll scatter bullets no matter your hardware. If you don't shoot well, accurate rifles are a waste of money. Still, because most shooters consider themselves crack marksmen, rifles that *can* deliver fine accuracy sell briskly. Some companies guarantee accuracy: 1½, even one inch at 100 yards.

I can't say how many rifles that don't drill tight groups are returned to the factory. Not as many as you might suppose, given the mediocre marksmanship of many customers. After all, if you return a rifle

that, in the company's tunnel checks out with ragged one-hole groups, you're left to explain the disparity. A smattering of rifles *do* get sent back, with notes from owners convinced the product is flawed. Patient technicians punch out additional groups, then offer telephone therapy. Convincing the incompetent that they are just that is a headache—which is why anyone would be nuts to guarantee *half*-minute groups. Yet after more than three decades as a celebrated guru of accurate rifles, Kenny Jarrett still stands behind the half-minute guarantee attached to every long-range sub-.33 rifle leaving his shop.

Jarrett, a fourth-generation soybean farmer from Jackson, South Carolina, grew up on the 10,000-acre Cowden Plantation, then owned by his uncle, J.M. Brown. After high school, Kenny went to work at Cowden. In the late 1970s, he bought a lathe and opened a gun shop.

Jarrett's perception of accuracy had already been molded by benchrest competition. Building a rifle that consistently shot winning groups, he found, was exceedingly difficult. Harold Broughton, a Texas gun maker and benchrest shooter, took a shine to Kenny and tutored him. Kenny still credits Broughton for setting him on track to build truly accurate rifles. Jerry Hart added barrel know-how to Jarrett's resumé. By 1979, Kenny had invested heavily in the gun business and given up farming. Favorable press in major gun publications gave him traction. The red beard and golf-ball wad of tobacco, his bib overalls and Bubba wit, all seemed an odd match to machine-work tolerances as fine as .0001. But that very incongruity helped sell stories about Jarrett rifles. It was the late Art Carter, I believe, who coined the term "beanfield rifle" to describe the deadly long-range effect of those guns on southern whitetails. Hunters took note and anted up. By the time Kenny's shop was a decade old, gross sales had topped $500,000 and he'd hired 13 people. The original 2,200-square-foot shop, of home-sawn cypress and cedar shakes, had sprouted four additions, nearly tripling the space. Meanwhile, prices of Jarrett rifles had risen to cover the overhead. In 1991, his least expensive rifle sold for $2,850, though the finish was by most standards rough. Accuracy was the Jarrett hallmark.

Kenny told me then that his success bucked predictions.

"I was warned early on that hunters just wouldn't pay for the accuracy demanded by benchrest competitors," he said. "But they do."

A top-rung competitor himself, Jarrett figured that, for many big-game hunters, accuracy remains the defining element of a rifle.

"You don't need a half-minute rifle to kill deer," he pointed out. "You don't need an expensive rifle to put bullets through bushel-basket vitals at ordinary hunting ranges. You pay for accuracy, because accurate is what a rifle should *be*."

Besides, he added, tight groups give you the confidence to make shots on game you'd have to pass with lesser rifles.

"Long shots," he said. "Beanfield shots."

For years, Kenny built rifles on actions the customer supplied, or he'd furnish a Remington 700 or, for the biggest cartridges, a Weatherby Mark V. After truing the lugs by surface grinding and hand fitting, he chased the receiver threads so barrel and bolt axes lined up perfectly. Kenny used Hart barrels for cartridges of .30-caliber and under, turning to Schneider tubes for bigger bores. He designed a switch-barrel system for the Remington 700.

Jarrett developed several of his own wildcat cartridges, from the .220 Jaybird to the .338 Kubla-Kahn, a .378 Weatherby Magnum necked to .33. One of his favorites is the versatile .300 Jarrett, on the 8mm Remington Magnum case. By the early 1990s, Kenny's shop held 68 chambering reamers. Seventy percent of his customers were then choosing wildcat rounds, "the .280 Ackley, especially."

McMillan provided all the early Jarrett stocks. At that time, Kenny didn't think walnut had a place on an accurate rifle. "Stability is crucial to accuracy," he insisted. "Walnut walks." He pillar-bedded all rifles and shot them to make certain they passed muster. In 1991, that meant ½-inch three-shot groups at 100 yards for rifles .25-caliber and smaller. The next year, Kenny started making his own barrels, button rifled in stainless steel.

Convincing the incompetent that they are just that is a headache— which is why anyone would be nuts to guarantee half-minute groups.

"We learned a lot right away, rejecting 27 percent of our barrels."

That figure later dropped to six percent, albeit the accuracy bar has been jacked even higher. Now Kenny demands half-inch groups from .264, .277, .284, and .308 bores, too. Once, after barreling a rifle several times and scrapping the tubes, Jarrett hacksawed the receiver and hung it over his workbench. No compromises.

Despite innovations and incremental improvements in product quality, the beanfield rifle business went flat during the 1990s. The flush of publicity that fueled early sales had died. Some customers came back with repeat orders (one fellow racked $46,000 in Jarrett rifles), but, for others, a single expensive, super-accurate rifle was all a marriage could stand. At the same time, Kenny was busy designing his own action. Unveiling it to me, he acknowledged he'd have been better off with an accountant at his elbow.

"It's *too* good," he shrugged. "I made it too expensive." Bleakly, he wondered if it would ever see production.

Not to worry. In 2004, I visited the Jarrett shop, where an electrical discharge machine (EDM) and a computer numerically controlled (CNC) mill were carving receivers from 515 stainless bar stock. This rifle mechanism boasts clever features like feed rails designed for specific cartridges; they're replaceable, not integral. A collar at the rear of the bolt ensures bind-free operation. Three evenly spaced lugs apply even pressure around the case head and permit low bolt throws.

Barrels for the Jarrett action and for Kenny's custom rifles on other metal are all rifled in house. Stainless barrels receive a copper bore wash to ease passage of the carbide rifling button. The copper must be later removed.

"That's one reason all our bores are hand-lapped," Kenny said. "We want to keep bore diameter within .0001, breech to muzzle. We air-gauge every bore to check. Tight tolerances bring high rejection rates, but, if a barrel gets chambered, we're sure it will shoot well. Of course, every rifle gets a proof target. We fire 40,000 rounds a year."

He pointed to 55-gallon drums full of brass. In the back forty, Jarrett posts targets as far as 1,000 yards.

Kenny's son, Jay, runs the stock shop, where composite shells are precisely fitted to the metal, and aluminum pillars are glued in with Marine-Tex, also used in the recoil lug mortise.

"Jay is one reason I've kept investing in the shop," Kenny told me. "Jay and my daughter, Rissa. She runs the office."

Jarrett's most popular cartridges are frisky in recoil, so Kenny designed his own brake.

"It works because it has lots of holes and just .001 clearance for the bullet," he explained.

He handed me a .300 so equipped. My three Ballistic Tips drilled a ½-inch group; recoil felt like that of a .270. He brought other rifles to the bench: a Tactical Rifle in .308, a long-barreled .243 Catbird (Jarrett's 6mm-.270) and Kenny's own .300, with the 200-grain Bear Claw loads he used to shoot a huge moose.

The first three-shot group from the .308 went under .2-inch. The first three-shot group from the Catbird measured .3-inch. At nearly .8-inch, the Bear Claws seemed naughty, but, to miss a moose with a rifle that delivers ¾-minute accuracy, you'd have to be shooting at more than 4,000 yards.

Zeros established, Kenny suggested we shoot long. The wind was up on the 600-yard range, and twice we had to staple backers blown off by gusts that swayed the pines and flattened the grass beneath them. Trees shielded bullets a bit over their first 350 yards of travel. Kenny called the quartering breeze, as I triggered three shots from the .300. Eight inches. I fired three from the .308, keeping them under five. Any thoughts that the tiny .243 Catbird bullets would be swept away by the gale were laid to rest by a four-inch group at 600 yards. Drop, of course, was another story.

"That's why our backer is as tall as an outhouse."

I settled into prone with a tight sling and fired another group with the .300, doping wind myself. Two bullets landed in the eight-inch target square, the third a hand's width out. A prone volley with another .300 Jarrett equipped with a 6-24x Swarovski scope delivered a grapefruit-size group in the center of the vitals on a life-size deer target.

"Addicting, isn't it?" Kenny grinned.

An accurate rifle impresses you the way a quick-footed sports car impresses you. But such a rifle puts your marksmanship on the line. Firing a Jarrett with Kenny at the spotting scope, you feel compelled to shoot your best.

The Jarrett product line is smaller than it once was, a result of prudent trimming and a focus on more efficient operation.

"Three of our rifles—Signature, Windwalker and Professional Hunter—account for 90 percent of sales," Kenny told me not long ago. We are a custom shop, and we'll continue to offer many options. But there's no sense listing catalog items that interest only a few people."

Jarrett's customer base is small.

"Of 1.3 million rifles sold annually in the U.S., we figure about 5,000 are custom-built," he said. "And our rifles are not cheap."

Still, Kenny has had tides of demand, and to ensure 90-day delivery, his shop capacity tops out at 200 rifles a year. He likes to think his rifles go to people who truly appreciate accuracy and who use them.

"Back in the 1980s, a local youngster saved his summer hay money for three years to buy a Jarrett rifle. I threw in a Leupold scope on that deal."

At the 2013 SHOT (Shooting Hunting and Outdoor Trade) Show, Kenny Jarrett introduced a new series of walnut-stocked rifles, his closely machined actions and barrels married for the first time to hand-checkered walnut. This Jarrett Prestige Series features barreled actions secured in a 6061 aluminum bedding block epoxied in place with pillar contact points. The block (or chassis) surrounds the magazine well. The barrel floats.

"We tried many sealants and finishes to make this stock absolutely waterproof," Kenny said. "We got there with multiple coats, starting with an epoxy base that penetrates and seals wood $3/16$-inch deep. I've submersed these stocks for days with no measurable change in weight."

In other words, there's no water up-take! Jarrett's new walnut-stocked rifles are handsome, with the long, slim grips I favor. Three wrist styles include standard pistol grip, Prince of Wales (round-knob) pistol grip, and a *straight* wrist!

Kenny Jarrett has shaved his beard and given up tobacco. But he still takes the measure of a rifle in tenths of an inch between centers.

"It's a good way to size up shooters, too."

Curt Crum, here in Coues deer country, builds long-range rifles with David Miller.

DAVID MILLER

"I may shoot farther than most hunters," says David Miller. "But I don't shoot farther than I can hit."

Depending on conditions, that can be far indeed.

"First, you need good equipment. I'm fortunate, because Curt Crum and I build rifles for a living. We've done it for more than 35 years, so we know how to make rifles accurate. We use the best barrels, install the best sights, and handload to ensure consistency in ammunition. We're obsessive about intrinsic accuracy, because it is the cornerstone of field accuracy. You can shoot only as well as your rifle."

David concedes that most deer hunters don't need a rifle that prints two-inch groups at 400 yards. But he and Curt aren't ordinary hunters.

"We focus on Coues deer, and we go for trophy-class bucks. You won't see many of those in a season—maybe only one. Those old deer will rarely let you get close, and your only chance to kill may come at a distance that demands a lot of you and your equipment."

While most hunters are digging for factory-loaded cartridges bought on sale five years ago, David Miller is sorting polished hulls by weight and reaming flash-holes. He spins bullets on his concentricity gauge and sets aside for practice those with unacceptable run-out.

"To get the best accuracy, you have to mind details. Accuracy is a measure of uniformity."

As for bullets, Curt and David favor long, sleek, Sierra MatchKing and Barnes Triple-Shocks. But they also sift them, again to ensure uniformity.

"Miking bullets to the fourth decimal and hand-weighing powder charges is tedious. But we know our ammo is as accurate as we can make it."

It's not unusual for Miller to reject more than half the bullets or cases in a given lot. He told me one batch of 500 match-grade bullets yielded only 50 that met his standards for hunting bullets. He uses a Bonanza Co-Ax Indicator to check run-out to .001, but admits that variation to .003 is hard to detect on targets. David says the Internal Concentricity Comparator, fashioned by Vern Juenko of Reno, is one of the best tools for sorting bullets by shape, weight, and concentricity.

"It can even detect voids in the bullet core."

Miller moly-coats his bullets, first cleaning them with denatured alcohol, then tumbling them two hours in a container of hard shot pellets and molybdenum disulfide powder. The steel pellets help drive the moly into the softer jacket. Then the bullets are tumbled for one minute in a cleaning mix of ground corncobs. After that comes a two-minute shaking in a jar of steel shot and carnauba wax, followed by a minute in the corncob mix for final polish. The bullets emerge slate-gray and slippery. David has found moly bullets shoot measurably flatter than uncoated bullets. With a 400-yard zero, 168-grain MatchKings from his .300 Weatherby rise only four inches above sightline at 200 yards. Moly delays fouling, too.

"My groups start opening up after 20 rounds with ordinary bullets," says David. "Moly-coated bullets deliver first-rate accuracy for up to 30 shots. And they make cleaning easier."

Early in his career, David specialized in gorgeous walnut-stocked bolt rifles. Then, to satisfy his own need for a long-range Coues deer gun, he built what he dubbed "The Marksman." A friend saw it and had to have one. Soon, Miller offered the no-frills, laminate-stocked Marksman to customers as a low-cost alternative to his custom Classic. Now, "low-cost" is relative. The Marksman will nick you as deeply as, say, a late-model used pickup. Ditto the synthetic-stocked Miller rifle that followed. But Miller makes no apologies, because he takes no shortcuts in building a rifle and insists on the very best components.

"We have only one standard for accuracy."

He guarantees minute-of-angle accuracy with factory loads. David and Curt will chamber a Marksman for wildcat rounds, "but we prefer standard cartridges. We don't tell the customer what he should want," he grins. "But we're good at making him want what we like to build."

The Marksman wears an uncheckered stock glass-bedded to the action. Save for paper-thin gaps on either side of the barrel, wood-to-metal fit appears skin-tight. A Harris bipod comes with every Marksman, as does David's own scope mount, machined from a solid steel bar.

Like the Classic, the Marksman is built on a Winchester M70 Classic action (Miller was one of several shooters who lobbied Winchester to bring back the Mauser-style extractor it had jettisoned to cut costs in the rifle's infamous 1964 makeover). Both rifles get extensive work to make them more beautiful, smoother in operation, and more reliable—and, of course, more accurate. The bridge is trimmed for easy loading, but most changes lie inside. The magazine is of David's design. It holds four magnum cartridges, not three. The follower has a detent so the bullet doesn't scrape it, and its shoulder is on the right so the first cartridge ducks easily under the left rail. The follower spring has less tension than most, but there's no trace of looseness. Parts on the Marksman move with the smooth precision of a Maserati gearshift.

Still, this rifle was designed for the trail. Its beauty derives from clean, graceful lines, impeccable fit and finish. The laminated stock is cut from David's own pattern. The medium-heavy 26-inch Krieger barrel has enough beef to mitigate muzzle jump and deliver accurate repeat shots in hot weather. David prefers to chamber for the .300 Weatherby Magnum.

"It drives 168-grain Sierra MatchKings at 3,400 fps. They shoot flat, buck the wind, and hit hard enough to kill little deer as far as we can see to aim at them."

To better equip the rifle for long shooting, David installs a Leupold 6.5-20x scope. It features his own range-finding reticle, a standard crosswire with two stadia wires below the horizontal wire. At 20x, they bracket 12 inches (the average depth of a Coues deer chest) at 400 yards. The Miller reticle includes two vertical lines either side of the center wire (12 inches at 20x at 400 yards) to help you shade for wind.

> To kill game far away, you must shoot well. David Miller and Curt Crum shoot very deliberately. To them, the idea of "If there's a bullet in the air, you have a chance" is just plain irresponsible.

Glassing for deer with a Marksman at your side is no different than glassing with a .30-30 in your lap. At least so it seemed to me, as the Arizona sun slowly warmed the desert.

"You don't walk for Coues bucks," David said. "You stay put and look carefully into places that might hold bedded deer. Then you look into them again. Don't waste time on big patches of brush you can't see through. Focus on smaller coverts; look for pieces of the animal. Scrutinize the edges of bigger clumps to catch deer moving around. We stay out all day, because Coues deer can get up and browse or stroll to the nearest water at any time."

David emphasizes that spotting a buck is hardly a guarantee you'll be able to stalk it. Ocotillo and other desert plants can hide these small deer as soon as you come off your vantage point. Shots from a hill or across a canyon or from a slope down to a flat can be long. Some are *very* long.

Our hunt was almost over before we spied a mature buck. Actually, I spotted him, moving slowly along the foot of a ridge a quarter-mile off. It was dawn; he was headed to bed. Even before David hissed, "Shoot!" I was prone, the Marksman steady on its bipod. Centering the second wire on the deer's chest to allow for drop from my 300-yard zero, I pressed the trigger. We paced 410 yards to the animal, perfectly hit.

The next morning, I grabbed a handful of cartridges and hiked into the desert to shoot the Marksman at paper. Groups from 100 to 500 yards included one three-shot cluster at 400 yards that measured one inch.

Intrinsic accuracy is not the whole trick. To kill game far away, you must shoot well. David Miller and Curt Crum shoot very deliberately. They can't abide the popular mantra, "If there's a bullet in the air, you have a chance." That's irresponsible thinking and leads to irresponsible shooting. David puts the onus on the shooter, not on luck.

"If you have a plan, you have a chance," he says.

David plans for hunting season by shooting a lot at long range.

"Because experience tells me I'll likely spot deer at long range, I zero at 300 yards and practice most from 300 to 500."

Once, hunting in Chihuahua, David spied a Coues buck in a place that denied him an approach. It was bedded far from the nearest place that offered a shot. Hiking there, David ranged the distance at 550 yards. Then, because the deer was hidden by brush, Miller waited. He waited for hours. Finally, the deer stood. David shot him, then fired again, scoring two lethal hits at double the distance most hunters might consider a long shot.

"It was farther than I like to shoot," says David. "Closer is always better. But there was no question in my mind I could kill that deer if conditions stayed favorable. I've shot this rifle at little targets out to 600 yards. I *know* where the bullets land and how big the groups are."

Crum and Miller stress the importance of practicing under different conditions, not just in wind, but under varied lighting and from every hunting posi-

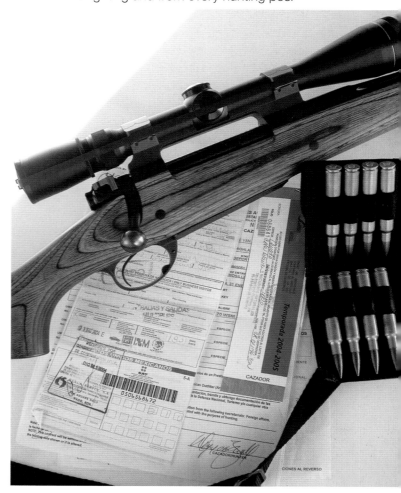

David Miller developed the M70-based Marksman rifle, in .300 Weatherby, for himself.

tion you might want to use. If you typically set up on a Harris bipod, employ it in practice—but the next shot you get may be in brush too tall for a bipod, so you're smart to also fire from a sit and kneeling. A sling helps you a great deal in these positions and in prone, even if you have a support like a backpack. Taut as it should be, the sling also affects the bullet's point of impact, because it pulls the fore-end away from the barrel and counters the natural rise of the barrel during recoil.

"Until you shoot at long range under specific circumstances, you can't predict the result of a shot at long range *under those circumstances*," says David. "And you're not qualified to take that shot."

There's no doubt in Miller's mind that shooting far before season has enabled him to take his best Coues deer. During the late 1980s and through the 1990s, he killed six bucks that scored into the Boone & Crockett records books. The *closest* shot at those six stunning deer? Four hundred and fifty yards! David attributes much of his success to diligent practice at targets too far off for most riflemen to hit without walking the bullets in.

"Just shooting is not useful," he says. "Every shot must be the best you can make it. Sloppy execution becomes habit. When Curt and I practice, we shoot as if one bullet was all we had. We know if we don't hit a deer fatally with that first bullet, it's a lost opportunity. We'll probably never see that deer again."

Oklahoma "Surgeon" rifle builder Preston Pritchett fires one of his heavy tack-drivers.

PRESTON PRITCHET

Prague doesn't get many visitors. Prague, Oklahoma, I mean. Not since super-athlete Jim Thorpe drew international attention in the 1912 Olympics has his hometown made news outside Lincoln County. Residents—all 3,500, if you also count the farms around Prague—find the obscurity comfortable enough. Oklahoma City is just 50 miles to the west, should they wish more excitement.

"We have oil," says Preston Pritchett. "And natural gas."

Corn and soybeans, hogs and cattle, too. Good deer and turkey hunting. But the real wealth lies underground.

"In 1984, oil prices fell and people shuttered their houses. But the drills have fired up again. Natural gas nets more than oil." He says the rigs can now reach 4,000 feet "from just about any angle."

Preston is not in the oil business. He operates a machine shop on 80 rural acres a few miles from town.

"I run a few cattle too," he says, "and play with rifles."

Actually, rifles have taken over most of the 55,000 square feet in his shop.

"We have three CNC mills and two manual mills, three CNC lathes and two manual lathes."

He points them out to me. I'm here for an afternoon, wedging the visit into business travel east. Preston was kind enough to fetch me from the Tulsa airport.

"We have this EDM (electrical discharge machine) that holds tolerances to half a tenth."

That's half a ten-*thousandth* of an inch, or 50 millionths. Even the CNCs here hew to ridiculously tight standards.

"I just checked one receiver and found it true within three-tenths over eight inches," Preston tells me.

Pritchett, 46, grew up in the area. He met his wife, Kathy, "in first grade, but didn't marry her until Valentine's Day, 1984." Daughters Nikki and Courtney followed. Preston apprenticed in machine shops until "the turn of the century," he grins. He started building his own shop the first of January 2001.

"Then I was hired out as a subcontractor for general machine work. That kept the wolf from the door."

He'd read about Kenny Jarrett, the colorful Carolinian whose long-range rifles had catapulted him to national prominence.

Wayne used this short Surgeon rifle in .223 to nip half-minute groups with several loads.

"I'm not after the spotlight," Preston assures me. "Just enough business to justify the rifles I want to build."

Those are super-accurate rifles for long-range enthusiasts.

You won't talk long with this big-boned, red-haired country boy, before spotting talent behind the unassuming smile. Listen and you'll want to listen more, because Pritchett knows how to manufacture rifles.

"We don't barrel actions from other makers," he explains. "We build ours from scratch."

"Tell me how." I'm listening.

"We make two actions," says Pritchett. "Long and short. The long one accepts cartridges as big as the .338 Lapua. The short one is for the .308 family."

Short-action blanks are cut on site from 2½-inch round bars into 10.6-inch lengths. Long blanks come from rectangular bar stock, 2½ by three inches in cross-section.

"Before machining, each 11½-inch magnum receiver weighs 19½ pounds," he says.

Pritchett and his crew of two equally savvy machinists mill rough contours before starting the EDM. On average, they spend four hours cutting the inside of a short action, five hours eviscerating a long one. EDM work burns camming surfaces and leaves a rail in the race that guides the left lug to smooth bolt travel.

Massive, precisely fitted parts contribute to Surgeon accuracy. Here, a recessed bolt head.

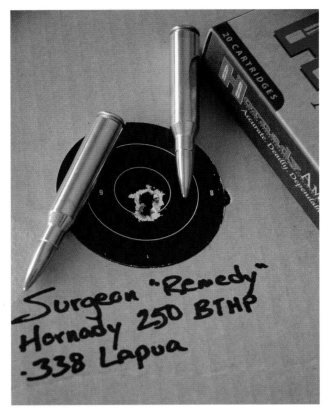

Each receiver wears an integral Picatinny rail, sloped to add 20 minutes of elevation on the short action, 30 minutes on the long action. That's so you can zero at long range without pushing the limit of the scope's elevation dial. A sight is at its optical best when the erector tube is centered. Building tilt into bases has become a popular way to ensure this with zeros beyond 300 yards.

"We cut the barrel shank threads and mill the action face and lug abutments while the receiver is secured in one fixture, to guarantee true and square surfaces."

Preston minds every detail that could affect accuracy. Machining is all done after heat-treating to 40 C on the Rockwell scale, so there's no possibility of heat warp.

"Then we de-burr the metal and tumble it in ceramic media. We finish actions in Cerakote, mainly olive and black, baking it on at 200 degrees. This makes for a handsome, very durable exterior."

Bolts on Pritchett's rifles are tapered, a tad bigger at the rear to reduce play in the race. Single-shots also have an enlarged area behind the lug to snug lockup. Preston learned that trick from benchrest shooters.

Wayne fired this three-shot .2-inch knot with a Surgeon Remedy in .338 Lapua.

Surgeon magnum actions are milled to fly-wing tolerances from rectangular steel billets. The integral rail is sloped to add elevation "gain" for long shooting.

Small-caliber Surgeon receivers are milled from solid round bar stock with integral lug, rail.

"Our bolts come from 4140 bar stock," he says. "They're one-piece; the handle is part of the body, so it won't ever come off."

Only the bolt knob is separate (it's threaded on). Bolts are heat-treated to a hardness of 60 C outside, 30 C inside. Bearing surfaces get "nitride," so they won't gall.

Preston designed his rifles to accept Remington 700 components. The bolt release is an exception, deriving from a Marine Corps release he modified so the pin would not break. Pritchett's .308 rifle has a Remington extractor; the .338 Lapua wears a claw he fashioned to fit inside the right-hand lug and throw cases in a low arc to clear scope knobs. While he favors Jewell triggers in "clean environments," he tells me they're less tolerant of dirt than are Remington triggers, which he also installs.

A unique product from Pritchett Machine is the Tri-Rail, a mounting device that fits in front of the integral recoil lug on his rifles, but can also be used in place of the standard recoil lug on a Remington 700.

"It provides three mounting surfaces for accessories like night vision equipment," he says.

A Surefire brake is standard on 20-inch barrels for most chamberings and on all barrels bored to .338 Lapua.

Preston favors cut rifled Krieger stainless barrels, rifled 1:11 for .308 bullets up to 175 grains in weight. He specifies a 1:10 twist for the .338 Lapua, "but a rifle ordered for military use gets a barrel cut 1:9.35." He can't say why, or if the slightly sharper spin makes a difference. "For other rounds, I'll advise the customer, but let him or her specify twist."

One of his favorite long-range rounds on the short action is the 6.5x47.

"It's essentially an abbreviated .260 Remington, with a .473 base, but a longer neck and sharper shoulder."

After installing his first 6.5x47 barrel, he punched a .148 group.

"It's hard not to like a rifle that stacks 'em in that tight!" he beams.

Preston insists that the crown is the most important part of a barrel. He turns his with a 45-degree inside taper that flattens to 11½ degrees, then meets the rifling at 45. When I ask him how he arrived at those steps and angle values, he shrugs, "The rifles shoot real well." He function-tests all of them, first at 385 yards, then at 1,000.

Because he emphasizes precision at long range, Preston Pritchett recommends Badger Ordnance 30mm scope rings. His rifles are heavy enough to absorb the ounces, and 30mm scopes are increasingly popular.

"We install McMillan stocks. They're painted and finished when we get them. We complete the inletting, then pillar-bed the metal with MarineTex."

He emphasizes that, though he can stock them for the field, most of the rifles he ships have a clearly tactical profile.

"They're patterned on sniper rifles." And just like every gun maker since North and Whitney figured out mass production, he'd like to see his rifles in the hands of U.S. servicemen. "We also target law enforcement agencies," he adds. Nonetheless, civilian sales have accounted for up to 95 percent of production.

Preston built about 100 rifles during 2004, his first year as a rifle maker. "We doubled that figure in 2005 and finished more than 300 actions in 2006," he tallied, conceding there's a limit to how many rifles he can build—and that he's closing in on it, unless he expands the facilities and hires more people. But he's still committed to his original goal of selling super-accurate rifles to advanced shooters.

"Our rifles aren't fancy, and they're not cheap. Our target clientele is really a small part of the shooting public."

He hopes orders from police agencies and military sniping units will multiply. Ten rifles have already found a home with the Oklahoma City Police Department. He says others have been shipped to the U.S. Secret Service.

After the shop tour, Preston explains why his rifles are not Pritchett by name.

"I call 'em Surgeon rifles, because a fellow named Surgeon was one of my first employees. An Army Ranger at one time, he could shoot very well and build good rifles." He points out that people trained as surgeons are expected to perform their tasks with utmost precision. "All the arrows seemed to point to that word." The moniker stuck.

Preston Pritchett lists four Surgeon rifles, with custom features available on all. He explained, "The Razor is our lightest rifle. Just 7¾ pounds. It's designed for hunters. We build a 12-pound Scalpel with a tactical stock, a 14-pound single-shot Laser with a target stock." These feature Pritchett's short action, for .308-length rounds. "The Remedy is a 16-pound repeater with our long action and heavy barrel. We chamber it mainly in .300 Winchester and .338 Lapua,"

Some weeks later, true to his word, Pritchett loaned me a Surgeon Remedy. It arrived in a sturdy

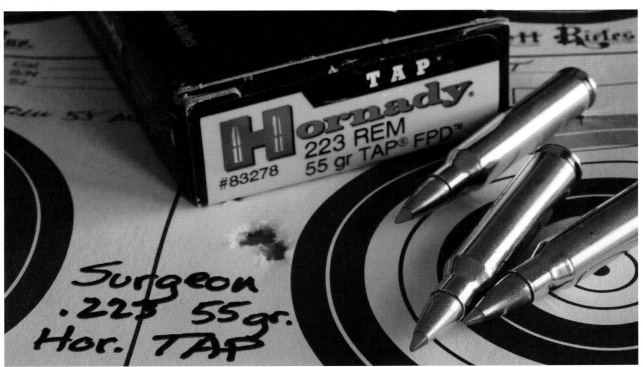

Hornady TAP ammo in a Surgeon rifle drilled this .3-inch group for Wayne.

A tri-rail on a Surgeon rifle accepts all Picatinny-friendly attachments, for long shooting.

polymer case. Like those I'd photographed at Pritchett Machine, the metal showed clean detailing under its olive Cerakote sheath. It was brand-new, but the bolt cycled as if polished by many firings. Vault-tight lock-up and a decided lack of wobble at the rear of the throw also reflected great care in finishing. The Jewell trigger tripped at 2¼ pounds. The five-round, single-stack detachable box slipped in and out with ease, but didn't rattle when seated. It fed .338 Lapua cartridges like a hound slicking up sausages. The tan and green McMillan stock had an adjustable cheekrest and buttplate. Narrow, even margins bracketed the floating barrel. My only criticism: the bottom metal stuck proud at the guard's rear, but lay below the stock surface in front of the magazine.

Of course, hitting small targets far away has little to do with cosmetics. I lost no time getting this Remedy to the bench. Preston had scoped the rifle with a Leupold LRT, a 4½-14x with a turret-mounted objective

dial and a mil-dot reticle. While this long-armed Lapua deserved exercise at 600 and 1,000 yards, I fired first at 100 yards for a zero and to test its mettle. Three Hornady-loaded 250-grain bullets later, I'm peering at one elongated hole. The group miked just over .2-inch.

Such accuracy doesn't show up often on my range. It's darned close to surgical precision.

■ ■ ■

I've been running 155 [-grain] Scenars at 2,980 fps. The rifle is topped with a 5-25x Schmidt & Bender PM2. To date I've taken 96 coyotes with it, 16 [at] over 500 meters. The longest shot so far, 1,120 meters.

So wrote a Surgeon customer in Montana, who added that he's put five bullets inside 2½ inches at 750 yards. Believable? Well, if he hadn't been shooting a Surgeon rifle ... .

PART 2:
RIFLES, OPTICS, AND AMMUNITION

SOPHISTICATED HARDWARE DOESN'T GUARANTEE HITS—BUT WITHOUT IT, THEY'LL COME HARDER!

Your rifle's barrel has a lot to do with its long-range potential. But there's no telling at a glance if it is carefully bored and rifled to exacting tolerances and finished by hand or if it came down the line, like a bottle cap, for installation on entry-level deer guns. You can resolve this mystery with some elementary detective work. Just go into this knowing that cheap barrels often deliver fine accuracy and expensive barrels can disappoint!

Neither target rifles nor hunting rifles these days wear the long, heavy barrels that dominated into the market hunting era. The huge charges of blackpowder used by buffalo hunters benefited from barrels longer than those on Civil War carbines. The advent of smokeless powder changed barrel requirements. The steel had to be thicker or stronger, to contain higher pressures, but the only advantages afforded by extra-long rifle barrels were incrementally higher bullet speeds, additional muzzle weight to steady your aim, and a longer sight radius for better aim.

At dusk you'll want low power, big front lenses, both in rifle scopes and binos. A 5mm exit pupil is wide enough.

High-velocity bullets prompted a shift from soft carbon steels to the "ordnance" steel employed in 1903 Springfields. Winchester's "nickel" steel was harder to machine, albeit more erosion-resistant. Later, Winchester pioneered chrome-molybdenum barrel steel. Stainless barrels emerged, in the 1960s.

Most hunting and military rifles wear chrome-molybdenum barrels, which is very strong. It takes hot and rust blues nicely, too. A lot of chrome-moly is designated 4140. Other four-digit numbers indicate a slightly different alloy. Stainless steel barrels dominate competitive shooting and are gaining favor among hunters, who like its rust resistance. (Indeed, 416 stainless barrel steel is not rust-*proof*!) It differs from the steel in stainless cutlery. High chrome content in barrel-quality stainless adds hardness (and makes bluing difficult). Sulfur makes it easier to machine. Super-accurate barrels can be fashioned from both chrome-moly and stainless steels. If you're shooting often in wet places, stainless makes sense.

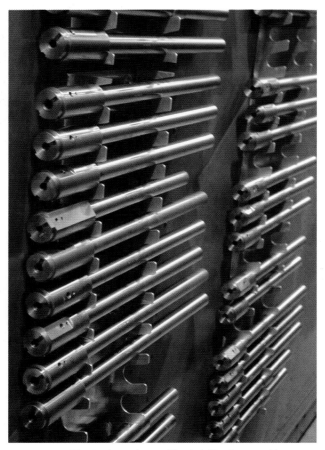

These barrels, at Black Hills Ammunition, are used for pressure testing and accuracy trials.

Current "fluid steel" barrels surpass those manufactured earlier for blackpowder, regarding both tensile strength and hardness. (Tensile strength is the force required to break a steel rod an inch in cross-sectional area by pulling at both ends.) Generally, hardening steel boosts its tensile strength. But a tensile rating of 100,000 pounds for a rifle barrel is worthless if the steel is so hard as to be brittle. Most makers target a hardness of 25 to 32 on the Rockwell C scale. Heat-treating leaves residual stresses in barrels that can be relieved by slow cooling after reheating the blank.

Barrel blanks are drilled and reamed much as they were a century ago. In fact, some of the deep-hole drills used on M1 Garand barrels in World War II are still in service! Most of these drills have a stationary bit mounted on a long steel tube, with a groove for cooling oil. The barrel rotates around it at up to 5,000 rpm, producing a bore commonly .005-inch undersized, so a reamer can finish the job and leave the interior smooth and uniform. Jeff Sipe, of The Montana Rifle Company, tells me bores to be chromed are bored and rifled to dimensions that allow for plating thickness. In many quarters, carbide bits and reamers have replaced tool-steel over the last decades. They deliver superior finish.

Rifling arrived late in the fifteenth century, when shooters started using lead because it cast easily and "slugged up" to fill the bore. Straight grooves preceded spiral grooves, which improved accuracy. Conical bullets required spin. A couple centuries later, the German *jaeger* rifle, with seven to nine deep, slow-twist grooves, inspired America's "Kentucky" rifle. Reducing the bore to .50-caliber or less yielded more shots per pound of lead. Frontiersmen speeded loading with rifling land-diameter balls in linen patches lubed with fat or saliva. The British and their mercenaries were handicapped by groove-diameter balls that loaded hard. Their rifles became unserviceable, when bores fouled. Broad rifling lands supported balls pushed under ramrod pressure. When breechloading became practical, narrow lands reduced friction on groove-diameter bullets.

During the 1830s, when percussion ignition began to replace flint, and big-bore Plains rifles edged out the elegant Kentucky in the West, conical bullets surged in popularity. Alvin Clark invented the false muzzle, in 1840, enabling competitive shooters to start paper-patched bullets square with the barrel proper.

Rifling twist or pitch or rate of spin is expressed as the distance a bullet travels while making one revolution. A 1:14 twist means the bullet turns over one time for every 14 inches of forward travel. If all bullets were the same weight and shape and traveled at the same speed, one rate of twist would work for all. But correct rate of twist varies. A patched round ball in a muzzleloader requires a very slow twist, while a long bullet in a smallbore rifle cartridge needs a quick twist to stabilize. Appropriate rate of spin might be 1:66 for a round ball in a muzzleloader, 1:32 for a conical bullet in the same rifle! Many muzzleloaders are rifled 1:48 as a compromise.

Centerfire rifles built for long-distance shooting with .264, .308, and .338 VLD (very low drag) bullets have steeper rifling twists than ordinary hunting rifles with those bores. Barrels for heavy, long-range .223 bullets have a very fast pitch, 1:8, even 1:7. Such a sharp spin is needed to stabilize 65- to 80-grain bullets, while a 1:12 twist may excel with standard 50-grain hunting bullets. Short, frangible bullets fired through a fast-twist barrel can sustain jacket damage, partly because they're light in weight and moving fast. Such damage can impair accuracy and terminal performance, even cause bullets to rupture in flight.

Determining how best to spin a bullet took a couple centuries of effort by talented people. In 1854, the British government hired Joseph Whitworth, a bright, young ballistician, to try various rifling types and twist rates. Standard twist in military rifles then was 1:78. Whitworth's experiments pointed to a twist of 1:20. Skeptics thought such a sharp spin would retard the bullet, but a hexagonal bullet of Whitworth's design flew flat and, at long range, drilled groups a sixth the size of those shot with ordinary patched balls. Their 500-yard deviation of 4½ inches from center trounced the 27-inch mean for the ball, and they penetrated more than twice as deep as balls from a slow-twist barrel.

Hexagonal bullets, though, were slow to load and expensive. William Greener's narrow-land rifling pitched in a twist of 1:30 stabilized smallbore (.40 to .52) bullets out to 2,000 yards. Gun maker James Purdey built two rifles featuring Greener-style bar-

Relatively steep rifling pitch is needed to produce groups like this with heavy .223 bullets.

rels, in 1856. He called them "Express Train" rifles, because of their power. "Express" became a descriptor of powerful British hunting cartridges.

Breechloading rifles, naturally, eliminated the need for bullets that could be loaded from the front. Bullets loaded from the rear could be made harder and longer and cast to full groove diameter. Hard bullets could be stabilized with shallower grooves and, thus, driven faster. They tolerated sharp twist rates. William Ellis Metford experimented with "gain twist," which gave bullets easy acceleration with slow spin forward of the throat; gradually steeper spin increased the degree of stabilization at exit. Metford used a 34-inch barrel that gave the bullet an exit spin of 1:17, but started it so gradually that the bullet turned over only once before reaching the muzzle! By the 1890s, gain twist and progressive grooving (deeper at the breech) were deemed of no practical value. But Metford also championed the wide, shallow grooves that have come to excel with jacketed bullets, and he developed segmented rifling, with rounded lands and grooves.

In 1879, Briton Sir Alfred George Greenhill came up with a formula for twist rate that works for most bullets in most loads: Proper twist, in calibers, is 150 divided by the length of the bullet in calibers. So, if you have a 168-grain .30-caliber bullet 1.35 inches long, divide 1.35 by .30 to get length in calibers (4.5). Then divide 150 by 4.5. Result: a fraction over 33—that's in calibers. Converting to inches of linear measure, you multiply it by .30. The final number is close to 10, a useful rate

> Charles Newton reasoned that, since a bullet bears on only one shoulder of a land, the other shoulder was unnecessary. His "ratchet rifling" failed at market.

of spin for most popular .30-bore hunting cartridges, from .308 Winchester to .300 Weatherby Magnum.

This formula works for most jacketed lead bullets, specific gravity 10.9. Note that bullet *length*, not *weight*, is at issue here. A 168-grain boat-tail spitzer with a long nose can equal the length of a blunt 200-grain bullet. Bullets of gilding metal, with no lead core, are, of course, much longer for their weight than are traditional jacketed bullets.

Rifling *configuration* also affects bullet flight. Early in the twentieth century, Charles Newton reasoned that, since a bullet bears on only one shoulder of a land, the other is unnecessary. His "ratchet rifling" put that principle in practice. It failed at market. The gun making firm of Marlin has famously used multiple, narrow grooves in its Micro-Groove barrels. They deliver good accuracy, but

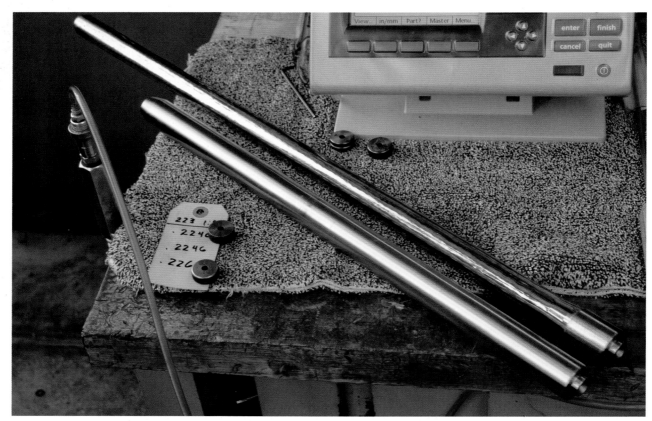

Barrels become longer in hammer-forging, a process that impresses rifling. Note the hammer marks.

SCHMIEDEDORN

This Blaser hammer-forging mandrel includes the chamber, as well as the rifling.

probably no better than traditional Metford-style bores with fewer grooves. Metford rifling has broad groove bottoms with the same radius as the bullet, plus flat-topped, square-shouldered lands. All else equal, barrels with shallow grooves typically shoot tighter than those with deep grooves, as they distort the bullet less. But shallow-groove barrels don't last as long.

Land size is a trade-off, too. Narrow lands distort bullets less and create less drag, but also burn away faster. Reducing the number of lands, a barrel maker can keep them wide while minimizing distortion and drag. While most rifle barrels these days feature four to six grooves (on average .004-inch deep in .30-caliber bores), U.S. soldiers carried two-groove Springfields in World War I. Marlin's early Micro-Groove barrels had 16, just .0008 deep!

Bullets can be spun right or left. Right-hand twist is most common, albeit P-14 Enfields had left-hand twist. At extreme yardage, right-pitch barrels nudge bullets to the right, left-pitch barrels to the left.

Rifling can be accomplished with a cutter, a button, or a hammer-forging machine. The cutter is the simplest method and dates to a Nuremburg shop, in the late fifteenth century. A hook in a hardened steel cylinder that just fits the bore is pulled through it on a rotating rod, the hook removing about .0001-inch of steel with each pass. After indexing so every groove is shallowly cut, the cutter is adjusted to deepen the bite. Broaches with multiple hooks in a step-tooth configuration speed the process. Rifling a barrel takes about an hour with one cutter. John Krieger's top-grade barrels are "single-point cut." He tells me this process imparts very little stress to the barrel steel.

Hammers flank two rifling mandrels on a bench near a Ruger hammer-forging machine.

A tungsten-carbide button is much faster. Mounted on the end of a high-tensile rod and rotated by a rifling head set to the desired rate of twist, the button is pushed or pulled through the finished bore by a hydraulic ram, "ironing in" the grooves. To prevent bulges, you must button rifle the tube before turning down thick walls. Dan Lilja says the smooth interior finish and uniform groove depth of buttoned barrels help ensure fine accuracy. But, as with cutters, buttons must move at a constant pressure through the bore.

Hammer-forging machines are mechanical beasts that pound the barrel around a mandrel that, like a button, features the rifling in reverse. Thick concrete floors shudder during this operation, which, in effect, kneads thick barrel steel like so much dough. Because a barrel gets about 30-percent longer in the process, blanks start short. Hammer-forging is fast, but leaves consider-

This chamber lap (used at Montana Rifle Company), ensures a smooth interior finish.

able radial stress in the barrel. It is also a more difficult process with hard steels, like 416 stainless.

Rifling must be concentric, with land corners free of irregularities. According to some shooters and barrel makers, *uniform* roughness in land and groove surfaces may actually prove a benefit, because a glass-smooth surface increases friction that can pull jacket material from bullets as effectively as do tool marks in a rough bore. According to some barrel gurus, surface ripple of 10 to 20 micro-inches delivers top accuracy. Some makers hand-lap freshly rifled barrels to ensure

Wayne's lapped McMillan barrel produced this group and many like it, in prone competition.

a properly smooth surface. Besides polishing, this operation relieves tight spots. "But lapping is no substitute for careful boring and rifling," says barrel maker Bill Wiseman. "It removes only .0002-inch or so and does not erase all tool marks." Final check of a lapped barrel is commonly done with a 75-power bore scope.

Champion high-power shooter David Tubb markets a kit called FinalFinish, an assortment of bullets coated with fine abrasives. You shoot them in a specified order through a new barrel to erase small machining marks. "The total amount of metal removed by FinalFinish is less than .0003-inch," claims Tubb, in his Superior Shooting Systems catalog. The company, headquartered in Canadian, Texas, also offers a FinalFinish kit for rimfires. Tubb insists that smooth bores better resist accumulating lead and jacket material and, so, deliver superior accuracy. They're easier to clean and needn't be cleaned as often. He also recommends the treatment in rifles with throats roughened by erosion, even if they've become worn ahead of the start of the lands.

John Krieger advises that every barrel be trimmed at least an inch at the muzzle when it is fitted to the rifle, because the tooling used in bore finishing can leave a slight flare at the ends. Krieger barrels are lapped to just under 16 micro-inch in the direction of bullet travel and held to a tolerance of .0005 over nominal groove and bore dimensions. But the dimensions are *uniform* to within .0001. Pac-Nor (a button rifle shop) and H-S Precision (with cut rifled barrels) specify tolerances of .0003 for the bore diameter. Pac-Nor limits variation in groove diameter to .0001.

Gauges used to check bore dimensions include the steel plug favored by ace barrel maker Bill Wiseman. The "star gauge" for 1903 Springfields registered land and groove diameters. Star-gauged barrels had a reputation for accuracy, but the use of a certain gauge doesn't guarantee a barrel is accurate. Compressed air delivers the most precise dimensional readings now. An air gauge is a probe that's moved through the barrel, with constant pneumatic pressure recording variations from specified dimensions. Ed Shilen's air gauge is sensitive to 50 *millionths* of an inch. Commonly accepted variation in bore diameter: .0002 for target rifles, .0005 for sporting rifles.

During the 1990s, several experimenters tried sleeved rifle barrels. Steel tubes with very thin walls were coupled with carbon-fiber jackets that added

Heavy barrels on AR-15 rifles like this S&W have helped improve their accuracy.

strength, but little weight. Sleeved barrels the diameter of varmint-weight steel barrels scaled half as much! Dave Smith, of Vancouver, Washington, was a pioneer in this field and patented a process for manufacturing composite sleeves.

"I used pre-impregnated epoxy resin and unidirectional graphite fibers," he explained. "Almost all the strength is in the fiber. I built the liners *into* the sleeve under high pressure. Freezing the liner and heating the sleeve is another method of joining them, but I don't like it because heat and cold induce stress."

Dave's work with rifle barrels resulted in a company, Accurate Composites, in Tualatin, Oregon. In 2003, a Minneapolis firm, Magnum Research, acquired all equipment from that plant, plus three patents for composite barrel manufacture. Dave still experiments with graphite compounds.

"They're incredibly strong," he affirmed. "Magnum-Lite barrels of my manufacture have been pressure-tested to 129,000 psi, or about twice the pressure generated from a Weatherby magnum cartridge."

Dave has applied his barrels to long-range shooting. One day, at the local Clark Rifles range, he showed me some of his artillery.

"I'm not really a competitive shooter," he chuckled, "though I've shot in rifle and pistol matches. Now I get my jollies breaking eggs at 300 yards."

A .223 on a Sako action wears one of his own Magnum-Lite barrels, a 29-inch tube with 1:12 twist.

Scoped with an 8-25x Leupold Long Range Target scope, it has landed five shots inside .33 at 100 yards.

"I once put four into .158," he grins. That load: 27½ grains H335 launching a 52-grain Sierra Match-King at 3,375 fps.

Another of Dave's rifles is a 7mm STW Rogue (with 35-degree shoulder). It's also based on Sako metal, with a 34-inch, three-groove, Magnum-Lite barrel rifled 1:10. Topped with an 8-32x Burris scope, "It was built to shoot 120-grain bullets, but prefers 168-grain MatchKings." A charge of 78 grains H1000 kicks them downrange at 3,160 fps. Dave once shot a .257 group—at 300 yards! Close behind is the .348 cloverleaf punched out by his 6.5-284 Nesika with a 32-inch Magnum-Lite barrel. Like the .223, it wears an 8-25x Leupold LRT.

"I use Lapua brass, Federal 210 primers, 60 grains of Ramshot Magnum powder, and 140-grain Berger VLD bullets," Dave recited from memory. "The chronograph tells me 3,174 fps."

Heavy barrels are not intrinsically more accurate than slender barrels, but thin barrel walls move more readily when bores get hot. D'Arcy Echols, who builds exquisite hunting rifles, insists lightweight barrels can shoot tiny groups.

"A .270 barrel gave us half-minute accuracy, though it measured just .544 at the muzzle." He adds that shots at game don't generate the heat that makes light barrels "walk."

Fluting has become popular, because it hikes cooling surface while reducing weight, but without sacrificing stiffness. Length affects barrel "spine," too, which is why single-shot pistols can be very accurate.

The barrel's crown (shape and finish at the muzzle) has a great effect on accuracy. The bullet's heel must exit squarely. A slanted or poorly finished crown, even a nick, permits uneven gas escape, tipping the bullet. My rimfire match rifle has an 11-degree crown, popular with target shooters. Recessing the crown shields the bores of hunting rifles that often meet dirt and rock or get shoved onto the gritty floor of a pickup. The common radiused crown serves almost as well. Muzzle brakes don't contact the bullet, but they do affect barrel vibration. The BOSS (Ballistic Optimizing Shooting System) on Winchester and Browning rifles is a muzzle weight you can adjust to specific loads.

Heavy barrels have less whip. Fluting reduces weight without compromising stiffness.

Wayne shot this group with a lightweight Kimber 84L. Slim barrels can be accurate!

Kimber
84 L
Black Hills
168 BTHP
.30-06

Cryogenic barrel treatment can improve accuracy. Pete Paulin, of Cryo Accurizing, told me that deep-freezing steel to relieve stresses dates to 1940. But it wasn't until 1992, when he solved the brittleness problem, did it become practical for barrels.

"Shooting changes barrel radii and length. Metal stressed in fabrication expands unpredictably. Cryogenic treatment dissipates stresses." At -300 F, the cryo bath is the ultimate cold shower. Paulin said, "Cryo may not make a bad barrel chew one hole, but it won't make any barrel shoot worse. And it *can* make a barrel shoot much better!"

Most well-known barrel makers now have web pages, and some offer barrel-making insights. If you want only to *buy* a good barrel, shop Midway. This shooter-supply outlet has paid attention to the results of benchrest competitions that test barrel accuracy. The logic: to sell shooters the most accurate barrels, stock those that garner medals. In the 2003 USRA-IR50/50 Nationals, 39 of the 87 top competitors used Lilja barrels. Of the best 20 shooters in 10.5-pound centerfire benchrest competition, 16 favored Shilen barrels. Shilen also ranked most popular in the 13.5-pound class. Hart barrels showed up almost as often on the heavy rifles and have for decades been a top choice of smallbore shooters. John Krieger's cut rifled barrels finished a close third in the latest postings. Douglas barrels appeared on both centerfire and rimfire lists, having produced high scores for half a century at National Match and 1,000-yard events.

Some barrels are less widely distributed than those on Midway's list, but also deliver top performance. Kenny Jarrett is known for rifle accuracy. So is H-S Precision. Both manufacture their own barrels. Ditto Preston Pritchett, who builds Surgeon rifles. Rick Freudenberg, near Seattle, competes at long range and installs barrels for shooters who demand teeny groups.

"I'm partial to Liljas," he says. "But many shops produce good barrels, chrome-moly and stainless. What matters is tight tolerances."

Tom Houghton at H-S Precision agrees.

"We manufacture our own cut rifled barrels from 416R stainless steel. We hold .0002 uniformity, breech to muzzle."

H-S Pro-Series 2000 rifles up to .30-caliber come with a half-minute accuracy guarantee. I've owned rifles by Rick and H-S Precision, rifles fitted with

A deep recess protects hunting rifle crowns from nicks that affect long-range accuracy.

Krieger, Shilen, and Lilja barrels. A McMillan barrel Vic Fogle installed on my Remington 37 handed me prone and benchrest titles—but the Douglas barrels on my hunting rifles have also nipped little knots.

While a truly accurate barrel justly commands a high price, some inexpensive barrels have shot stellar groups. At an IBS (International Benchrest Shooters) match on April 27, 2008, John Lewis punched a group at 600 yards that measured just .386-inch! That's roughly .065-minute of angle! His .308, shooting 155-grain Lapua bullets, was a home shop project. John got the barrel, with 1:14 twist, secondhand—*for $50*. These days, good barrels abound!

Competitors approve an 11-degree target crown, here on Wayne's McMillan-barreled 37.

HOW DEEP THE THROAT?

A long-throated rifle is said to have "free-bore," but there's no measure to define it. Weatherby rifles, noted for their long throats, enabled Roy to achieve top bullet speeds.

The rifle's throat (the unrifled bore ahead of the chamber) can be parallel or tapered. Funnel-shaped throats, from blackpowder days, are generally less conducive to accuracy than are parallel throats .0005-inch over bullet diameter. A tapered throat offers no initial support to bullets, unless they're seated almost to the lands. A parallel throat that lets the bullet slide like a piston provides more guidance. John Burns, who builds long-range rifles for GreyBull Precision, prefers not to "short-throat." He says "It's better to keep throat diameter as snug as practical. And uniform." Because bullet diameters vary, parallel throats must permit some bullet clearance.

A long-throated rifle is said to have "free-bore," but there's no measure to define it. Long throats let you seat bullets out to boost case capacity or, with standard seating, give them a running start. Weatherby rifles, noted for their long throats, enabled Roy to achieve top bullet speeds. D'Arcy Echols builds rifles in .300 Weatherby with a shorter .125 throat, because he's found that his long-range handloads shoot more accurately in them. His rifles are so marked; for any load, a shorter throat usually means higher pressures. D'Arcy adds that rifles hurling bullets with long shanks need long throats to keep pressures in check.

Forward of the throat is the leade, the tapered rear section of the lands. Most barrels have a leade angle of 1½ or two degrees. Three degrees is considered steep and can increase pressures.

CLEVER DESIGN, TIGHT TOLERANCES, AND CAREFUL MANUFACTURE GIVE SOME RIFLES—AND YOU!—THE EDGE.

A rifle built for long-range target shooting is distinctive in form. But profiles and mechanisms of target and hunting rifles have changed since the nineteenth century, when Remington built a Creedmoor version of its Rolling Block. David Tubb, a competitor with many national rifle championships to his credit, uses a modular rifle of his own design. To the uninitiated, it might resemble a "ray gun" from a science-fiction film. It differs a great deal from hunting rifles, because it was not engineered to be shouldered quickly or carried through thickets or shoved into saddle scabbards. But Tubb's rifle *is* supremely accurate, and it is easy to shoot accurately from prone, with sling or bipod.

While rifles for long-range shooting have evolved from black-powder muzzleloader to dropping-block single-shot to bolt-action repeater, requisites for accuracy at distance have remained much the same. But besides accurate barrels and precisely machined actions,

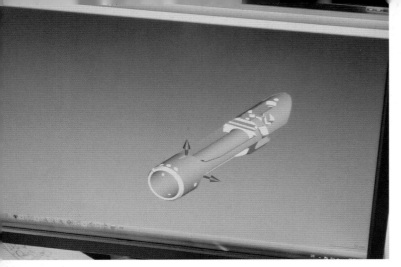

Computer-aided design speeds development of rifle actions and the tooling to make them.

hunting rifle and remains steady long enough for a shot. It has great *inertia*; it won't bounce to each beat of your heart or hop at each muscle tremor. You don't work as hard to lift a modern sporter, but it doesn't go to sleep as readily and you must work harder to keep the quivers at bay. You'll have no luck ironing out jiggles that continually jerk your sight off-target. Modern bolt rifles built for long shooting and precise hits on bull's-eye targets have the muzzle-heavy tilt of early blackpowder rifles, albeit barrels now are shorter, so the pendulum effect is reduced.

rifles to be fired without bench support must also be crafted with an eye to balance.

When next you have the chance, shoulder a muzzleloading rifle from the mid-nineteenth century. Whether Kentucky or Tennessee (Southern) in form, or a Plains rifle from the Hawken era, it will likely have a long, heavy barrel. Aim it. You'll find it hard to hold for more than a few seconds without tiring, but also that it steadies more quickly than does a lightweight

The advent of metallic cartridges changed standards of accuracy at distance, though not as much as it changed the form of the rifles used in competition. Rifle makers from all quarters scrambled to show themselves worthy at distance. Among the best-known target rifles on the eve of smokeless powder was the Ballard, absorbed in 1881 by the Marlin Firearms Company. Six years earlier, John Malon Marlin had begun production of Ballard match rifles. The wonderful Ballard Creedmoor A-1 Long Range Rifle No. 7 had a 34-inch full- or half-octagon barrel cham-

Craig Cushman has adjusted this rest so the rifle *naturally* points at the target. Crucial!

The 1898 (top) and 1894 Swedish Mausers rank among the best actions in battle rifles of their day. Wayne likes them in hunting rifles, too.

bered for the .44-100-25/8 (Sharps and Remington) round, sparked by a Berdan primer. The stock was of fancy checkered walnut. This dropping-block single-shot wore a Marlin Improved Vernier tang sight—*graduated to 1,300 yards*. The front sight comprised a spirit level and a bead and aperture disks. While this rifle sported a shotgun butt, Ballard and other makers also served a flourishing schuetzen market.

Originating in Germany, schuetzen competition spawned a special single-shot rifle, one with a deeply hooked buttplate and provision for a palm rest. These features helped the shooter support his heavy rifle offhand, as matches were shot standing. Carefully machined Vernier tang and globe front sights afforded precise aim. Double set triggers reduced pull weight and rifle movement during let-off. Ballards, unlike some rifles of that era, had chambers throated to permit breech loading of the bullet. Thus, bullets could be sized properly to take the rifling. During the transition from muzzle- to breechloading firearms, some target shooters inserted a cartridge from behind, but a hollow-base bullet from the front. Powder gas upset the skirt of the hollow-base missile, pressing it into the rifling and sealing pressure behind it.

The schuetzen game faded before World War I. During its brief heyday, many outstanding target rifles appeared, based on the likes of the Stevens 44½ and Winchester High Wall. Harry Pope and other gun making gurus experimented with bullet and rifling design. Their work influenced the bolt-action rifles and smokeless ammunition that followed. Stevens match rifles, for example, featured barrels rifled with six right-hand grooves .12 wide and .0025 deep, the lands being .03 wide. In the words of Major Ned H. Roberts, this design "gave especially nice accuracy." Such rifles and their lead bullets were held to high standards established and challenged by 10-shot groups, not the three- and five-shot strings commonly recognized today. Most shooting was done at 100 and 200 yards with iron sights, though scopes like the Malcolm presaged a shift to optical sights.

In the Stevens-Pope catalog of 1902, a .32-caliber rifle was fired 130 times at a 100-yard target, in 10-shot strings. The largest group was three inches across, the smallest 1$^7/_{16}$. Then a group "was shot at 200 yards machine rest, with as perfect bullets as we could select, another of same holding with bullets badly mutilated at the point; these two grouped closely, a three-inch circle holding all."

Many modern rifles would fail to match that performance.

The Short Magazine Lee Enfield saw England through both World Wars. A great battle rifle!

A new trigger is a smart investment when turning infantry rifles into sporters. Here, a Timney on a 1917 Enfield).

During the first decades of the twentieth century, the German 1898 Mauser, British Short Magazine Lee-Enfield (SMLE), and U.S. 1903 Springfield bolt rifles introduced high-velocity smokeless rounds to long-range competition. Still, all were *service* rifles, developed for soldiers. The Springfield evidently made a splash on the line; comparisons spawned the observation that Germans had built a hunting rifle, the British a battle rifle, the Americans a target rifle.

For all its attributes, the Springfield was far from perfect. Winchester combined the best of its action with that of the Mauser, then refined the results to produce the Model 70, in 1937. Though a hunting rifle by design, it also appeared in target versions, the Bull Gun specifically for long-range (1,000-yard) shooting.

The Model 70 proved immensely popular, and Remington's Model 30 languished. Big Green's later 40X target rifle and Model 700 hunting rifle would again make the company competitive, but not until the early 1960s. The 700's debut, in 1962, made news. So did Winchester's 1963 overhaul of the Model 70, but *that* update drew universal outrage from shooters. Remington's new flagship bolt-actions got a welcome, if unexpected, bump at market, as a result. Since then, the Browning A-Bolt and X-Bolt, Ruger 77 Mark II, and Savage's line of rifles on the 110 action have served many thousands of hunters. Some of these bolt guns deliver very fine accuracy.

GreyBull Precision re-barreled, restocked, and scoped this Remington 700 action, ever popular.

The Jack O'Connor Tribute Rifle shows the lines and Model 70 action the celebrated *Outdoor Life* writer favored.

If, instead of a hunting rifle, you're on the prowl for a super-accurate long-range target rifle, the field gets smaller. Some companies—Cooper and H-S Precision, for example—stake their reputations on top accuracy, even in lightweight models suitable for sporting use. Nesika Bay rifles, proven in benchrest competition, are now manufactured by Dakota. I routinely got one-hole groups from a Nesika rifle bored to a .22 wildcat. Kelbly's, of St. Lawrence, Ohio, supplies the steel-core alloy actions pioneered by Ralph Stolle in the 1960s and '70s. Stolle Pandas, long and short versions, are stiff but relatively lightweight, thanks to a wrap of 7075-T651 aircraft-alloy sleeve around 4140 steel. An F-Class Panda, for that new target game, has an integral Picatinny rail with a 20-degree elevation gain, to assist your scope's elevation dial at 1,000 yards. The Kodiak is essentially a slim Panda. Kelbly's notes it's a great choice for a custom sporter. The all-steel Atlas is another option from that family.

With generous weight limits, sensitive triggers, and stocks proportioned for shooting from prone or

Patrick Holehan built this .25-06 for Wayne, on an early M70 action. Accurate can be pretty.

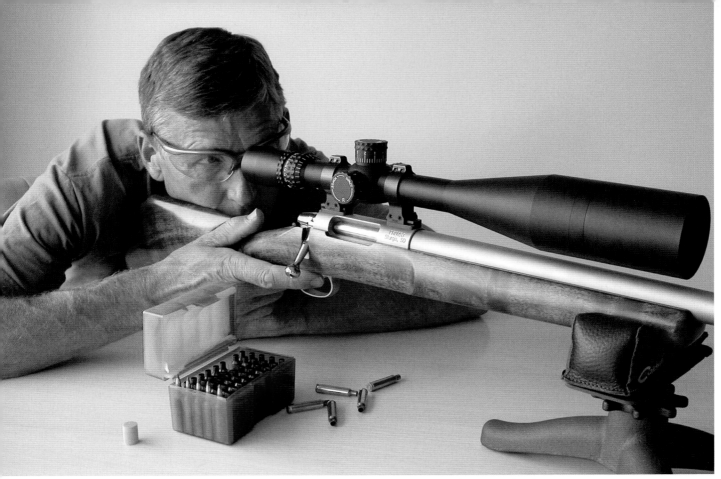

The benchrest pedigree of Nesika bolt rifles comes through even before you check targets.

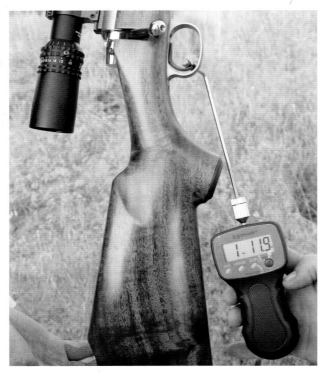

This super-accurate Nesika has a clean trigger pull of about 1¾ pounds. Perfect!

the bench, target rifles can be made more inherently accurate than hunting rifles and, just as importantly, easier to shoot well. Hunting rifles designed for long reach, on the other hand, incorporate more compromises, because they must be both more rugged and portable and are commonly barreled to powerful cartridges not known for fine accuracy. Heavy recoil from potent cartridges in rifles of modest weight also affects marksmanship.

Expert gunsmithing can make a tack-driver of a bolt-action sporter—and add hundreds of dollars to its cost. The improvements will be largely invisible. You can't tell at a glance if an action has been trued so barrel threads and bolt race are concentric, or if locking lugs have been lapped for full contact, or if the bolt face is square with the bore axis. You can't see pillar bedding or the alloy block cradling the receiver, or the rail adding rigidity to the fore-end. You can't distinguish a high-quality barrel from a reject, even by looking through the bore. Indeed, a big part of the gunsmith's job—and that of custom rifle-makers—is to work their magic without showing they

Wayne shot these one-hole groups with a Dakota/Nesika rifle in .20 Tactical. Hoo boy!

have. Add to this the fact that, to ensure a rifle performs well on the trail, the smithy can't stray too far from traditional form. Dimensions and weight must hew pretty close to those of production-line rifles that sell by the truckload to people who will never shoot far.

So, if you can't see the changes that transform a hunting rifle into one for targets, how do you tell? Cycle the bolt of a tuned rifle, and you should sense something special. Press the trigger, and all doubts will vanish.

Even an exceptional marksman will have trouble hitting with a trigger that's gritty or hard to pull. Problem triggers give you the most headaches when you shoot off-

Some sporting rifles, like the Cooper 52, 54, and 56, are built with special attention to accuracy.

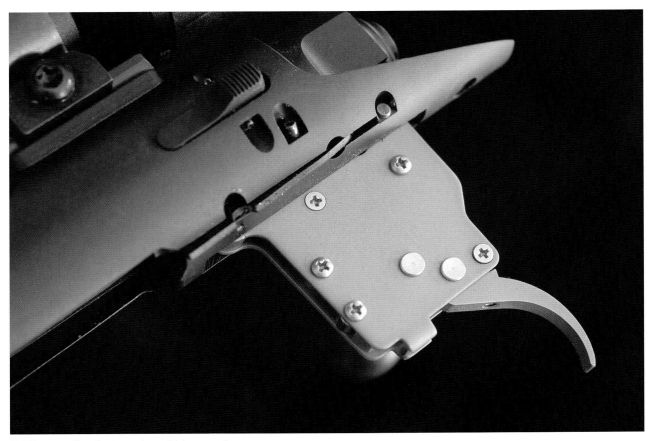

Ed Brown rifles feature Jewell triggers, for riflemen serious about long-range precision.

A washer-style recoil lug and headspace-setting barrel nut cost little and yield fine results.

hand. An inconsistent trigger is perhaps the worst kind. If your trigger can't be adjusted for a crisp, consistent let-off, you'd do well to replace it.

Pull weight gets a lot of attention, but a stiff pull can feel light if there's no perceptible creep. If the break is like that of a tiny icicle, and exactly the same each time, weight matters little—within reasonable limits.

What's reasonable? Three pounds has long been the standard for hunting rifle triggers, though, in recent years, many factory-installed triggers are adjusted heavier. I've found some unyielding to seven pounds. As the weight of the *trigger* approaches that of the *rifle*, the odds increase that you'll move the rifle before the trigger breaks. Contrary to common thought (driven no doubt by class-action attorneys), lightweight sporters are best equipped with sensitive triggers, again, within reasonable limits; accidental discharge is not a function of trigger pull. It results from careless handling.

While a clean, predictable, three-pound trigger should be light enough for precise shooting, I prefer a two-pound trigger on hunting rifles; some rifles in my rack wear triggers that break at less than a pound. My competitive career on the small-bore prone circuit has no doubt colored my views on triggers. Through a 20x scope, every ounce of trigger pull becomes a hop of the crosswire on a buckshot-size X-ring. Getting a trigger to break at a wish became a holy grail among those of us vying for top score. In those days, the best triggers came from Carl Kenyon. A rifle so equipped seemed to fire itself. A Kenyon trigger could be adjusted to break at a couple ounces. The Remington 40X was then available with a two-ounce trigger.

A trigger can be *too* light for accurate shooting. Muscle twitches and even blood pulsing through your trigger finger move it. I like to contact a trigger before a shot, not resting my finger, but feeling some slight resistance. Sensitive triggers that release at my heart's beat or a muscle tremor spook me. One rifle, owned by a colleague, had such a light trigger that, if he eased the muzzle from horizontal to vertical, the weight of the trigger alone would release the sear! Most remarkable: this trigger was so finely made that it performed consistently at that level! It was impractical for me.

Because hunting rifles may be used in a variety of climates, where temperatures can affect the dimensions and, thus, the contact of trigger parts, you must accept a somewhat stiffer pull in sporters. How *much* stiffer depends on the trigger design. Two pounds is not unreasonable, though few factory triggers will go this low.

An exception is Savage's AccuTrigger, about a decade old, as this is written. Savage CEO Ron Coburn put his engineers to work designing a trigger that would deliver a light, crisp pull, but that would not release accidentally even if the rifle were dashed against stone. The AccuTrigger employs a central blade that depresses very easily, releasing the trigger proper to move under light pressure. If the blade is not depressed, the rifle will not fire (you can't grab the edge of the trigger and discharge the rifle, much as it is with the central blade mechanism on a Glock pistol). Variations on this design have cropped up under other names. Savage is to be applauded for designing (and installing on even its more affordable rifles), a safe trigger that lets you fire with very light pressure.

Few hunting rifle triggers now are fully adjustable, though there's a trend toward giving shooters more control over pull weight. A fully adjustable trigger typically has three adjusting screws, one each for over-travel, sear engagement, and weight of pull.

Many safeties, like this on a Surgeon rifle, engage the trigger mechanism, not the bolt.

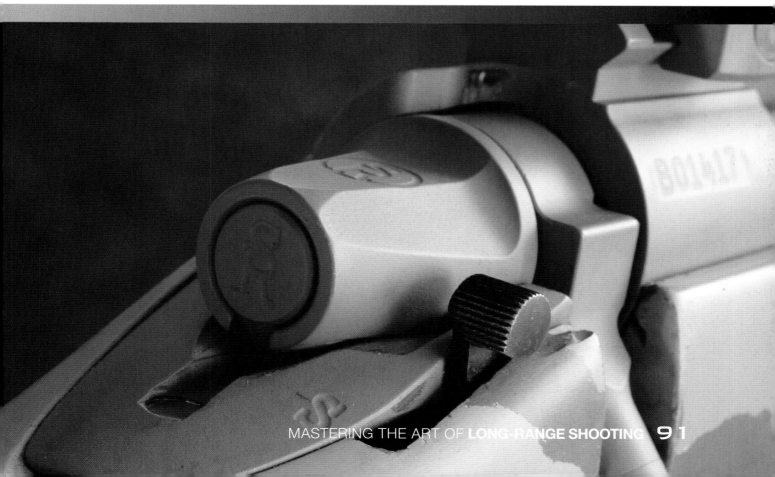

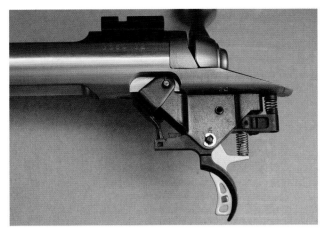

Savage's AccuTrigger safely gives you a light, crisp pull. Similar designs have followed.

Over-travel, the movement of the trigger after it releases the sear, is the least important of these three trigger features. Shooters who prefer the sensation of trigger break without movement reduce over-travel to a minimum, but a caution: You *can* adjust out *all* trigger movement, so the over-travel screw bears against the trigger before it's moved far enough to release the sear. You'll detect this right away, and can correct it by loosening the over-travel screw. Dust and lubricant, even shifts in temperature, can change over-travel settings, too, even if slightly. If you're within a gnat's eyelash of stopping the trigger short, you may find at the most inopportune time that your rifle won't fire! I like to give triggers enough over-travel to feel. A small amount of trigger movement past sear release won't affect the shot if your pull is smooth.

Sear engagement is much more important. A rough feel to the trigger pull or long "creep" before sear release should send you to the shop bench or a gunsmith. (Military two-stage triggers are designed with a measure of creep before the trigger engages the sear.) Sadly, sear engagement is impossible to adjust on many rifles without voiding warranties, disassembling the trigger, or getting out an Arkansas stone. Until recently, Remington M700 sear engagement has been screw-adjustable (though that and the other trigger screws on this rifle were shellacked in place to discourage tinker-

H-S Precision makes all its own parts, machining and finishing receivers in these steps.

ing). Sear engagement on Model 70 Winchester is not so readily altered; you must hone the sear lip on the trigger. Go too far, and the rifle will not hold cock—try to correct *that* error, and you change trigger geometry. The latest Remington and Winchester triggers do *not* let you adjust sear engagement.

Fortunately, pull weight is easier to adjust. The trigger's finger-piece bears against a return spring that counters the pressure of your finger. Reduce spring pressure and you reduce pull. The spring isn't all you feel, though. Pressure of the sear against its contacts adds resistance. Some triggers, when adjusted so the trigger spring is free, still give you plenty of pull. The problem with removing all spring tension is that, after the sear releases, the trigger will not return forward. You need *some* tension on the trigger spring. Timney's replacement triggers offer an affordable option to factory triggers you don't like.

Lock time is another component of field accuracy, especially when you're shooting offhand. The shorter the time between sear release and primer ignition, the better. You want the bullet on its way before your rifle can wobble off target! Set triggers, both single blade and double set, seldom give you the shortest lock time. A set trigger delivers a "de-fault" pull that will feel quite normal. The single set design affords a lighter pull, when you nudge the blade forward. Clicking into place, it brings weight to a few ounces. With a double set trigger, you can shoot normally using only the front trigger. Pulling the rear trigger doesn't discharge the rifle, but sets the front trigger to break at a lighter pressure.

In addition to structural refinements and a worthy trigger, super-accurate rifles commonly have non-standard parts. Most of these are commercially available and can be retrofitted to popular bolt rifles. David Tubb, for example, sells SpeedLock kits for Mauser, Remington, Ruger, Savage, Weatherby, and Winchester bolt rifles. It includes a lightweight alloy striker with a tip of heat-treated 4140 steel, plus a resilient spring made of "the same Chrome Silicone alloy used in the manufacture of valve springs for Indy car engines." Those springs endure a million high-temperature compression cycles in one afternoon, so Tubb reasons that a CS firing pin spring will serve a shooter for many years!

The term "speedlock" dates to the 1920s, possibly earlier. Military rifles of the day were altered by gunsmiths to reduce lock time. Strong springs, lightweight strikers, and short striker travel kept lock

This modern CNC center at Montana Rifle Company produces finished rifle actions.

McMillan's modular rifle, new in 2013, offers versatility and fine long-range accuracy.

The Czech firm CZ built this box-fed "tactical" rifle around one of its sturdy bolt-actions.

times to a minimum. In his Superior Shooting Systems catalog, David Tubb notes, "Flight time of most bullets through the barrel is 1.0 to 1.5 milliseconds, while the lock time of most conventional bolt-action rifles varies between 2.6 and 9.0 milliseconds … . A SpeedLock Systems firing pin cuts lock time approximately 31 percent. Combined with a SpeedLock CS Spring, lock time is reduced another eight percent."

That spring is important, insists Tubb.

"When a factory Remington 700 firing pin spring has lost half an inch of free length, it has lost over 25 percent of its original power. This amount of set can occur in less than one year, even if the rifle is not used. Our CS springs are rated for 500,000 compressions with a loss of no more than a quarter inch."

Because of its superior resiliency, Tubb's CS spring can be made lighter than ordinary springs, so it's faster. Because it is stronger for its weight, it can also be smaller in diameter, minimizing or eliminating contact (friction) with the bolt body.

Trigger pull weight gets a lot of attention, but, if the break is like that of a tiny icicle, and exactly the same each time, weight matters little—within reasonable limits.

Expert marksman David Tubb cycles the bolt on his own trim action, here barreled to 6 XC.

BENCHREST SHOOTING

Experiments to test and improve the inherent accuracy of rifles led, in the mid-nineteenth century, to a sport that has since grown. Benchrest games began as a non-competitive diversion for shooters, fueled partly by Joseph Whitworth's "fluid steel," a stronger barrel metal than was available before 1850. Ponderous rifles designed to deliver top accuracy and ballistic performance appeared before the Civil War. For years, their use was limited to the Northeast, where factories applied to firearms design what gun enthusiasts learned at the bench.

After the 1930s, as benchrest competition became popular, shooters demanded of their rifles and handloads ever better accuracy. Single-shot bolt-actions in various weight classes fired ammunition whose components had been individually weighed. Bullets went under the calipers. Cases endured several "uniforming" operations; the same hull might be used for many firings. The winning scores in benchrest competition were group measurements at 100 and 200 yards. Rifles shooting "in the ones" were drilling five-shot groups under .2-inch!

Then, competitors started stretching the range. During the Vietnam era, Mary Louise DeVito fired a 1,000-yard group measuring less than eight inches, a world record—and the competition was just heating up! In 2003, Kyle Brown put 10 shots into 4.23 inches at 1,000 yards. That coup, too, has since been eclipsed. The best five-shot 1,000-yard knot to date was fired at an IBS event by Tom Sarver, at Ohio's Thunder Valley range, July 7, 2007. Launching 240-grain MatchKings with 85 grains H1000 in his .300 Hulk (a shortened, necked-down .338 Lapua), Sarver kept his group to an incredible 1.403 inches! Equally amazing—he fired it in the Light Gun competition and put every bullet in the X-ring, for a record

The bag must support the fore-end in the same place each shot. Protect the bag from the swivel stud.

CHAPTER SEVEN
—STOCKS DON'T GROW ON TREES

SYNTHETIC STOCKS LACK THE BEAUTY OF WALNUT. BUT, AT LONG RANGE, BEAUTY IS AS BEAUTY DOES.

The problem with rifles that have lots of inertia is that they have lots of inertia. A super-accurate rifle can be a liability on a hunt. Years ago, chasing elk, I met a fellow toting a tactical rifle in .338 Lapua. It wore an enormous scope that brought the setup's total weight to more than 16 pounds. He conceded it wasn't ideal for hikes into deep canyons, "But it shoots accurately." Well, if rifle weight prevents you from going where your quarry lives, you'd best choose lighter artillery, even if it is marginally less accurate. Unlike prairie dogs, big game doesn't live in towns you can penetrate via a Suburban hauling a collapsible shooting bench.

Much of a rifle's weight lies in its steel parts, the action and barrel. But the stock contributes, too, and it's most responsible for a rifle's bulk. Benchrest shooters commonly touch only the trigger to fire, so that the rifle is unaffected by inconsistent pressures at grip, fore-end and comb. On a hunt, however, or if you're on the 300-meter line in Olympic competition, you must hold the rifle.

The stock plays an important role. If it fits you—*if the rifle wants to point where you're looking*—it will give you control that's all but unconscious. If the stock doesn't fit or doesn't help you transfer the rifle's weight to your frame, you must force the rifle onto the target and fight to hold it there.

Deficiencies in fit are magnified by distance. Slight rotation of fore-end or grip as you crush the trigger, slippage of the butt on your clavicle, pressure of your cheek against an ill-fitting comb—all can cause a miss. That's why stocks on rifles for competitive bull's-eye shooting have myriad adjustments. Most are impractical for hunting rifles, though a cheekrest adjustable for height and a buttplate you can move to change pull length make sense on rifles already heavy. Such furniture does add ounces to the buttstock.

One thing competitive shooters needn't fret about are changes in stock wood. Target shooting is typically done in good weather, and the firing is concentrated into a few hours. A wood stock won't likely "walk" during one match, though it might between matches in different environs.

Hunters must consider shifts in wood pressure with changes in temperature and, especially, moisture. As atmospheric moisture varies, wood fibers lose and absorb water. This process can be reduced by stock finishes that truly seal the pores. But, over time, moisture has a way of entering and leaving even well-finished stocks. The subsequent shrinking and swelling affect stock dimensions and the pressure of wood against metal; it is not an even pressure. Fore-ends also bend with changes in moisture, affecting barrel vibrations and accuracy. One solution: replace walnut with inert synthetic compounds that do not absorb moisture or otherwise move in response to their environment.

In 1959, Remington announced a four-pound .22 rifle with a Nylon stock. The next three decades put more than a million Nylon 66 autoloaders afield. Lever- and bolt-action versions appeared briefly, in

Synthetic stocks have kept a lid on the cost of utilitarian rifles—and put smiles on young faces!

the early '60s. At that time, these racy Remingtons sold for $25.75 to $49.95.

Synthetic stocks were clearly in the cards for centerfire rifles. Yet the shift from walnut has come slowly. Early on, shooters dismissed "plastic" as cheap. Well, it was—inexpensive, that is. That's why manufacturers left it on their to-do lists. In 1964, you could still get a Fajen semi-finished walnut stock for $6.45! Double-A fancy figure ran the tab to $30. Meanwhile, the new M-16 infantry rifle was derided as a "Mattel" by soldiers enamored of the Garand and M-14. But anyone supplying or installing stocks then had to know prices would vault. "You can't manufacture walnut," shrugged a pal who built custom hunting rifles. "You gotta wait for it to grow." Demand would soon outstrip supply.

Top-grade walnut *blanks* have now hit the $1,000 mark. Cheaper hardwoods, notably beech, have shown up as surrogates. On commercial sporting rifles, walnut routinely shows as much figure as a wagon tongue. Still, the plainest wood has character a chemical product can't match. And, because no two blanks are the same in color or figure, a wood stock makes a rifle unique. Wood is organic. It *complements* polished steel. Wood can be finished to deliver an almost sentient glow, and refinished wood can give a battered rifle new life. I've dug deep to buy rifles with time-blackened wood, just to steam out the scars, touch up flat diamonds, and release the sunny streaks and swirls hidden by age, oil, and stains.

I'll concede there's a place for stocks that come from moulds. Weeks before this writing, I was stumbling about over snow-sheathed rock, above timber that might have sheltered me from the sleet. I'd fallen twice in creeks and so often on slides I'd lost count. My Dakota 97 rifle, of stainless steel and with a costly synthetic stock, actually seemed to revel in the adventure, bouncing off various hard surfaces much more gracefully than did I.

After descending the mountain in the dark and tending my many bruises, I found this .30-06 had none. There was no checkering to chip. The paint, whatever it was, seemed unfazed. One of my spills had jarred the scope's reticle eight minutes off zero— but the rifle looked like new, and it had downed a fine billy at 400 yards.

These days, you'll find more synthetic rifle stocks than walnut. Some (not all) come cheaper

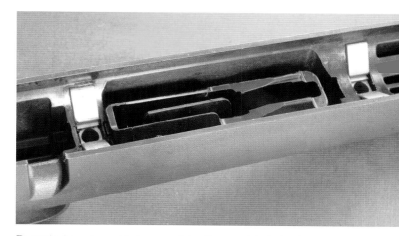

Ruger's American rifle has an injection-molded stock, ingenious alloy bedding blocks.

than walnut. Some (not all) weigh less. Almost all endure knocks better than wood. Synthetic materials don't absorb moisture like wood, so they don't "walk" or shift pressure at bedding surfaces when wet. They *do*, however, move with changes in temperature, which can affect point of impact at distance.

These days, "plastic" isn't the right word to describe synthetic stocks, though it applies to some. Zytel has gone the way of the Stegosaurus. So, too, Tenite, the material commonly used to imitate ebony in the fore-end tips of my youth. Perhaps those materials hide under other monikers now. Fiberglass also has a diminished role in marketing rifle stocks, though it still appears in many upscale models. Fiberglass weighs more than its popular successors. "Kevlar" is a trade name, yet common in the stock trade. Perhaps oddly, it seems to have faded in advertising. Most stocks now are of injection-molded polymers (plastics, with the mould seam typically evident on the comb and belly), or comprise "hand-laid" shells of fiberglass and/or carbon fiber material (lightest in weight and most expensive) around a foam core.

If austerity appeals to you, you'll want an injection-molded stock. Fred Choate knows as much as anyone about this type. Over the last four decades, the company founded by his father, Garth Choate, has produced many thousands of injected-molded stocks. Still headquartered in Bald Knob, Arkansas, Choate builds aftermarket stocks for commercial sporting rifles by Harrington & Richardson, Heckler & Koch, Marlin, Mossberg, Remington, Savage, and

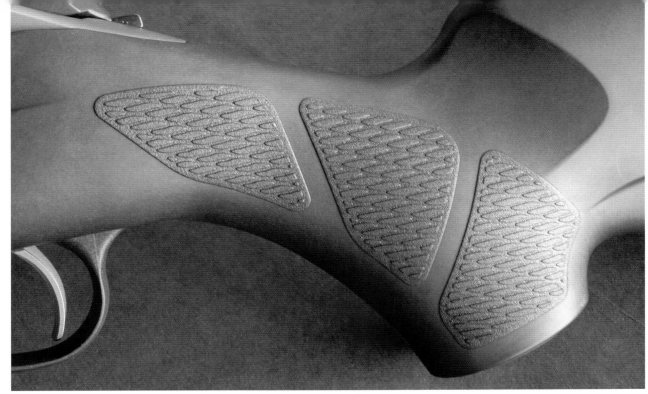

Besides checkering, synthetic stocks can offer other gripping surfaces. Here, a Tikka T3.

Thompson/Center. Fred says the firm has moulds for "a couple of hundred different stock configurations." Fashioned of tool steel, these moulds are costly; each can weigh as much as a piano. Fortunately, some moulds work for more than one rifle, just by changing cores. Still, Choate inventories more than 150 moulds. High volume justifies that huge investment. Modest per-unit price to shooters and manufacturers fuels high volume. So does the quality of Choate products. About 70 percent of the company's output is OEM (original equipment manufacture) for factories. The rest go to shooters and gunsmiths installing them as replacements.

Each Choate stock begins as a tub of extruded pellets. "It looks like rabbit food," says Fred. "The buckshot-size pellets are 20-percent fiberglass, 80-percent polypropylene. We add dye for color. It's easy to make eye-catching stocks." Then, reading my mind, he chuckles, "Yep. Boring, lifeless and redundant, black still sells best. By far."

The pellets enter the mould through a gate under the rear of the fore-end cavity. Heat turns them to goop the consistency of honey. Clamped to seal 500 tons of pressure, the airtight mould cooks its polymer quickly and at very high temperature. A 60-degree water bath cools it. Removed from the mould, the stock goes to a CNC machine, which cuts the groove for the bolt handle.

"We can do that on either side," says Fred. "Lefties are no problem for us. Building left-hand rifle *actions* is a bigger commitment!"

Butt-pads, swivel studs, and grip caps come next. (Recoil pads are injection-molded, too.) Any checkering is already molded in. So, too, bedding blocks.

"We sold stocks to Savage as early as 1989," Fred recalls. "Varmint rifles were the first with a bedding block and a rail. Now we run two shifts to make bedding components."

Fred adds that Choate also has its own investment casting operation, where it produces bolt handles.

One noteworthy development in molded rifle stocks came at Savage, in 2009, six years after the company unveiled its revolutionary AccuTrigger.

"We found a way to economically incorporate an alloy rail/bedding block in the molding process," says CEO Ron Coburn, who has shepherded the firm since 1987. This metal spine, of 6061-T6 aluminum, extends through the magazine web, so it accepts the rear guard screw, too. A third screw, forward of the front guard screw, engages a small alloy wedge, which, as it is tightened, crams the washer-style recoil lug against its abutment in the bedding block. In addition, the sides of the block, around the magazine well, are designed to spring .010-inch before the receiver bottoms out, "so the stock applies constant pressure to the receiver," explains Chris Bezzina,

Savage's Director of Engineering. My tests with Savage bolt rifles equipped with AccuStock show it improves accuracy.

Another way to make synthetic stocks is to hand-lay composite shell materials in an open mould. Foam fills the core. These stocks weigh less than injection-molded stocks. They also cost more, because the materials do. Moulds for hand-laid synthetic stocks, however, are less expensive, because they needn't bottle extreme pressures. But there's more work to a hand-laid stock after the mould swings open.

Not long ago, I visited H-S Precision, a South Dakota firm known for both its hand-laid synthetic stocks and for super-accurate hunting rifles. H-S manufactures every major component of its rifles—the action and barrel as well as the stock—in-house. Stock shells combine carbon fiber, fiberglass, and Kevlar in a resin. Tom Houghton, who runs the business started decades ago by his father, explained that the core is of "reaction injection-molded foam." He scooped a gob of black mud into a tall paper cup. While we watched, the substance grew fast, climbing out of the cup to form a big bulb the consistency of rubber. It looked like a licorice ice cream cone.

"The heat of reaction forces this pudding into all stock crevices," Tom told me. "It forms a tough core that's firm, but also resilient. To add even more strength, we install a full-length bedding block in each stock. Unlike most rails, ours run back into the grip! We think the extra rigidity makes our rifles more accurate."

Fly-wing tolerances distinguish the best custom walnut stocks. But H-S fits its synthetic stocks to barrel and receiver as if to make the bond airtight! H-S stocks sold as OEM and aftermarket components get the same attention to detail, with dimensions for snug drop-in fit and "no zero shift, in and out." H-S makes stocks for heavy-barreled varmint and tactical rifles, as well as for sporters. A .223 in my rack has an H-S prone-style stock with an adjustable cheekrest. The company's folding stock (the butt swings against the receiver, for easy stowage), is clever indeed. H-S offers 20 standard colors and half again as many for custom orders. Its aftermarket stocks are carried by Brownells, Cabela's, and Midway USA.

Bell & Carlson, long a prominent name in synthetic stocks, hand-lays its Medalist and Carbelite models. A two-part urethane skin covers a shell of fiberglass, carbon fiber, and Kevlar. The urethane foam core includes a reinforcement of chopped fiberglass strands. The Medalist boasts an integral bedding block CNC-machined from 6061-T6 aluminum. Like H-S, Bell & Carlson fashions its stocks for drop-in fit. At nearly two pounds, a typical Bell &

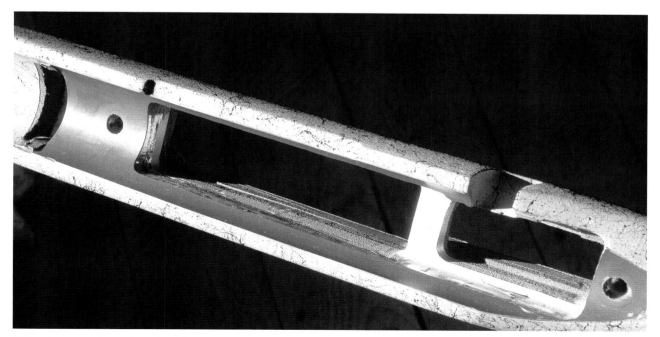

A clean job of glass bedding in this hand-laid H-S Precision stock promises accurate shots!

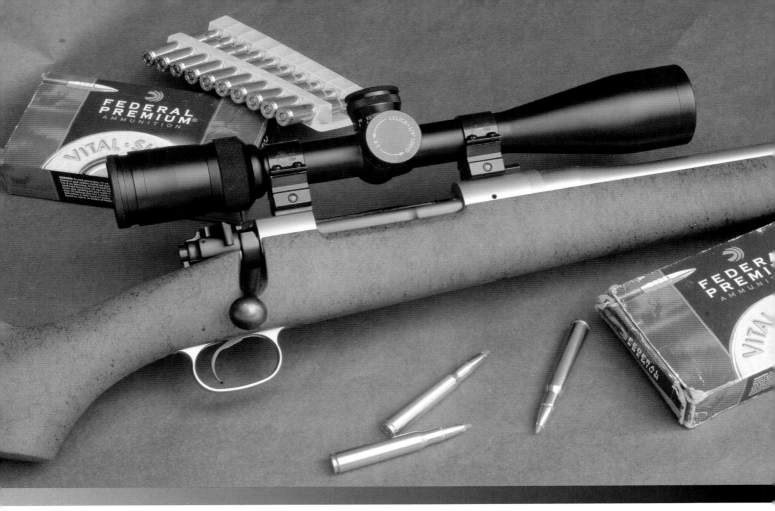

Dakota's 97 Outfitter wears a high-end, hand-laid stock precisely fitted to the metal.

Carlson sporter stock weighs more than some hand-laid models. But the company notes that its stocks are "solid throughout" and stronger. Steel swivel stud cores are molded in (the alloy spine in Medalists holds the forward swivel). Among eight textured stock finishes, seven have black webbing on a colored base. Eleven camouflage finishes and B&C's willingness to grow its mould inventory bring steady OEM business.

The Montana Rifle Company has, at this writing, a new facility and a fresh line of hunting rifles. A clone of the early Winchester Model 70, each investment-cast Montana 1999 action is wedded to a barrel made by Montana Rifleman, next door. Brian Sipe started that operation and still runs the barrel shop; son Jeff markets completed rifles.

"We're pleased to have Bell & Carlson stocks on our new XWR rifles," he beamed, during my last visit. "They have the alloy rail. They're trim and nicely contoured." He handed me a .280, which promptly flew to my shoulder. The first B&C stocks, decades ago, wore oversize butt-pads that reduced felt recoil

at some cosmetic cost. The company's latest stocks are sleeker, but mitigate kick as effectively. The .280 had a lean, hungry profile. "We glass-bed each action," said Jeff.

Now, 17 rifle makers install B&C stocks, including not only Montana and its ilk—Cooper, Nosler and Kimber—but also Browning, Remington, and Winchester. GreyBull Precision, which builds accurate long-range rifles, relies on Bell & Carlson stocks. I've used them with great success in the field and shooting at gongs as far as a mile off. The stability of B&C's material, with a V-block machined by GreyBull, give the 2½-pound varmint-style GreyBull stock an edge on distant steel. Still, it's slim enough for big-game hunting. I have one on a Magnum Research 6.5 Creedmoor with a carbon-fiber barrel. The outfit looks like it weighs 10 pounds, but actually scales eight. Don Ward, who manages the GreyBull shop, told me, "Wade Dunn, at B&C, kindly piggy-backed our stock on a Remington 700 mould, to reduce cost." GreyBull stocks have two swivel stud holes in front, two in back, plus a spot for a monopod to level the rifle from the rear.

Perhaps best known of all the firms producing synthetic stocks is McMillan, in business since 1986. The McMillans once produced fine rifle barrels, too. My Remington 37 wears one; it brought me a couple prone championships. But changing interests within the family have narrowed the focus of this Arizona manufacturer. Kelly McMillan stated it simply, saying, "We produce rifle stocks and high-performance sporting rifles on our own actions." No embellishment there. But McMillan sets a high bar in the important areas of design, materials, tolerances, and finish. McMillan hunting rifles show exceptional workmanship, and McMillan stocks are the go-to standard for gun builders like Preston Pritchett, whose Surgeon rifles drill tiny groups far away. McMillan built the first M40 sniper stocks for the U.S. Marines, in 1975.

Dick Davis has an insider's knowledge of McMillan stocks and a shooter's enthusiasm for them. In 2003, he fired a world record benchrest score, with a 146/150 aggregate at 1,000 yards. His Nesika Bay rifle wore a 1:12 Schneider barrel chambered in 7.82 Patriot, a short-action Lazzeroni cartridge. Three of his 15 Berger VLD bullets landed in the three-inch X-ring. Almost all the rest punched the seven-inch 10.

"We use hand-laid fiberglass in our stocks," says Dick. "Eight-ounce S-weave cloth with a resin binder. We prefer graphite (carbon fiber) to Kevlar. While Kevlar is strong, and useful when it's loose and flexible—as in tires and body armor—it's not so good in stocks. Graphite is a third stiffer."

McMillan's lightweight Edge stock is all graphite, the five-ounce material as stout as eight-ounce fiberglass. It also costs eight times as much! Dick doesn't advise it for trim rifles with harsh recoil. "Graphite works best on mountain rifles."

A lightweight hand-laid stock suits this Remington 700ti (titanium), a very accurate '06!

Both walnut and synthetic stocks hold the receiver better if glass-bedded at the recoil lug.

During McMillan's stock manufacture, an air bladder with up to 80 pounds of pressure establishes the cavity. The bladder is pulled after the shell sets.

"Fill matters as much as the shell," says Dick. "We tailor fill to the application and often use different fill in different places. The buttstock and fore-end get lighter, more flexible material than the area near the action, where you need strength. We put denser fill in sniper-style stocks, where weight matters less, to secure the furniture."

Dick says, "You won't find an alloy rail or bedding blocks in McMillan stocks, because the fiberglass is strong and hard enough to ensure a stable platform. It doesn't need reinforcement, not even to stand the bump of the .338 Lapua or .50 BMG." Besides husky material, McMillan claims super-tight tolerances. CNC mills with carbide cutters hold 'em to within .001-inch over 30 inches! Still, Dick insists, "To get skin-tight fit, you *must* glass-bed."

Metal pillars have appeared on rifles for decades, to ensure against malfunctions caused by wood compression with repeated cinching of the guard screws. "We don't install pillars in our fiberglass stocks, because fiberglass doesn't compress easily," says Dick. McMillan's lightweight Edge stock *does* include pillars "because the fill is lighter." It's important that, when pillars are used, the screws don't touch them. During recoil, the stock around the action well flexes, shortening the distance between guard screws. On McMillan rifles, screws .248 in diameter slide into pillars with an I.D. of .311—ample clearance.

No maker of synthetic stocks has more color and finish options than McMillan. The firm offers 27 hues in 300,000 combinations for its gel-coat finishes. You can specify the colors and percentages

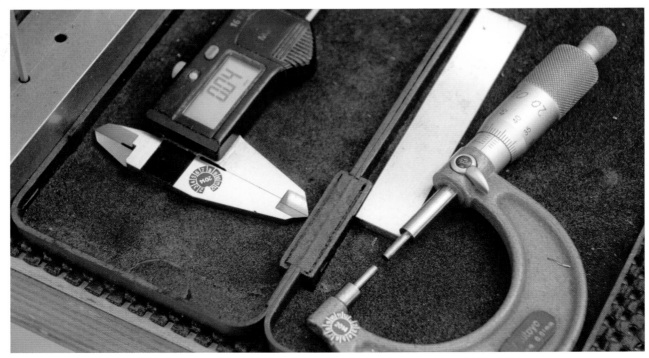

Internal bedding blocks make precise measurements, as important in stocks as they are in actions.

Wayne shot this gemsbok with a synthetic-stocked Blaser R93. Blaser offers wood, too.

of each. A gel-coat stock gets its colors and patterns before the fiberglass cloth reaches the mould. Both are part of the material; they're not painted on. McMillan has six solid colors for shooters who prefer paint.

McMillan supplies stocks for an astonishingly long list of manufacturers. They fit more than 200 types of rifles, foreign and domestic. The most popular metal? The 700 Remington. But McMillan caters to a broad clientele, including riflemen with actions by Hart and Hall, Stolle and Stiller. He and Kelly McMillan emphasize that almost all their stocks are made to order.

"For one-hole groups, you can't have a stock that squirms," Dick declares. "McMillan stocks are heavier than some. But they're very stable."

Just a few years ago, synthetic stocks went mainly to sportsmen. Before that, benchrest shooters drove the business. Now the market favors so-called tactical or sniper rifles—think varmint rifles with .30- and .33-caliber bores. Through this evolution, the number of synthetic-stocked big-game rifles has climbed steadily. Ditto aftermarket stocks for hunting rifles. From inexpensive injection-molded to the best hand-laid models, these surrogates are tough, if not pretty. They shed water better than wood. Recoil won't split them. They're the best choice, hands down, for rifles designed for the long shot. You might even find a few synthetic stocks attractive—that is, if you've never seen figured walnut.

CHAPTER EIGHT
—OPTICS WITH REACH

YOU CAN HIT ONLY AS WELL AS YOU CAN SEE. BUT MAGNIFICATION IS NO PANACEA. HERE'S WHAT'S TO KNOW.

A spotting scope *moves* things. It pulls things tiny with distance right into your hand. But the "Big Eye" is cumbersome too. On a hunt, you must weigh the benefits of detailed looks at distance against the various costs of making them.

"Good grief! Drop tines!" My pal had pushed me aside for a peek. "What a deer!"

It was indeed. As it made its way across slope, through thin aspens, it didn't get smaller. We eased down our side of the canyon to gain yards. The buck slipped onto a trail angling across our front. In the shadow cast by a Douglas fir, I set up the tripod again.

"Two bucks now." Both were extraordinary animals. We watched them slide, ghost-like, toward the canyon's head. Then a third animal emerged. By the time they'd come even with us, four more bucks had joined the trio. At 320, maybe 350 yards, Jim had the shot. But there was no place to steady the Sako.

Before optics, shooters used tang sights with small apertures to boost sight radius, precision.

The muzzle bobbed wildly. I hesitated. Two of these deer were record-book bucks. At last I said, "Best not shoot." Jim was already lowering the rifle. No matter the prize, a risky shot is a risky shot. That first deer, with its heavy beams and myriad points, is still the finest I've ever seen in the wild. Without the Big Eye, we'd not have seen the antlers so well—or perhaps not have spotted the buck in the first place.

Spotting scopes date way back. In 1608, Dutch spectacle maker Hans Lippershay lined up a pair of lenses on a distant weathercock. A huge chicken appeared, as if by magic! A year later, Galileo Galilei built his first telescope. With it and later versions, he discovered four of the moons orbiting Jupiter and distinguished individual stars in the Milky Way

Galileo's first telescopes had a convex objective lens and a concave ocular lens, so the focal point of the front lens lay behind the rear lens. Johannes Kepler changed Galileo's design to put the image inside the tube. The image was upside down there, but, since these men were viewing stars, upside down

didn't matter! Later, engineers would devise an erector system to right the image. Early 'scopes delivered a fuzzy image, a result of "spherical aberration," or the failure of light rays to meet at a common point along the lens axis. With no way to refine lens curvature, makers of early telescopes just increased focal length. Some versions had lenses *several hundred feet* apart! Tubes were both impractical and unnecessary. Compound lenses would eventually correct spherical and chromatic (color) aberrations.

By the time target shooters used spotting scopes to see bullet holes at 600 yards, and hunters took them afield to find bighorn rams, magnification had become an industry. Bull's-eyes and animals at very long range popped, sharp-edged and super-sized, from a tube no bigger than a rolled-up newspaper. Four hundred years of progress in optics have put close images in a rucksack, and the last 50 years have delivered refinements early astronomers could not have imagined. Still, the Big Eye's function is the same as it was in the seventeenth century: to help us see better.

In spotting scopes, you'll sacrifice brightness and resolution for light weight and a slim profile.

Magnification is one assist. But bigger images aren't sufficient if image quality suffers as a result of the enlargement, or if the image gets dim. In fact, magnifying a recognizable object too much can make it unrecognizable! And the ability of lenses to transmit usable light diminishes as you increase power.

The first requisite of a magnifying optic is that it resolve images clearly. Resolution is a measure of the level of detail you see through a scope. High-resolution optics can distinguish fine detail, separating small objects that, to the naked eye, appear as one at distance. Comparing the resolution in scopes the old way is like taking an eye test at the optometrist's office. Indeed, a 1951 Air Force resolution chart works the same as the optometrist's. Sets of three horizontal black bars separated by white spaces of equal width and paired with three vertical black bars are numbered by size. Eight groups of six pairs of bars, each of diminishing size, zero through seven and one through six, are keyed to a table

showing levels of resolution in seconds of angle. A minute of angle (an inch at 100 yards), is about the limit of resolution for unaided human eyes. A second of angle is a sixtieth of a minute of angle.

Given good lenses, boosting magnification improves resolution. So does increasing lens diameter. At high power, a small lens won't deliver a picture clear or bright enough for you to distinguish what big glass would make plain. A man named Rayleigh came up with a constant that, divided by objective lens diameter in millimeters, yields maximum resolution in seconds of angle. Here's how it works.

Say your spotting scope has a front lens diameter of 60mm. Dividing 60 into the constant, 114.3, yields a resolution of 1.9 seconds of arc. That figure determines the useful magnification limit of your eyepiece. As your eye can resolve 60 seconds, you divide that by 1.9 and get 31. So, for that scope, magnification of 31x is the usable top end. More power will make the picture bigger, but not clearer; you won't see any more detail. If you bought a bigger scope—say, one with an 80mm objective—you'd hike the power limit to about 43x (114.3/60 = 1.4; 60/1.4 = 43).

All this to say that you're wise to pick an eyepiece of reasonable power. A 20-60x eyepiece may seem wonderful, but the top third of that range is practicably unusable! Even if Rayleigh was off his rocker, 40x is a practical maximum afield, where wind and mirage make still images shimmy, and where you're often short of light.

High magnification means dim images at dawn and dusk. Light transmission is commonly expressed as the diameter of a scope's exit pupil—that pencil of light making its way to your eye from the ocular lens. Calculate EP by dividing objective diameter by magnification. For example, our 60mm scope with 20x eyepiece offers an exit pupil 3mm in diameter. The bigger the lens, the bigger the exit pupil, if power stays constant. Increase magnification, and the exit pupil shrinks. A bigger exit pupil brings more light to your eye, which can dilate to 7mm in total darkness. As you age, your pupil becomes less flexible, and 6mm may become a more practical maximum. In dim hunting light, 5mm dilation is more likely.

In bright light, your eye doesn't dilate, it constricts. A tiny exit pupil gives you as broad a shaft of light as your eye can use under brilliant sun. At dusk, a generous objective lens helps you. But the biggest spotting scope practical for field use, one with an 80mm lens, delivers a 5mm exit pupil only at 16x!

Lens quality and coatings matter a great deal, and the best are expensive. The price spectrum for spotting scopes reflects real differences in scope and image quality. Still, optics that offer fine resolution and efficient light transmission shouldn't require a second mortgage. You'll get them now, even with mid-priced scopes, provided you insist on fully multi-coated lenses. That means all air-to-glass surfaces are coated with compounds that reduce light loss due to reflection and refraction. (Uncoated

Viewd from outside, anti-refelctive, anti-refractive coatings have color. You don't see that color when aiming—only a brighter image!

A high-quality bino is more useful than a big, powerful bino; 8x is easier to steady than 10x.

lenses shed up to four percent of incident light at each surface.) You might also consider ED (extra-low dispersion) or APO (apochromatic) or fluorite lenses. They're commonly available on top-quality scopes.

While, in my view, most big rifle scope objectives deliver fewer benefits than liabilities, you'll get real value from added lens surface up front in a spotting scope. I prefer 80mm lenses, but 65mm scopes by the likes of Swarovski, Leica, Zeiss, and Nikon are great alternatives, where weight matters.

Another useful feature on spotting scopes is variable power. For hunters, 15-45x is ideal. Keep it at the low end to quickly find an animal you've spotted with your naked eye or binocular. Once on target, you'll appreciate a choice of magnification to match distance and wind and light conditions. I've used a fixed 25x Bushnell while guiding hunters. It also served me well on the smallbore circuit, showing .22 bullet holes in targets 100 yards off without undue distortion in mirage or disturbing movement in wind. For hunting, Leupold's 12x-40x adds versatility. A

David Tubb spots with a powerful binocular. It's actually easier on the eyes than a spotting scope.

15-45x is more useful than any 20-60x afield. Higher power makes sense only at long-range paper, from a very steady support, and then only occasionally.

Spotting scopes for hunting should have a straight eyepiece. Angled eyepieces excel on the rifle range, because you can set up the scope close to your eye and peek at bullet holes without getting out of position. In the field, however, angled oculars slow you down when you're trying to find a distant animal. It's easier to align a straight tube. One useful device on a spotting scope is a sight—a blade, or a little tube on the top or side of the scope—so you can align the optic quickly with your naked eye.

Some scopes have two focus adjustments with different "gearing." One lets you quickly change focus across great distances. The other is "fine," so you can easily put an object in sharp focus without the frustrating forward-and-back dialing you might find necessary with ordinary adjustments, especially when your fingers are cold and either you or the scope aren't steady. A good idea!

You'll need a tripod. Like front glass, the bigger, the better, though, for hunting, cost and weight eliminate studio-quality camera or video tripods. Because

This 18-45x65 is a fine spotting scope for hunting and properly fitted with a straight eyepiece.

you might also use a tripod to advantage under your cameras, get a versatile model, with rubber feed so you can put it on surfaces that might be damaged by spikes. Make sure a multi-purpose tripod is tall enough for use without stem extension when you're shooting offhand. I like lever-lock adjustments for

More convenient than the traditional front sleeve is an AO dial on the scope's turret.

"Gain" is slope on a scope base (here a Surgeon), to extend range without more dial clicks.

their speed. Bogen/Manfrotto squeeze-grip heads help bring the scope onto an object quickly and instantly lock it there. Among field-worthy tripods, I'm sweet on those by BOGpod. Want a tripod for the bench? Get one developed for Benchrest competition. Steady, in both rifle rests and spotting scope tripods, is worth its price.

Because the laws of physics apply to rifle scopes as they do to spotting scopes, you should have little trouble picking a sight for long shooting. But remember that a rifle scope is for aiming, not viewing, and that its weight and bulk become one with the rifle's. It must also endure recoil. Many shooters choose scopes that are unnecessarily powerful.

Too much magnification handicaps you in several ways. It shrinks the field of view, so you won't find the target as quickly as with less. On a hunt, you may not see the huge buck in the shadows to the side of the most obvious animal. High power reduces exit pupil diameter, so, in dim light, the target image won't be as bright. The magnification that makes that target bigger also bumps up the amplitude of reticle movements due to muscle tremors and heartbeat. Reticle quivers you might not even notice at 2½x become violent dips and hops at 10x. At 20x, you'll see so much chaos in the tighter field, the target may bounce in and out of view as you try to tame that reticle. A scope helps you when it shows movement you can control. It's a liability as

The powerful Nightforce scope on this T/C rifle is optically superb, but also bulky, heavy.

Too much magnification can be a liability. For big game, 8x may be all you need—ever!

it amplifies movement you can't. Instead of applying gradual pressure to the trigger, you wear yourself out fighting the jitterbug image in your sight. As eyes and muscles tire, an accurate shot becomes impossible.

Magnification also shows you mirage, a good thing on days when mirage is light and the target is in reasonable range. But, on hot days, when you're aiming over great distance, the target may appear as a dim, shapeless object stuck below the surface of a raging river.

In general, the least magnification that gives you a clear target image is the best magnification. I use 4x rifle scopes for most big-game hunting and think it adequate to 300 yards. A 6x works fine for me at 400. Of course, you'll want more magnification for small animals like prairie dogs. Deliberate shooting at paper bull's-eyes and steel gongs brings out powerful glass. I've used 16x, even 20x, scopes to advantage in good light, when there's time for a solid position and precision trumps all else. In smallbore matches, a 20x Redfield served me well. I needed

that much power to hold on a .22 bullet hole at 50 meters, or shade to the bottom-right quadrant of an X-ring the size of a bottle cap at 100. I've used 25x to good effect on bull's-eyes, but am inclined to think 20x would have served, too. Higher power is very hard to use.

These days, variable scopes offer wide four-, five-, and now six-times power ranges; that is, the highest magnification is four, five, or six times that of the lowest. So, instead of the 3-9x that once awed sportsmen with its versatility, you can get a 3-12x, a 3-15x, or a 3-18x. Or bump up to 4x on the bottom to get 20x or 24x on the top. Such scopes feature 30mm tubes. These may or may not have a bigger erector assembly (the tube with lenses and magnification cams held inside the main tube). Those with erector assemblies of standard size for one-inch scopes give you more windage and elevation adjustment. That's an advantage at long range, though a scope performs best with its optical axis close to its mechanical axis.

Incidentally, you'll do well to get a scope with resettable dials, so you can leave them at "0" and easily track any changes you make to compensate for drop at long range. High target knobs, convenient at the range, are vulnerable to damage on a hunting rifle and a nuisance in cases and scabbards. Mid-height knobs make sense, if you expect to use them a lot and aren't horse-bound afield.

Keep objective lens diameter modest. The 42mm is big enough unless you insist on very high power. Remember that, with a variable scope, big glass up front enhances brightness only at high magnification. At 7x, a 42mm lens delivers all the light your eye can use in the dimmest conditions. In bright light, your eye won't be dilated. The 3mm exit pupil of a 14x scope with a 42mm objective is enough.

Optical sights (here a Kahles) are complex, require close manufacturing tolerances.

"Four times" magnification on this 4-16x Meopta yields a wide power range, useful for away targeting.

Wayne's 4x rifle scope on this Ruger No. 1 rifle complements an 8x binocular. These optics are used differently!

The locking cap on this NightForce scope lets you reset zero—and adjust for another load.

Schmidt & Bender's elevation dial shows where the reticle is in relation to optical center.

A top hunting rig: here, a Schmidt & Bender Summit scope on a Weatherby Vanguard Back Country rifle in .30-06.

For long shooting, you'll want an adjustable objective, so you can focus the target and eliminate parallax at the target distance. Parallax appears as the apparent movement of the reticle when you move your eye off the scope's optical axis. Every scope is set for zero parallax at a certain distance, typically 100 or 150 yards in sights designed for centerfire rifles. At that range, you can move your head up and down or sideways behind the scope, and the reticle will stay on target. At other distances, you may see the reticle off-center when it really isn't, that is, it wouldn't be if your eye was directly behind the scope. Adjustable objectives let you zero out parallax. Traditional AO scopes have a sleeve on the objective bell. A knob on the left-hand side of the turret is more contemporary and easier to use.

As for reticles, simple is good. For long shooting, a "range ladder" on the lower stem of a standard crosswire or a plex can provide useful aiming points. You'll want them beyond 400 yards or so. While a fine crosswire yields precise aim, it can cost you a shot if it's not easy to see in dim light. Avoid jungles of tics and hashmarks and multiple lines that clutter your field. They slow your aim. Picking the wrong intersection has caused many a miss—and the more marks

you see, the more likely that mistake! The mil-dot is as complex a reticle as I like. Shooters who learn to use it can do well at distance.

While most reticles in scopes marketed Stateside have second- or rear-plane reticles, the standard in Europe has been first- or front-plane reticles. Both have advantages and drawbacks. A rear-plane reticle stays the same apparent size (crosswire thickness) throughout the power range of a variable scope. This is good, because most hunters don't want the reticle to grow in thickness as they boost power for fine aim at distance, nor do they want one that gets thin and hard to see when they dial down for close shots in timber. On the other hand, a first-plane reticle stays the same size *in relation to the target* as you change magnification, so you can use it as a rangefinding device at any power without recalculating.

Before committing to a scope, consider its weight and dimensions. Besides adding to your burden afield, heavy scopes can slip in their rings under stiff recoil. A long eyepiece can force placement of the scope too close to your eye. Scopes with little "free tube" between bell and eyepiece limit your options for ring location.

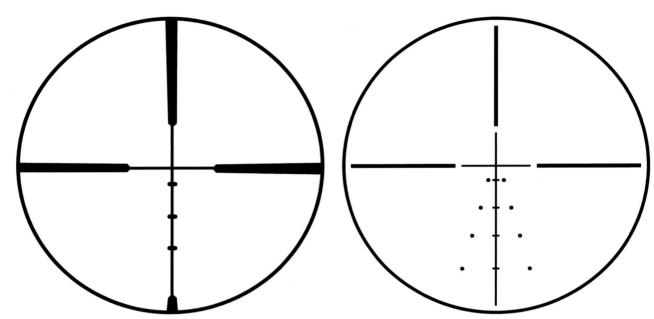

Burris' Ballistic Plex, with intelligently placed tics, is a useful ranging reticle for hunting.

This "ballistic" reticle is as complex as Wayne accepts, with tics for drift as well as drop.

The Burris Eliminator, a laser rangefinding scope, has a lighted aiming point that corrects for drop at long range.

WHAT'S A MIL?

The mil-dot reticle gets a lot of attention these days. "Mil" has nothing to do with "military." It's an abbreviation for "milliradian," a sliver of a circle. An angular measurement, a mil spans 3.6 inches at 100 yards, or three feet at l,000 yards. In a reticle, a mil is the space between ¾-minute dots strung vertically and horizontally along a crosswire. With a mil-dot, you have both a rangefinder and a way to compensate for drop and drift.

To use this reticle as a rangefinder, divide target height in mils at 100 yards by the number of spaces subtending it. The result is range in hundreds of yards. For example, a buck three feet at the back (10 mils at 100 yards) appears in your scope to stand two dots high. Divide two into 10 and you come up with five: the deer is 500 yards away. You can also divide target size in yards (in this case, one) by the number of mils subtended (two) and multiply by 1,000 to get the range in yards.

A mil-dot reticle works only at one magnification. In variable scopes, that's usually the top number, though some very high-power variables identify another setting. For short shots with a mil-dot reticle, you just ignore the dots and aim as with a crosswire.

Mil Dot Master is a slide rule-like device (an analog calculator) that helps you employ mil-dots more effectively. Get it (and instructions) from Mildot Enterprises, POB 1535, Los Lunas NM 87031.

A long-range shooter pauses to consult his Mil Dot Master. It helps you aim precisely!

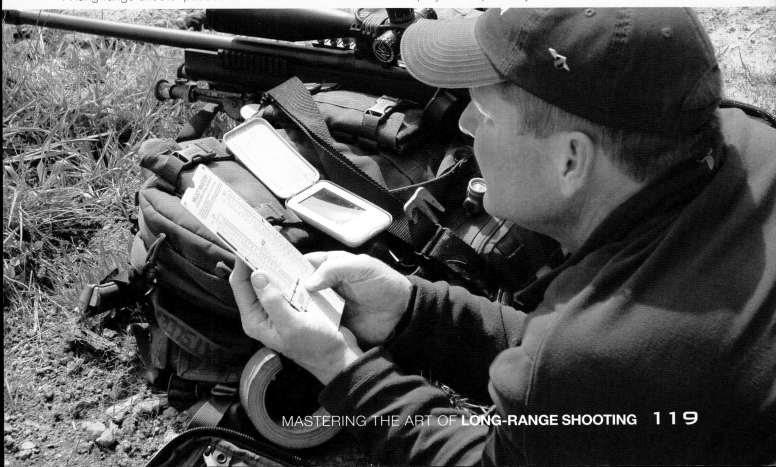

POWER MATTERS LESS THAN EFFICIENT FLIGHT AT DISTANCE. THESE LOADS LOOK GOOD GOING LONG.

THE MILD ONES

The Remington 700 was borrowed, so I checked zero on the GreyBull scope dial. It had been cut for the handloads in my ammo box, and, at a setting of "2," my bullets drilled center at 200 yards. I trotted the paper out to 300, dialed to "3," and shot Xs again. In the dead-still air, those 55-grain .22-250 bullets drifted not at all. The mild recoil made accurate prone shooting easy.

"Let's try steel rodents." John Burns dragged a couple of them from the pickup. They looked like giant prairie dogs. "Don't let the size fool you," said John. "We'll plant them long."

Long for my .22-250 and his .243 was, by mutual agreement, 500 yards. We took alternate shots, he off a bipod, me with my Latigo sling. I managed to best him with five consecutive hits to his four. One of my bullets struck a bit low, but the others blasted a baseball-size group in the rodent's middle. Following up with an exploding "Tannerite" target the size of a deck of cards, we each missed a couple shots. My next bullet brought flash and smoke and, a second later, a satisfying *boom*.

The 6.5 Creedmoor (left) and old 6.5x55 are easy to shoot well, adequate past 600 yds.

as hunting rounds—the .243 Winchester and 6mm Remington—can surely be adapted to long shooting. They're best sized (and the necks turned) to specific chambers with long, minimum-diameter throats that accept long bullets. The 6mm, derived from the mid-size 7x57 Mauser hull, needs a .30-06-length rifle action to be useful at distance, as VLD bullets can't be seated deep enough to cycle in short receivers. The .243, though designed for short actions, also benefits from more front-end room, if you're to tap its potential with VLDs.

Alternatives for precise target work are the sixes developed for benchrest shooting. These date to the 1960s, when wildcatters necked down the .308x1½, a Frank Barnes creation. Remington's Mike Walker standardized 6mm BR dimensions, in 1978, whereupon Remington started supplying brass. These hulls had thin walls, to make neck forming easy, and were designed to take Small Rifle primers. The short, fat cases followed development of the .22 and 6mm PPC, wildcat rounds on the petite .220 Russian. Lou Palmisano and Ferris Pindell used their consider-

I nailed John's with another. Burns conceded the day—but he'd soon get his revenge.

While I've missed my share of targets and bowed to many a competitor, I seldom trade a rifle of light recoil for one with bigger bullets. Of course, under some conditions and at extreme range, you can benefit from the wind-bucking heft of bullets from cartridges with mulish kick. You will either endure the battering, or install a brake that makes your head ring and blows cavities in the dirt, hiding your target and a barrel beefy as a truck axle behind billows of dust. Other lads revel in violent guns; the concussion must be addicting. Me, I'll stay with smallbores whenever practical.

"Small" is relative. While heavy-bullet .223 loads in fast-twist barrels perform well at 600 yards, and .22-250 ammunition reaches farther, neither is truly a long-range option. The bullets are just too small and wind-sensitive, ballistic coefficients too low. A short step up to 6mm (.243) adds distance without boosting recoil very much at all. The "sixes" designed

A .223 with 69-grain bullets performs to 600 yards, but require a reasonably fast twist.

The .25 Souper (.308 case) falls between the .243 and .260. It's a fine long-range deer

able experience as benchrest competitors to pioneer the PPCs, during the 1970s. By the late '80s, these cartridges were winning most of the major matches. It's no coincidence that Remington's first 6mm BR factory loads (100-grain bullets at 2,550 fps) arrived a year after Sako began loading PPC ammunition.

The 6mm BR case (including the Norma version, with identical hull dimensions but a 1½-degree throat specification instead of the original three-degree angle for the Remington), holds 10-percent more fuel than the PPC. The 6mm BR kicks 70-grain spitzers out at 3,200 fps. Norma's handloading manual lists a 100-grain bullet at 2,850. But, for long shooting, you'll want something like a 105-grain Berger LTB at 2,800, or a 107-grain Sierra MatchKing Norma at 2,780. For such bullets, 1:8 rifling works best. Another light-recoiling 6mm is the 6x47 Swiss Match, developed, in 2001, by necking the .223 to .243. Two more: the 6mmX and the 6mmXC. Texas marksman David Tubb brought both to prominence.

"I wanted a 6mm that would drive a 107-grain at least 2,950 fps," David said.

The .250 Savage necked to 6mm—called the 6mm International—was an option. But Tubb got more case capacity forming a .250 case in a chamber cut by a .243 Winchester reamer stopped .132 short of standard .243 length. The hull came within the eight-grain capacity of a .243's. He liked the result, but tweaked it by steepening shoulder angle from 20 to 30 degrees. Result: the 6mmXC. With that cartridge, Tubb won three consecutive High Power Rifle Championships at Camp Perry (2001 through 2003).

Twin to the 6.5 Grendel, the .264 Les Baer Custom adds reach to the AR-15 rifle.

The .260 Remington, essentially a 6.5-308, has less powder capacity, but is better suited to short actions. It was wildcatted long before Remington adopted it, in 2002. *Outdoor Life's* shooting editor Jim Carmichel developed his 6.5 Panther in the 1980s, his purpose to nip tight groups at long range. With a relatively lightweight (12-pound) rifle so chambered, Carmichel entered an IBS 1,000-yard match and fired a seven-inch 10-shot group. That performance, he wrote, caught Remington's eye, and the 6.5 Panther became the .260 Remington.

Hunting rifle chambers for the .260 won't yield the best results at distance; nor will ordinary match

Dave Emary headed Hornady's design of the 6.5 Creedmoor. It got him this buck at 300 yards.

The 6.5mms launch heavier bullets that better buck the wind. Since 1894, the 6.5x55 has served Scandinavian marksmen on the battlefield and the target range. No doubt, more of Sweden's moose have been taken with this native round than with any other cartridge, though magnums have lately chiseled at its popularity. With sleek bullets, the mild 6.5x55 acquits itself remarkably well at distance. But there are more effective choices now. One, the 6.5-284, excels at 1,000 yards. Gary Rasmussen, who has won many long-range matches, began using a 6.5-284 in the late 1990s, after a fellow competitor on the Palma Team put it high on the scoreboard. Gary's .30-338, hurling a 220-grain bullet around 2,850 fps, showed no real accuracy advantage over the 6.5-284 with a 140-grain bullet at 2,950—and it kicked a lot harder! Rick Freudenberg, a Seattle-area gun maker who has built rifles for me, supplied Rasmussen with a competition rifle. Both advise checking for throat erosion (good advice if you're shooting *any* fast smallbore bullet).

Sarah Forbes killed this hartebeest and two other big Namibian antelopes with a shot apiece from her New UltraLight Arms in .260.

Wayne's 6.5 Creedmoor, by Magnum Research and GreyBull Precision, is a nail-driver!

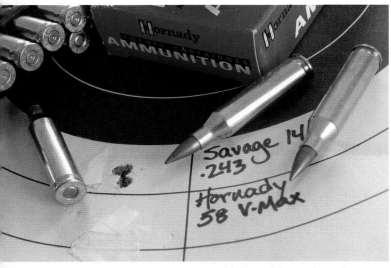

Light weight and modest cost didn't keep this .243 Savage 14 from shooting one-holers!

bullets. Very Low Drag profiles, justly favored by long-range marksmen, may require sharper twist than the standard 1:9, which is sufficient for most boat-tail game bullets. The .260 will drive 140-grain MatchKings over 2,800 fps, equaling the performance of the slightly longer 6.5x55.

Another target cartridge with impressive credentials at extended range is the 6.5x47 Lapua. Like the 6x47, this short-action cartridge uses Small Rifle primers, which many shooters insist deliver more uniform ignition than Large Rifle primers. Introduced by its namesake Finnish ammunition firm in 2006, the 6.5x47 hull is 4mm shorter than the .308's. It operates at slightly lower pressure (55,000 psi versus 62,000), and launches a 140-grain bullet at about 2,670 fps. Not long ago, I engaged a well-known rifle maker to barrel a Model 700 Remington to 6.5x47. Feeding inconsistencies in the early stages caused us to switch to the .260 Remington. Like many short rounds that will cycle through actions designed for

Karen killed this fine Oklahoma buck with a DRT bullet from her .223 S&W rifle.

6.5 Creedmoor on a long 700 action. Its carbon fiber barrel had a stainless core rifled by Kreiger. GreyBull Precision provided the stock and a 4.5-14x Leupold. Prone with a sling, I was soon hitting plates at 500 yards. In New Mexico, my hunting partner called a coyote across a mesa. At 250 yards, the dog collapsed to the bite of my 129-grain SST. That rifle also toppled an elk with one shot at longer range than I'd ever before killed an elk. Civil, accurate, and potent, the 6.5 Creedmoor challenges the .270 Winchester at the muzzle. Downrange, the high ballistic coefficients of the 6.5's 129- and 140-grain bullets give it an edge. Truly versatile, the Creedmoor has more sauce than a 6.5x55. Its 1.92-inch case accommodates VLD bullets in short magazines better than does the superb, but under-sung, .260 Remington. Light recoil and efficient burn suit it to compact, featherweight hunting rifles. Pressure is 60,190 psi, standard rifling twist is 1:10.

Wayne used a light-recoiling 6mm Remington to take this Coues buck at 220 yards.

the .308 clan, the 6.5x47 with a long, tapered bullet does not stack on or move from the follower exactly the same as a cartridge longer in the body and with a hunting bullet.

Among smallbore cartridges with headline status these days, the 6.5 Creedmoor ranks among the most unlikely—and the most useful! It emerged from the house of Hornady in 2008, brainchild of senior ballistician Dave Emary, who tapped competitive shooters like Dennis DeMille for ideas on 1,000-yard cartridges. A long-range marksman himself, Emary necked the .30 T/C hull (another Hornady product), to .264. The compact case kept overall length within limits imposed by short actions. Dave applied powder technology from Hornady's then-new Superformance Ammunition, to get blistering velocity.

The 6.5 Creedmoor is more than a flat-shooting, light-recoiling target cartridge. It's also ideal for deer and antelope. Not long after it hit shelves, Todd Seyfert, at Magnum Research, shipped me a rifle in

6.5 CREEDMOOR EXTERIOR BALLISTICS

120 A-Max (Hornady)	Muzzle	100 yds.	200 yds.	300 yds.	400 yds.
Velocity, fps	2910	2712	2522	2340	2166
Energy, ft-lbs	2256	1959	1695	1459	1250
Arc, inches	-1.5	1.6	0	-7.1	-20.5

129 SST (Hornady)	Muzzle	100 yds.	200 yds.	300 yds.	400 yds.
Velocity, fps	2950	2756	2570	2392	2221
Energy, ft-lbs	2492	2175	1892	1639	1417
Arc, inches	-1.5	1.5	0	-6.8	-19.7

140 A-Max (Hornady)	Muzzle	100 yds.	200 yds.	300 yds.	400 yds.
Velocity, fps	2710	2557	2409	2266	2128
Energy, ft-lbs	2238	2032	1804	1596	1408
Arc, inches	-1.5	1.9	0	-7.9	-22.6

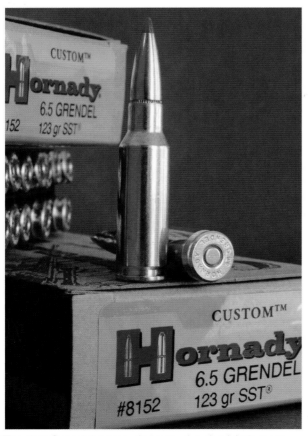

The 6.5 Grendel came along to give the M16 more reach, more punch. It delivers both!

It won't stay with a Lapua at 1,000 yards, but the 6.5 Creedmoor is fun to shoot and cheaper.

Jason used a Winchester M70 Featherweight in .270 WSM on this South Dakota buck.

Amber used a 7mm-08 on this outstanding warthog. Mild recoil makes for good shooting!

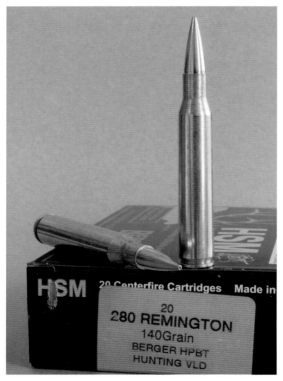

Sleek bullet noses hike ballistic coefficient. Factory loads now feature them, for long reach.

MIDDLE MAGNUMS

If you're shooting beyond 1,000 yards, you may want more velocity from 6.5mm bullets. Of the few truly fast-stepping rounds in this class, the 6.5x284 may be the best choice. Another option, though, is the .264 Winchester Magnum. With greater case capacity, it boasts even more speed and flatter flight. Current factory loads are pretty anemic—certainly less frisky than those at the .264's 1959 debut. But my handloads have easily wrung 3,300 fps from 140-grain bullets in 26-inch barrels. That's nearly 10-percent more zip than factory charts list now and 100 fps faster than original claims.

Largely because marketing gurus at Winchester didn't do the .264 justice, the 7mm Remington Magnum that followed three years later barreled over it like a freight train. Still, I'm sweet on this hot 6.5. It has treated me well afield, and at targets very far away. In fact, I've used it at a mile … .

The Suburban bounced over low Wyoming hills, wound through washes, then climbed a grassy grade. John pulled up on a knoll. Afoot, we made our way to the shadow of a tall bluff. There we spray-painted a steel plate big as a chest freezer. We descended, then lurched in low gear across the landscape to our ridge-top firing point, a crow's mile off

The Remington 700 John had tuned wore a Greybull/Leupold 4.5-14x scope on a base angled to add elevation to the dial. He'd loaded VLD bullets in the .264 Magnum hulls. I bellied onto the mat, John set up his spotting scope.

The wind didn't have a Wyoming push. Still, it tossed the mirage gently to and fro and curled it up from the broad swale in front of my muzzle. Nothing to fret over at 200 yards. Or 400. You'd have to pay attention at 600. At a mile, those zephyrs became a real issue. Even John's ambitious handloads weren't immune. Those VLD bullets spent more than two seconds in flight!

Chasing the shots, as John called the strikes on the bluff, I was frustrated by frequent shifts in air currents. During its 1,760-yard journey, each 140-grain missile had to negotiate several wind conditions, many invisible because the mirage vanished as the ground dropped away. Even through the powerful scopes, distance over the last half of the bullet's flight limited our view of both mirage and moving grass.

If memory serves, I scored on the fourteenth shot. The sound of the hit was five seconds getting back. A few minutes later, John landed a bullet on steel with his fifth shot. It was my turn to concede the day.

Shooting a mile, you need precise drop data, as a bullet's arc approaching the target is frightfully steep. "Flat" is decidedly relative, because even ballistically gifted .264 VLDs and heavier match bullets from the mighty .300 Winchester, .338 Lapua, and .50 BMG dive sharply well short of a mile.

What about the 7s? Well, the 7mm Remington Magnum only got more popular as the .264 faded. In surveys I've taken among elk hunters, only the .30-06 is more popular than this 7mm Magnum. The big 7's instant success took a lot of shooters by surprise, because Roy Weatherby had fashioned his excellent, nearly identical 7mm Weatherby Magnum in the early 1940s—and, apart from Weatherby, no commercial rifle maker then offered Weatherby chamberings. Like the 7x64 Brenneke that appeared in 1917, and the similar .280 Remington that arrived 40 years later, the 7 magnums were designed for the hunter. Ditto the 7x61 Sharpe & Hart and 7mm Vom Hofe SE, both from the mid-1950s.

The .264 Winchester and 7mm Remington Magnums are excellent for long shots at deer.

At 500 yards, prone with a sling, Wayne hit all five shots with a .22-250 Remington 700.

Wayne killed this Idaho elk at 330 yards with a pal's rifle in 7mm WSM loaded with 140-grain AccuBonds.

Scott Downs used a GreyBull Precision rifle in 7mm Remington Magnum on this fine buck.

In 1983, the 7mm STW arrived for shooters who wanted a flatter-shooting 7mm. It emerged as a wildcat derivative of the then-new 8mm Remington Magnum. Gun writer Layne Simpson, credited with bringing the cartridge to life, told me there was no interest from Remington at the time. "The marketing staff may have thought it would siphon sales from the 7mm Magnum," he said.

U.S. Repeating Arms (corporate name for Winchester's firearms enterprise then), actually chambered for the 7mm STW before Remington. At first, the name circulating at Ilion was 7mm Remington Maximum. But Layne had dubbed it the STW—Shooting Times Westerner—after the publication that trumpeted the round. The 7mm STW's full-length 2.85-inch hull holds significantly more powder than the 2.50-inch 7mm Remington Magnum's.

My tests showed the 7mm STW to be a stellar performer. Shooting factory-loaded 140-grain Core-Lokts in a Winchester Model 70 Sporting Sharpshooter, I recorded higher average velocities than the advertised 3,325 fps. Several rounds sped over the screens in the mid 3,400s—and drilled half-minute groups. A pal reported getting an occasional three-inch group at 500 yards with his Hart-barreled Remington in 7mm STW.

Randy Brooks at Barnes Bullets generated the STW data below in his company's test tunnel. He seated those X-Bullets .1 off the lands to keep pressures within reason and achieve best accuracy.

powder weight, type	7mm STW bullet weight, type	muzzle velocity (fps)
80.5 N204	100 Barnes X	3827
80 H4350	100 Barnes X	3843
88.5 Vit N165	100 Barnes X	3862
86 H1000	120 Barnes X	3444
76 IMR 4350	120 Barnes X	3457
81.5 Win WMR	120 Barnes X	3494
76 Norma MRP	140 Barnes X	3218
74 H450	140 Barnes X	3229
73 RL-19	140 Barnes X	3242
80 H5010	160 Barnes X	2972
72 Win WMR	160 Barnes X	2984
87.5 AA 8700	160 Barnes X	3053

The STW wasn't really new. Warren Page, long-time shooting editor at *Field & Stream*, favored 7mm wildcats. The powerful 7mm Mashburn was based on the .300 H&H Magnum case blown out. The wildcat 7mm-.300 Weatherby, adored by 1,000-yard benchrest shooters since the 1940s, is similar. These differ only in minor details from the 7mm STW. According to Layne, Remington adopted the 7mm STW, partly because the firm was selling lots of 8mm Magnum brass and few 8mm Magnum rifles. Remington eventually concluded 8mm cases were turning into STWs inside RCBS dies! In 2000, Remington followed the STW with its 7mm Ultra Mag, a more capacious rimless round with marginally more oomph.

There's no magic in the 7mm STW or the 7mm Ultra Mag. Kicked from either of these big hulls, a bullet simply flies flatter and hits harder than the same bullet from a 7mm-08, 7x57, .280, or any other short 7mm magnum. At 300 yards, either delivers what a .280 carries to 200. But, at long range, both are better served by heavier bullets than loaded in ordinary hunting ammo, provided those hefty missiles have VLD profiles.

Of course, the marketing gurus have their say in load development. If you boost bullet weight, you must reduce velocity, and velocity is what sold the big 7s in the first place. But a signal advantage of big cases is their ability to drive heavy bullets fast. In the 7mm UM, Remington has the ideal engine for long 160-grain bullets. I mentioned this to Remington management. "We'll probably use 175-grain bullets, not 160s," was the response, "and they'll be standard soft-points."

Now, this didn't make sense to me. The leap to 175 grains from the 7mm standard of 140 is *huge*. Adding that much weight to a hunting bullet means increasing shank length significantly, which eats into the powder capacity. A longer shank also hikes bore friction, thus stacking more resistance on a bullet already hard to move for its greater mass. A 175-grain VLD load would be a dandy at long range, but it might also require a sharper than usual twist.

"If I need a 175-grain big-game bullet," I said, "I'll go to a .30-caliber cartridge that can drive a 180-grain bullet more efficiently."

"A good argument," Remington conceded. "But we have a huge stock of 175-grain 7mm bullets."

THREE HUNDREDS

As bores increase in size, you can boost bullet weight ever more easily. That is, you can add 20 grains to the weight of a .30-caliber bullet without sacrificing as much speed as you would adding 20 to a 7mm bullet. The additional weight has less effect on the bullet's length and bearing surface, so pressures aren't as sharply affected.

Both the .308 Winchester (7.62 NATO) and the .30-06 have acquitted themselves well at distance. The .308 remains a favorite for black bull's-eyes at 600 yards and for sniping with standard-weight rifles. But a .30 magnum trumps both. I've been using various renditions for three decades. My first elk rifle, a Henriksen-built Mauser, was chambered in .300 Holland. Since then, I've shot elk with other rifles in that chambering, and rifles bored for the .300 Weatherby, .300 Winchester, and .308 Norma Magnums, and the .300 Winchester Short Magnum and .300 Remington Short Ultra Mag. A Ruger 77 Hawkeye in .300 Ruger Compact Magnum took a moose. One of my biggest elk fell to a .30-06 Improved, a magnum

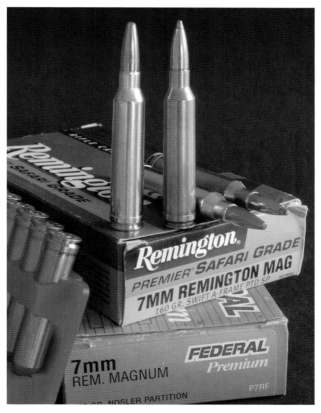

Remington's 7mm Magnum, brilliantly sold, deserves its huge popularity with hunters.

in performance, if not name. A .30-.338 Model 70 by Rick Freudenberg is in the bullpen for next fall.

The first big .30 came from the drawing board of brilliant inventor Charles Newton. Dubbed the .30 Adolph Express, for gun maker Fred Adolph, the rimless round booted 180-grain bullets downrange at 2,880 fps—in 1913, that was fast indeed. But few hunters were ready for such muscle. To riflemen of that day, the .30-06 packed the power of Zeus. Besides, Newton's .30 had no home except in Newton rifles. Western Cartridge Company dropped the loading, in 1938.

Meanwhile, the .300 H&H popped up in Western's catalog. This long, belted round progeny of the .375 H&H was designed for Cordite powder. Know also as the "Super .30" at its 1925 U.S. debut, the .300 H&H duplicated .30 Newton performance. Custom rifles from Griffin & Howe and British shops kept it alive, until Winchester chambered the Model 70 for it, in 1937, two years after Ben Comfort won the 1,000-yard Wimbledon Match at Camp Perry with a .300 H&H. The Holland's 2.85-inch hull limits it to very long actions, like magnum Mausers, the Model 70, and Remington's later 721 and 700 (Comfort used a reworked 1917 Enfield). The Super

The .300 H&H (left) sired the first commercial short belted .30 of note, the .308 Norma.

Cartridges get bigger, game doesn't. Recoil impairs accuracy. Precision trumps power.

The .300 Ruger Compact Magnum cycles in short actions, performs efficiently in short barrels.

.30 got a tepid welcome, compared to Winchester's fast-stepping .270, announced the same year. Its fortunes rose, then gradually slid, as newer, shorter .30s came along.

The .300 H&H has been revived of late. Graceful in profile, it feeds with unparalleled ease and recoils with less vigor than you'd expect. Some rifles in .300 H&H have yielded fine accuracy on my range. A pointed 180-grain bullet generates 3,315 ft-lbs at the muzzle and brings more than 1,700 to 400 yards. At one time, you could buy .300 H&H ammunition with 150-grain bullets at nearly 3,200 fps, and 220s at 2,620. The 180-grain spitzers make most sense for hunters. They fly 15-percent flatter than those from standard .30-06 loads and deliver a 10-percent advantage in wind. Competitive shooters have found handloads with 178- to 190-grain HPBTs put the .300 H&H in league with the more popular .300 Winchester Magnum.

Oddly enough, the first .30-bore cartridge on a short magnum case hailed from Norma, of Sweden. The hull measures 2.56 inches, slightly longer than that of the .338, so it was not interchangeable with the .30-338 (a logical wildcat fashioned by shoot-ers tired of waiting for Winchester to unveil a .30 magnum). Norma blunted its own entry into the U.S. market by first selling only cartridge cases. A year and a half later, ammunition appeared, an "re" on the headstamp signifying reloadable Boxer-primed brass. Browning alone among the American gun companies

The .300 Winchester Magnum is the best-selling belted .30, a superb round at long range.

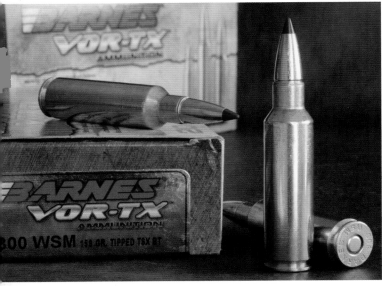
Barnes loads the popular .300 WSM with accurate, flat-flying Tipped TSX bullets.

listed a rifle in .308 Norma, the lovely Mauser High Power. Had not Remington, then Winchester, come up with alternatives, the .308 Norma might have gained a foothold Stateside. From a design standpoint, many shooters consider it a superior medium-bore cartridge.

Winchester's .300 Magnum arrived, in 1963, partly as a response to Remington's 7mm Magnum. Riflemen expected a necked-down .338. Winchester, instead, delivered a belted case with the same head, but a length of 2.62 inches. Its short neck fell shy of bore diameter. Case capacity exceeded Norma's, but .30-06-length actions limited useful capacity by requiring deep bullet seating. Still, the .300 Winchester Magnum quickly ate market share away from the 7mm Remington Magnum.

For more than two decades, the .300 Winchester and 7mm Remington Magnums satisfied hunters seeking more reach than they could get from

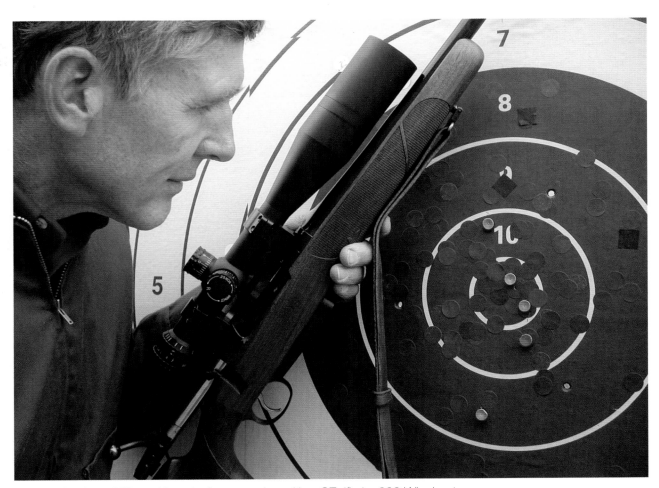
Wayne checks a 600-yard target after a session with a CZ rifle in .300 Winchester.

Long shots from one ridge to another reward well-practiced hunters with .30 magnums.

a .270 or .30-06. Then, Don Allen unveiled the .300 Dakota on a shortened .404 Jeffery hull. At 2.54 inches, the Dakota case is slightly shorter than the Winchester's, but it holds more powder and performs like the .300 Weatherby Magnum.

As if we didn't have enough .30 magnums, Weatherby announced, in 1996, the .30-378, based on the gigantic .378 Weatherby case. By early 1997, the rifle plant in Maine was scrambling to fill orders—10 times as many as Weatherby had expected! Fifteen years later, the .30-378 remains a strong seller, factory-loaded with 165-grain Nosler Ballistic Tips at an advertised 3,500 fps, 180-grain Barnes X bullets at 3,450. Given a 300-yard zero, these bullets strike less than four inches high at 200 yards, a mere 7½ inches low at 400. They carry well over a ton of energy to 500 yards. The only .30 to challenge its performance is John Lazzeroni's 7.82 Warbird, a rimless round fashioned from scratch. These .30s require super-size actions.

Janice killed this lovely hartebeest with well-placed shots from her Remington 700 in .300 WSM.

This blue wildebeest fell to Wayne's .30-06. Open country, but a close approach!

Retumbo powder and Weatherby's giant .30-378 Magnum excel at extreme range.

In 1998, not to be left out of the .30 magnum game, Remington brought out its .300 Ultra Mag on the .404 Jeffery hull. The Ultra Mag is about as big a round as the 700 action can stand. Its rim is slightly rebated to fit bolt faces for the .532 H&H head common to most belted rounds. Though it has 13-percent more case capacity than the .300 Weatherby, you won't get 13-percent more velocity from the Ultra Mag. As case volume grows, efficiency declines. There's negligible difference between the .300 Ultra Mag as loaded by Remington and the .300 Weatherby loaded by Norma. The Ultra Mag boots a 180-grain Nosler Partition at 3,250 fps; the Weatherby launches 180-grain Partitions at 3,240. Remington followed its first .30 magnum with other Ultra Mags, then trimmed the case for short actions to compete with Winchester's WSMs. I probably shot the first elk killed with the .300 Remington Short Action Ultra Mag, a round a tad smaller than the .300 WSM. I still find it a most fetching all-around cartridge.

The .300 Winchester Short Magnum arrived in 2000, the first of a family of WSMs. Its 2.10-inch case was short enough to work in rifle actions designed for the .308 Winchester. But, with a base .555 in diameter (and a .535 rim), the WSM hull was wider than a .308's. Capacity essentially matched that of the .300 Winchester Magnum. So did ballistic performance. The .300 WSM quickly earned a following and, at this writing, remains the most popular of modern short, rimless magnums.

Arguably even better is the .300 Ruger Compact Magnum, introduced by Hornady in 2008. It is more than a thinly veiled copy of the .300 WSM or .300 SAUM. It and the companion .338 RCM were developed to wring magnum velocities from 20-inch barrels. Inspired by the 2.58-inch .375 Ruger, the .300 and .338 RCMs share its .532 head and base. Shoulder angles are 30 degrees; case capacities average 68 and 72 grains of water to the mouth. For comparison, Remington .30-06 hulls hold 67 grains of water, Winchester .300 WSM cases 79 grains. Ruger Compact Magnums cycle through WSM magazines, and you can sneak four RCMs into most three-round WSM boxes.

Mitch Mittelstaedt, who headed the RCM project, explained that, with new proprietary powders, his team was able to "tighten" pressure curves so that the .300 RCM matches traditional .30 magnums from ordinary barrels, but doesn't lose as much enthusiasm in carbines. Tests showed velocity losses of 160 to 180 fps when .300 WSM barrels were lopped from 24 to 20 inches; RCMs gave up only about 100. With chronograph guru Ken Oehler, I chronographed .300 RCM loads from the 20-inch barrel of a Ruger M77 carbine. The Oehler 35 indicated 2,840 fps with 180-grain bullets.

Terri downed this fine gemsbok with one shot from her .300 Winchester Magnum.

Short and potent, from left: Remington .300 SAUM, .300 Ruger Compact Magnum, and .300 Winchester Short Magnum.

Early Model 70 Winchesters in .300 H&H were barrel-stamped simply ".300 Magnum." Seventy years ago, no more identification was needed, because the .300 Holland & Holland had no competition. Now, .300 magnums come in many shapes, sizes, and performance levels. For long-range shooters, the big .30s drive rocket-shaped bullets flatly. They drill through wind that would bend the paths of .224 and .243 bullets. They strike tough game with authority far beyond the range at which most of us can shoot accurately. Still, most .300 magnums fit affordable rifle actions and can be fired without inducing nosebleed. They are the most versatile family of cartridges for the long shot.

Wayne shot this group with an early Weatherby Mark V in the powerful .300 Weatherby.

ADDING REACH WITH .33S

Cartridges launching .33-caliber bullets date at least as far back as 1902, when the .33 Winchester appeared for the 1886 rifle. It thrust a 200-grain round-nose bullet at 2,200 fps. Around 1908, the British gun maker Jeffery announced two .333 Nitro Express rounds, a flanged (rimmed) version for double rifles and a rimless counterpart for repeaters. As with the .33 Winchester, bullets miked .333. The flanged .333 faded in the 1940s, but the rimless round remained popular and may have contributed to development of the wildcat .333 OKH, just before World War II. Charlie O'Neil, Elmer Keith, and Don Hopkins followed with the belted .334 OKH on the .375 H&H hull. The steep-shouldered .333 OKH Belted came later; it used .338 bullets, as did the .338-06, which Art Alphin eventually convinced SAAMI to bless as an A-Square round.

The most important .33 of the twentieth century is surely the .338 Winchester Magnum. Like almost all other .33s, it was designed for hunters. Announced in 1958, it followed, by two years, the firm's first short belted round, the .458. Winchester dubbed its Model 70 .338 the "Alaskan." Bullets from this .33 fly as flat as those from a .270, but, of course, hit much harder. Ballistically, Winchester's .338 is a short step behind the .375 H&H (though, to the uninitiated, the two belong in separate classes).

Four years after the .338 Winchester came the .340 Weatherby Magnum on the full-length H&H case. I scrounged a Weatherby Mark V in this chambering and carried it up a cold Montana mountain. In a wooded draw, I came upon a small group of elk. The bull took my 250-grain soft-point and dropped as if jerked to earth. The .340 is a leggy cartridge with a seductive profile. It has roughly 250 fps on the .338 Winchester and shoots flat enough for a 300-yard zero. It can drive 225-grain bullets to 3,100 fps; they carry a ton of energy to 500 yards and pack enough recoil to frighten the fainthearted. Weath-

Handloading, Wayne found this recipe a winner in his .338 Norma, on a Remington 700.

erby's Mark V is currently the only rifle chambered to this round. Its substantial weight and a stock comb intelligently designed to move away from your face make the .340 seem almost civil.

The .330 Dakota, on a shortened .404 Jeffery case, ballistically matches the .340 Weatherby. So does the .338 Remington Ultra Mag. It appeared, in 1999, as a line extension, the .300 UM preceding it.

John Lazzeroni's 8.59 Galaxy was one of the first modern ultra-short magnums. It's a fat, squat round that beats the .338 Winchester Magnum, nearly matching the most ambitious .340 loads. John developed this and his other high-octane cartridges from scratch, but concedes he could have saved himself much trouble by starting with the .404 Jeffery, which sired the Dakota line.

Truly Herculean .33s arrived with the .338-378 Keith-Thompson (Elmer Keith and R.W. "Bob" Thompson), in the 1960s, shortly after the debut of the .378 Weatherby Magnum. Commercial production of the K-T, as the .338-378 Weatherby, came in 1998. Factory ammunition by Norma, under Weatherby's label, hurls 250-grain Nosler Partitions at 3,060 fps. The only hunting round to match it: John Lazzeroni's long-action 8.59 Titan.

Dave Kiff's fine machining shows on this bolt face. The Lapua case has a broad base!

Overlooked but a fine hunting round, the .338 RCM all but matches the .338 Winchester ballistically.

Long shooting with a .33 means heavy bullets, stiff recoil. These Sierras excel at distance.

The most talked-about big .33 nowadays, the .338 Lapua, was designed, in 1983, as a sniper round. While the Finnish Lapua firm is best known Stateside for rimfire target ammo, this potent cartridge has the makings of a truly great round. Shorter than a .416 Rigby, it has roughly the same size head. On my scale, the case weighs half again as much as a .340 Weatherby's. A 250-grain bullet powered by 89 grains IMR 4350 and Federal's 215 primers clocks 2,900 fps—and is still well shy of pressure ceilings. Tests at Quantico Marine Corps base have yielded half-minute groups at 1,000 meters. The .338 Lapua appeals not only to snipers, but also to sport shooters, who can now buy affordable rifles from several firms.

At 2.724 inches, the Lapua's hull is long enough that, when capped with a sleek bullet of five or more calibers, the cartridge exceeds the length of ordinary magazines. So Texan Jimmie Sloan shortened the hull to 2.50 inches, the length of a common short belted magnum like the .338 Winchester. At 107 grains of water, case capacity shrank 6.5 percent from the 114 grains of a Lapua hull, but deep-seating bullets in .338 Lapua ammunition to fit repeating bolt-actions had gobbled much of its interior anyway.

In June 2008, the U.S. government reiterated its desire for a long-range precision sniper rifle to supplant the Mk 13 (.300 Winchester) and M40 and M24 (.308) rifles then issued. About that time, Norma acquired, from Sloan, the rights to his shortened .338 Lapua and soon put the hull into production. Loaded with a leggy 300-grain Sierra MatchKing seated normally, the round fit the magnum-length magazine of Remington's 700 action. Not long thereafter, I snared a batch of brass from Norma.

"Okay," said Rick Freudenberg, a gun maker in Everett, Washington (www.freudscustomrifles.com). He agreed to rebarrel my 700 Remington with a 26-inch cut rifled tube supplied by John Krieger (twist 1:10). Dave Kiff, at Pacific Tool & Gauge (www.pacifictoolandgauge.com) came up with a new bolt. The .338 Norma has the same case head as the Lapua, a bigger rim than the .532 of belted magnums. I could have asked Rick to open the 700's magnum bolt face, but Kiff's bolt, with an M16-style extractor, was a better option. It's a beautifully made bolt, with as much beef around the head as the action permits.

For extreme range, you need a big rifle, a better bench—like this one, by Wally Brownlee!

My friends at GreyBull Precision volunteered to fit the metal with one of their synthetic stocks, designed for the prone shooting I'd planned for this rifle. Don Ward, at GreyBull, also suggested I use one of the 4.5-14x50 Leupold scopes he equips with a range-compensating elevation dial. Third-minute clicks make the GreyBull modification ideal for shooting at extended ranges.

When Rick Freudenberg phoned to say my rifle was finished, I found my way over the Cascades to retrieve it. The medium-heavy barrel (.720 at the muzzle) put the point of balance of this nine-pound rifle (scoped) at exactly the right spot. Adjusted to 2½ pounds, Remington's trigger didn't need replacement.

I had penciled out data for starting loads, reasonable estimates from 40 years of handloading and charges that had proved out in magnum .30s and .33s. New Norma cases were so well-finished, I skipped the pre-loading prep necessary with brass of lesser quality. I didn't neck-size or turn necks, or bevel case mouths or de-burr flash-holes. I simply gathered powders, bullets, and a carton of CCI Mag-

A Winchester Model 70 Alaskan drilled this tight group for Wayne. Fine accuracy!

num Large Rifle primers and laid all out on the bench. Redding dies, a Lyman scale, and my ancient Herter's press turned out a loading block full of shiny cartridges. Even the long 300-grain MatchKings did not intrude unduly into the powder space; there'd be no need to compress the slowest powders. A trip to the range with my Oehler 35 chronograph yielded fine groups, with bullet speeds predictably on the shy side of full throttle. I got no sticky hulls or extruded primers. Some loads were obviously mild. To the right is a synopsis of the results.

I was surprised Barnes's 285-grain TSX bullets keyholed, a sign of bullet instability, commonly caused by rifling twist not steep enough. There were no problems with the 300-grain MatchKings, though close inspection showed the 285 Barnes bullets to be slightly longer. I suspect I can bump velocity 300 fps with the 285s, and that boost might straighten them out. If not,

.338 NORMA, REMINGTON 700 WITH PACIFIC TOOL BOLT, KRIEGER 26-INCH BARREL

Charge, powder, bullet	Velocity	Std. dev.	Group size
86 H4831 250 MK	2820	4	2570
79 H4350 250 MK	2810	2	.6
85 AA3100 250 A-Fr	2814	5	0
87 RL-22 250 A-Fr	2839		18
92 R Big Boy 250 Sce	2736	3	.7
87 VV N165 250 Sce	2778	9	.8
94 R Mag 250 Pt Gold	2766	12	
91 AA8700 285 TSX	2507	16	keyholed
86 H1000 285 TSX	2669	17	keyholed
82 RL-22 300 MK	2618	11	
90 R Mag 300 MK	2625	24	.4
81 Nor MRP 300 MK	2537	5	
90 VV N570 300 MK	2761	22	.4

Wayne readies his Remington-based .338 Norma, a rifle with great reach and precision.

I'll know to specify a 1:9 twist next time. The excellent accuracy of 250- and 300-grain MatchKings at speeds within 150 fps of reasonable maximums leaves me thinking this rifle will shoot most bullets of these lengths well. While Swift A-Frame and Nosler Partition bullets did not in this session print groups quite as small as the MatchKings, I hardly expected them too. Besides, a hunting-style .33 spitzer with a

The .338 Lapua kicks! A Lead Sled from Midway USA tames this Surgeon. Note the stout scope rings.

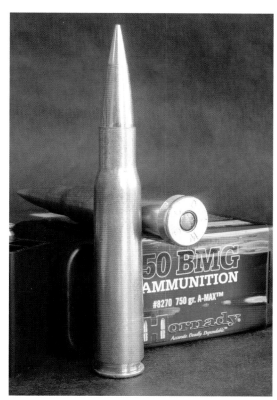

Browning's .50 BMG does its best downrange with sleek (C=1!) Hornady A-Max bullets.

payload of nearly 2½ tons is doing just fine, if bullets nip into a minute if angle—that's cake-pan accuracy at 1,000 yards. Then, too, long bullets often stabilize some distance downrange and shoot tighter (in minutes), far away than they do at 100 yards.

THE MIGHTY BMG

Few long-distance shooters could wish for bigger bullets (or more recoil!) thank the .338 Lapua's. For those few, there's the .50 BMG (Browning Machine Gun).

Developed by John Browning for his fearsome, tripod-mounted infantry weapon, in 1918, the .50 BMG, in standard military form, heaves a 661-grain .510 spitzer around 2,700 fps—the speed the .30-06 delivers with the 150- to 180-grain bullets that have dominated in that cartridge since its inception 12 years before the .50's. An important cartridge in both World Wars, the .50 BMG awed soldiers from all quarters. Examining .50-caliber Brownings seized by Rommel, in Tobruk, German Field Marshal Herman Goering remarked, "If we'd had these, the Battle of Britain would have turned out differently."

Recently, the .50 has become a sporting round and the ultimate sniper's tool. Thanks largely to Ronnie Barrett, who has designed bolt-action and auto-loading .50s for use from the shoulder, the round is now the namesake of a club: the Fifty Caliber Shooter's Association. Its 600-yard matches for various weight classes draw riflemen obsessed with long-range precision. At this writing, Lee and Sheri Rasmussen have captured most of the records. Lee's Heavy Gun group of 1.955 inches, fired in July 2009, is the smallest on the chart. Group measures and scores (the best are 50-5x for single targets across the board), enter six-target match aggregates. Lee holds the aggregate record for group size (5.416, Unlimited Gun) and score (298-19x, Heavy Gun).

Competitive shooters and snipers have triggered a flow of match-quality bullets and ammunition. Hornady's 750-grain A-Max load clocks 2,815 fps and leaks speed reluctantly. At 500 yards, it's moving at nearly 2,400 fps! Lapua's sleek 750- and 800-grain Bullex-N missiles perform similarly. The ballistic coefficients for these bullets are astounding: .960 and .980 for the Lapuas, a listed 1.050 for the Hornady!

Some years back, I attended a Tactical Long Range Class sponsored by Barrett, which supplied its .50-caliber rifles. The venue: The NRA Whittington Center, south of Raton, New Mexico. A shooter's cornucopia of rifle, pistol, and shotgun ranges, the Center sprawls across the eastern hem of hills shadowing a great, dry basin. Instructors Jon Weiler and

A .50-caliber enthusiast tries out a "home-built" rifle at 500 yards—not far for a .50!

Ryan Cannon, both with service in the 82nd Airborne, got started right away.

"We'll use M33 ball ammo. Its 660-grain copper-jacketed bullet has a soft steel core," said Jon. "It starts at 2,700 fps from our 29-inch barrels. Expect two-minute accuracy—that is, 12 inches at 600 yards." Jon scrolled quickly through a Power Point ballistics summary. "Some of the ammo is de-linked machine gun fodder. A lot of BMG is manufactured off-shore." He said these cartridges vary, one to the next, "in case dimensions and hardness." He passed around a fired hull with the rim badly bent. "This one's soft."

After lunch, Jon talked about the Barrett M82.

"The Army calls it the M107." He added that for my benefit. The other students, mostly soldiers and law officers seemed to know. "It's a short-recoil self-loader with a 10-round detachable box magazine. The barrel is button rifled, lands pitched 1:15. The Leupold Mark IV scope sits 2½ inches above bore line. A revolution of its elevation dial moves impact 15 minutes. To find the target quickly at 300 yards, bottom the dial, then turn it up 22 clicks." He advised us to keep a light coating of high-pressure grease on the barrel extension and bolt head. "The trigger pulls eight pounds and is not adjustable. You'll get used to it. When you fire, hold the trigger back for a count of two to ensure follow through."

Next, he delivered a monologue on distance.

"Shooting far, you must contend with variables most riflemen never think about. Like air density. Cold air is denser than warm. Air at sea level is denser than air in the mountains. As humidity goes up, air density goes down—strange, but true." He emphasizes the importance of "dope," an acronym for "data of previous engagement." Accurate data, he said, is the first step to hitting far away. "On the line, always record conditions and results. Most data is standardized for shooting at sea level at 59 degrees Fahrenheit. Hot and frigid weather, and high altitudes, can affect your bullet at extended range."

Jon reviewed ballistic coefficient, reminding us it changes with speed. "The most accurate bullets don't always have the highest C values. A football is aerodynamic," he pointed out. "But it's very unstable."

We began shooting early the next morning, 15 rounds to zero at 200 yards, then 20 each at 600, 800, and 1,000. I joined the pit crew first, plugging

and pasting to the rhythmic thump of rifles hundreds of yards away, the crack of their bullets close overhead. Relay One took all day to finish.

I abandoned the pits early to photograph the line against New Mexico's red evening sun. The gaping gills of the muzzle brakes hurled amber dust high over the prone marksmen and the spotters on their flanks. Brass cases the size of whisky flasks wink as they spin forward through the haze. The rifles, hard against the sand-filled feed sacks in the shooters' armpits, shuffle reluctantly to the cycling of the bolts.

"Call those shots," Jon snapped "Keep your body behind the rifle! Talk to him, Spotter!"

Many bullets found the 10-ring at 600 yards, fewer at 800. At 1,000, mirage and undulating wind flags merited even more attention. The spotting scopes show rippling bullet wakes hooking into the black bull's-eyes. I had little experience shooting .50s; on the other hand, wind is wind, and its harsh treatment of my bullets in smallbore matches was clear in memory. When, the following day, our pit crew got to the firing line, I hunched over a spotting scope, marking up the log book, coaching my partner as best I could.

A big brake, sturdy bipod, and heavy rifle make even the .50 BMG manageable by petite shooters.

Leupold and other scope makers offer optics and dials especially for long shots with .50s.

"Hold 10-ring at nine o'clock."

"You mean three o'clock, don't you?" Jon had come up behind us. "It's a four o'clock wind."

I conceded that was so, "But he's set up for that. The mirage at 1,000 has slowed. I see big waves. Wind is putting on the brakes. He'll leak right if he holds center." Age gives you some prerogatives, such as telling young, bright people with better eyes that your call is correct, if counterintuitive. "Conditions same," I repeated, my eye still in the scope. "Hold 10-ring, nine o'clock."

Boom! Seconds later, the target sank. It rose with the white plug near center at six o'clock. "An X. Good call," Then Jon strode to the next firing point.

When I bellied down with the M82, I found its stout bipod is more than an accessory. Without it, the rifle would be as useful as a chair without legs. And without the toe bag, I would have hardly endured a 20-round string. Recoil and the great weight of the rifle's butt quickly make themselves felt.

"Lie on *top* of the bag." Jon was back. "Take some sand out, if it won't conform to your body."

Getting that simple bag to behave under my bicep proved as big a challenge as mastering the long, hard trigger pull. "You're doing well." Jon put a rosy spin on my mediocre shooting. At 1,000, I leak a couple to the edge of the last scoring ring, 30 inches from center. "Two-minute ammunition," he consoled.

Recoil from this .50 was not brutal. *Thank that reciprocating bolt and that hulking brake*, I thought, wiping my eyes as I came off the mat. Faces stained by dust and a black film of powder residue marked all the riflemen who'd just fired, the price exacted by brakes on rifles fired prone.

The last day, we arranged a war zone in the pits. Cardboard silhouettes on long poles represented people. Painted various colors, the full- and half-size cutouts are designated friendly and hostile by hue. Shooters had to identify them at a glance. With the first relay on the 300-yard line, we in the pits hoisted the faux targets briefly at random places. Then we marched around with them, crossing hostile silhouettes with friendlies.

"It's like this over there," said Ryan. "In Afghanistan, I mean. Little time to shoot. A high risk of collateral damage."

A tight schedule denied me the last day of tactical shooting with the Barrett M82 to 1,700 yards. "That's about as far as we can correct for elevation on a Mark IV, when the scope base has 27 minutes of gain," explained Jon on the eve of the exercise. I figured it was farther than snipers, even those with the most accurate .50s and match-quality ammunition, would likely fire in combat. And certainly as far as they could expect to hit man-size targets.

I was wrong on both counts.

Successful shooting at distance requires careful observations, calculations between shots.

THE ULTIMATE LONG-RANGE ROUND?

The .338 Norma (left) and parent Lapua are champs at four-digit yardages. Snipers agree!

The .338 Lapua dates to 1983, when Research Armament Industries, in the U.S., outlined plans for a sniper cartridge driving a 250-grain .338 bullet at 3,000 fps. The sleek FMJ missile would penetrate five layers of body armor at 1,000 meters (1,094 yards).

RAI chose the Rigby case, for its modern rimless design and great capacity. But the .416 was born in a gentler time and configured for a maximum pressure of 47,137 psi. The new .338 would exceed that limit. To guard against unacceptable case stretching and possible separation, the Rigby's hull would get a thicker, harder web. RAI contacted BELL (Bell Extrusion Laboratories) of Bensenville, Illinois, to make the brass. Alas, the first batch didn't meet specs. In 1984, after building a test rifle and procuring bullets from Hornady, RAI looked to Lapua for help in pushing the project forward. Shortly thereafter, financial difficulties forced RAI out. The .338-416 project was officially cancelled.

Lapua found it worth pursuing. Partnering with Accuracy International, a young British firm, Lapua changed the dimensions and composition of the Rigby hull to brook pressures exceeding 60,000 psi. Not only was the web thicker, brass hardness was engineered in a gradient from hard to soft, base to mouth. Lapua designed a 250-grain FMJ bullet, designating it the "LockBase B408." The .338 Lapua was registered, in 1989, with the CIP (Commission Internationale Permanente pour l'Epreuve des Armes a Feu Portatives). Europe's CIP is the equivalent of SAAMI (Sporting Arms and Ammunition Manufacturers Institute), in the U.S. Both organizations provide manufacturing standards for the firearms industry.

Data for the .338 Lapua specifies a maximum pressure of 60,916 psi (piezo measure). During its development, the 300-grain Sierra MatchKing was not yet in production. Lapua's 250-grain LockBase VLD bullet, and the 250 Scenar, met the 3,000-fps target, generating about 4,890 ft-lbs at the muzzle. A hunting load hurling a 250-grain Nosler Partition clocked 2,940 fps. Current loads with 300-grain Sierra Match-Kings exit at 2,710 fps. Lapua's 300-grain Scenars reach 2,750 fps, carry 5,000 ft-lbs.

The .338 Lapua (left) has a big advantage downrange over the .300 Winchester and .30-06.

PUTTING UP WITH MAGNUMS

The problem with high-octane .30- or .33-bore cartridges is that they kick. Fast bullets mean fast recoil, according to this formula: V = bullet weight (grains) /7,000 x bullet velocity (fps) + powder weight (grains)/7,000 x powder gas velocity (fps). Powder and its gas figure in because, like the bullet, they are "ejecta" and cause recoil. Gas velocity varies, but Art Alphin, in his A-Square loading manual, says 5,200 fps is a useful average. The "7,000" denominators simply convert grains to pounds so units make sense in the end. For a 180-grain bullet launched at 3,000 fps from my 8½-pound .30-338 or .308 Norma rifle, I'd calculate recoil this way: 180/7,000 x 3,000 + 70/7,000 x 5,200 = 8.5 x V. That simplifies

to (77.143 + 52) 8.5 = V = 15.19 fps. Then I can calculate recoil using the first formula: KE = MV2/GC. The result: 8.5 (15.19) 2/64.32 = 30.49 foot-pounds of recoil, half again as much as from a .30-06. But the increase in felt recoil may be less noticeable if the rifle has a straight comb and a forgiving recoil pad. Your hands help absorb recoil, too, if grip and fore-end are properly shaped. Heavy rifles absorb more recoil than light rifles.

Oh, yes, two more things. On hard-kicking rifles, you'll want to install scopes well forward. Recoil becomes more noticeable if the ocular ring bangs your brow. And, on shoulder-fired rifles with the muscle of the .338 Lapua, a brake is almost essential.

Chrystal didn't feel the kick, when she downed her first African game. Thank the brake!

Recoil is one reason many hunting cartridges aren't listed in this chapter. A .338 Winchester will shoot far. But, if you need a .338, the Norma and Lapua are superior. The .340 Weatherby, which can match these ballistically, has a longer hull, and VLD bullets would preclude its use in many rifles. A VLD from a frisky .300 would perform as well at distance as a shorter .338 bullet. A problem for some rounds is simply their diameter. The .270 and 8mm bores, for example, haven't enjoyed the attention from bullet makers that has benefited the 7mms, .30s and, increasingly, the 6.5s. "Match" reamers and barrels are also easier to find for bullet diameters commonly used in 600- and 1,000-yard competition.

The target is a half-mile off. That heavy, braked 6.5/284 barrel on this Montana rifle stays down in recoil.

CHAPTER TEN
—TRAJECTORY

YOU NEEDN'T SEE A BULLET FLY TO KNOW WHERE IT WILL HIT—IF YOU KNOW ABOUT EXTERIOR BALLISTICS.

SPEED AND FRICTION

To the first riflemen, bullet travel was no mean mystery. Bullets flew too fast to see. Conjecture about their path was wild and rampant. In 1537, Trataglia, an Italian scientist, wrote a book in which he described that path as an arc. Though this seems obvious to us, it was not so then. The arrow's visible arc notwithstanding, some people envisioned a bullet flying almost straight until its energy was spent, at which point it dropped abruptly to earth!

Trataglia also experimented to determine the launch angle that would give a bullet its greatest range. He found this angle to be near 45 degrees—much steeper than the angle you'd choose to give your .270 its greatest reach. But Trataglia's conclusion was valid in its day. For very low velocities, gravity has a far greater effect than air resistance on bullet flight. Modern high-speed bullets, in contrast, are influenced less by gravity than by drag.

A century after Trataglia's studies, Galileo published his explanation of a bullet's arc. Dropping cannonballs from the Leaning Tower of Pisa was only one of many trials he ran, as a ballistics consultant for the arsenal at Venice. Galileo decided that the acceleration of a falling body was a constant and that, as a result, bullet trajectories must be parabolic. This was a great discovery! However, Galileo concurred with Trataglia in assigning 45 degrees as the launch angle for maximum range. His experiments did not take into account the drag variable because, again, projectiles then were very heavy, very slow. Compared to the acceleration of gravity, drag on a cannonball dropped from a window mattered not at all!

In 1740, Englishman Benjamin Robins invented a pendulum-like device to measure bullet speed. The pendulum had a heavy bob of known weight. After weighing the bullet to be clocked, Robins fired it into the pendulum. By noting the height of the swing, he was able to calculate impact velocity. A series of measurements with .75-caliber musket balls showed velocities between 1,400 and 1,700 feet per second. People of that day were skeptical: how could anything travel so fast? When Robins increased the firing distance, his results drew even more criticism. To explain readings at the greater range, he concluded that air resistance was 85 times as strong as the force of gravity! Now *that* was a hard concept to sell! It was, of course, true.

Benjamin Robins may have cited some support for his findings. Sir Isaac Newton, who had died only 15 years before Robins began his experiments, had come up with important observations in the fields of physics and mathematics. One of them was the universal law of gravitation, which specifies that the force of gravity varies with altitude. Newton's fundamental laws of mechanics and his development of calculus (at the same time Leibnitz was working on calculus, in Germany), were crucial pieces in the complex puzzle of ballistics. Newton showed that drag increases with the density of the air and the cross-sectional area of a projectile. He also demonstrated a relationship between drag and the *square* of the projectile's speed. As he had no way to measure the speed of musket balls, he could not know that drag increases dramatically when projectiles approach the speed of sound (about 1,120 fps).

The first chronographs were clumsy pendulums. Now electronic eyes clock bullet speed.

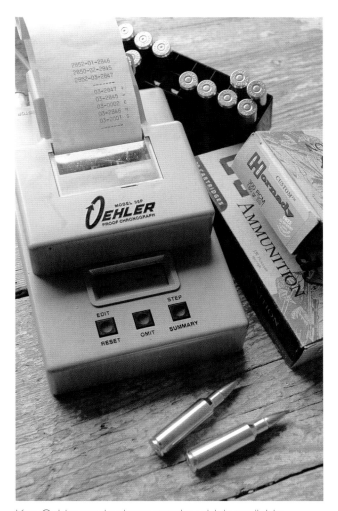

Ken Oehler made chronographs widely available. They help you sift loads, predict arcs.

We no longer measure velocity with pendulums, but instead with electric eyes that register the passage of a bullet's shadow as it breaches a known distance. That device is a chronograph. While chronographs are a century old, it wasn't long ago that Texan Dr. Ken Oehler did shooters an enormous favor by designing and building the first chronographs for consumer use. Before the Oehler instruments, chronographs were found only in the laboratories and shooting tunnels of ammunition companies; they were fixed in place and very costly. Consequently, shooters had to take factory-generated ballistics charts at face value and hope their handloads delivered the pressures and bullet speeds listed in loading manuals. Now, every long-range rifle enthusiast I know has a chronograph. Portable and easy to use, many cost less than an ordinary rifle scope. A chronograph is vital to understanding what your bullets are doing downrange!

Consumer chronographs have screens—electric eyes—installed a short distance apart on a bar or even directly on the electronic box housing the device's "brain." The chronograph measures the travel time of the bullet between screens. As you could clock a bicycle over a quarter-mile and compute speed in miles per hour, so you can use a small sliver of a bullet's flight to determine its starting velocity in feet per second. The greater the span between screens, the more accurate a chronograph's reading. The brain must be precisely calibrated for the span.

You'll get plenty of information from an Oehler chronograph, not just bullet speed, but average (mean) speed for a string of several shots. The range of velocities, slowest to fastest, shows up as extreme spread (ES), which is useful, because you want consistent ammo. If a load delivers good accuracy and velocity, and ES stays within 20 fps, I'm satisfied. Some loads produce lower ES values than others that perform similarly.

> Bullet velocity varies not only with powder type and charge and bullet weight, it's also influenced by chamber, throat, barrel dimensions, and bore finish. A tight chamber reduces energy leak. So does a tight throat.

Another number you get from a chronograph is standard deviation (SD). This statistical term probably arrived in the late 1890s. American statistician Karl Pearson is credited with the formula. Side-stepping the math, which had me in a headlock through my PhD program, I'll summarize standard deviation as the positive square root of the variance. What's variance? It's simply the sum of the squares of the deviations from the mean of chronograph readings, divided by a number that's one less than the number of shots. A high standard deviation indicates a lot of spread in your data, that is, lots of variability among readings. A low SD indicates most of your velocity readings are clustered close to your mean. There's more to milk from standard deviation. With it, build a bell curve that shows how your velocities group around the mean and, for any given velocity range, the percentage of shots likely to fall in that range. You'll get a rogue reading occasionally. Any reading more than 2½ times the SD from the mean is best tossed out.

Bullet velocity varies not only with powder type and charge and bullet weight, it's also influenced by chamber, throat, and barrel dimensions and bore finish. A tight chamber reduces energy leak. So does a tight throat. But a long throat that allows the bullet to move before engaging the rifling and permits long seating of the bullet to increase powder space enables handloaders to "heat up" loads, thereby boosting velocity.

Barrel length also affects bullet speed, but differently for different loads. For any given load, the only way to tell for sure how much velocity you'd gain with a long barrel or lose with a short barrel is to chop it shorter an inch at a time. One such exercise conducted by A-Square with a pressure barrel in .300 Winchester Magnum, measured velocities at one-inch increments from 28 to 16 inches. At top right are some of the resulting speeds from two loads: 70.5 grains IMR 4350 pushing a 150-grain Nosler Ballistic Tip, and 78.0 grains RL-22 behind a 180-grain Sierra Spitzer.

barrel length	150-grain velocity	180-grain velocity	velocity loss, 150/180
28 inches	3346	3134	2570
26 inches	3268	3089	78/45
24 inches	3211	3016	57/73
22 inches	3167	2966	44/50
20 inches	3108	2930	59/36
18 inches	3014	2874	94/56
16 inches	2903	2748	111/126

Velocity loss per inch of barrel length varies from a low of 22 fps to a high of 56 fps for the 150-grain bullet, and 18 fps to 63 fps for the 180-grain bullet. That range could be expected to vary with other .300 Winchester Magnum loads. Certainly it would with other cartridges. Note that *rate* of velocity loss increases substantially, as the barrel is lopped to less than 20 inches. (Variability in the data prevents conclusions as to differences in loss rates between 150- and 180-grain bullets.) Rule of thumb: Unless you cut barrels short enough to invade the "working" part of the pressure curve, estimate 30 fps per inch of barrel for most centerfire rifle loads similar in size and case/bore ratio to the .300 Winchester. If the barrel is cut very short, the bullet exits when the volume of expanding gas has an effect on raising pressure greater than increasing volume behind the bullet has in lowering pressure.

Changing components can also affect pressures and velocities. Substituting magnum primers for standard primers, for example, can boost pressure by several percentage points; you can expect a smaller change in velocity, however. At full-power levels, increasing pressure (by whatever means) kicks velocity up a little, but not proportionately. Similar changes occur when you substitute cases with smaller powder chambers (thicker walls or webs). Pressure goes up and velocity follows, but not at the same rate. Switching bullets, you may see no significant change in velocity. However, if the new bullet has a longer shank and generates more friction in the bore, or is seated closer to the lands on takeoff, or is very slightly larger in diameter, or has a "sticky" jacket, pressures will climb. Remington's choice of Nosler Partition bullets for its first .300 Ultra Mag loads no doubt disappointed the folks at Swift, who were already supplying A-Frame bullets to Reming-

ton. The rationale: A-Frame jackets were softer, bore friction higher. To push 180-grain bullets as fast as they wanted, Remington engineers turned to Noslers.

BALLISTIC COEFFICIENT

It's helpful, at times, to think of a bullet not as a rocket, but as a piece of shrapnel. This mindless sliver of lead, spinning madly and relying only on momentum once it's free of the muzzle, must rip through powerful forces we know collectively as air. Air is not a void. It is like water—it offers resistance. If you dip your hand in water, you feel a little resistance, but not much. Swimming, you feel more resistance. A belly flop from the seven-meter board will wake you up with more resistance still.

Looking through a high-power target scope as you launch a .22 rimfire bullet downrange, you'll see the path of this slow projectile as a hook, the steep trajectory fore-shortened in the lens. That track illustrates clearly that a bullet striking center is out of line for a center hit for nearly its entire flight! Alternatively, thinking of bullets as curve balls thrown by a pitcher can help you put them in the middle of distant targets or in the vitals of game far away. You'll shoot better at distance, when you stop thinking in straight lines!

Beginning around the mid-1700s, ballisticians in Europe worked hard to describe, mathematically

Clicking to the distance makes sense only with repeatable dials and after much practice.

Both bullets are sleek, but dimensions, shape, and weight of the .50 give it a far superior C.

"Slippery" bullets like the TSX give great reach to cartridges traditionally used close up.

and precisely, the flight of high-speed bullets. But accurate measurements of drag eluded them until the late 1800s, when chronographs were invented in England and Germany. By this time, conical bullets were in widespread use and cartridge firearms were supplanting muzzleloaders. Around the middle of the nineteenth century, ballisticians hit upon the notion of a "standard bullet" that could be used to develop benchmark values for drag and other variables affecting bullet flight. The flight characteristics of other bullets might then be computed using a constant factor that defined their relationship with the standard bullet. Thus was born the descriptor we know as ballistic coefficient, expressed as "C." In mathematical form:

$$C = \text{drag deceleration of the standard bullet/drag deceleration of the actual bullet.}$$

Though this relationship is *exactly* true *only* when both bullets are of the same shape and density, it's useful in comparisons of most modern bullets of similar form.

By the end of our Civil War, ballisticians around the world were hard at work determining drag characteristics of standard bullets. The best-known studies were conducted by Krupp, in Germany (1881) and by the Gavre Commission, in France (1873-1898). Around 1880, an Italian ballistician named Siacci discovered a short alternative to the laborious calculus in determining a bullet's trajectory. He found that, after using calculus to plot the path of a standard bullet, he could determine, with simple algebra, the path of any other bullet with a known C.

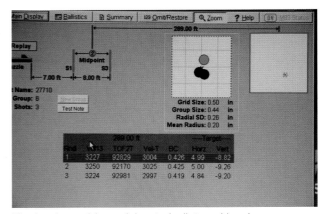

Electronics add precision to bullet and load tests. Weatherby's lab ran these figures.

The Gavre Commission's tests were perhaps the most extensive, including velocities up to 6,000 fps and data from several countries. But variations in atmospheric conditions caused inaccuracies in the Gavre drag figures. Krupp's work proved more fruitful. The standard Krupp bullet, a flat-based conical, was three calibers long, with a two-caliber ogive. Shortly after the Krupp data were published, a Russian colonel named Mayevski developed a mathematical model that showed the drag deceleration of this bullet. U.S. Army Colonel James Ingalls used Mayevski's work as the basis for his Ingalls Tables, first published in 1893, then revised in 1917. The Ingalls Tables describe the behavior of a standard Krupp bullet, which is close in form to most hunting and target bullets used at distance today.

Still, the actual C for other bullets had to be determined before the standard-bullet data could be used to project *their* flight paths. One way of determining C is with firing tests, comparing the ballistic properties of the object bullet with those of the standard bullet. Another method, developed by Wallace Coxe and Edgar Beurgless, at DuPont, in the 1930s, is essentially a matching exercise. The object bullet is compared to bullet profiles on a chart of many profiles and, when a match is found, the chart provides a number by which to calculate C. While this method is popular because it is so convenient, ballisticians at Sierra Bullets have reported discrepancies of up to 10 percent between comparisons and firing tests. Because drag increases with speed, you can't expect shooting tests of the same bullet at different speeds to yield the same C. For the same reason, tests of different bullets at different speeds are invalid for determining C.

The advent of analog computers during the 1940s made ballistics calculations easier, just as the weapons of the Second World War demanded more detailed plottings of trajectories. The digital computer later eased the burden of calculating complex arcs, such as those of bombs dropped at high altitude.

In 1965, Winchester-Western published ballistics tables that grouped small arms bullets into four families, each differing from the others in shape and each having its own drag function: "G1" drag applied to all bullets not described in the other categories; "G5" drag was for sleek boat-tail bullets that set up little air resistance and friction; "G6" drag was for flat-base spitzer (pointed) bullets with full metal jackets. These shapes covered almost all rifle bullets in common use by hunters and target shooters. The "G" descriptor, incidentally, was chosen in honor of the Gavre Commission.

Few shooters and hunters have the equipment and facilities for finding C in firing tests. A simple math formula is an alternative:

$$C = w/id2$$

In this formula, "w" is the bullet weight in pounds, "d" is bullet diameter in inches, and "i" is a form factor reflecting bullet profile. The higher the C value, the flatter the bullet will fly and the better it will conserve speed and energy. The standard bullet has a C of 1.000. Most hunting and target bullets carry C values of .200 to .600. A flat-nose .45-70 bullet has a C around .200, as does the standard 170-grain flat-nose .30-30 bullet. A flat-base spitzer of medium weight for the caliber, such as common 100-grain .25s, 140-grain 7mms, and 165-grain .30s, have ballistic coefficients of .350 to .400. A tapered heel or a more streamlined nose hikes C. The heaviest VLD bullets (say, a 240-grain .308) have C values higher than .700.

The effect of C on bullet drop is less than its effect on drag (which, by increasing flight time, also contributes to drop). Sierra tables show that a bullet with a ballistic coefficient of .600 driven at 3,000 fps drops about 58 inches at 500 yards. A bullet with a C of .400, fired at the same velocity, drops 65 inches. That's a pretty small disparity, given the 33-percent

At 1,000 yards, a .30-06 zeroed at 200 yards prints 328 inches low. That's 27 *feet*. So much for those campfire champs who say they topple game routinely at a half-mile by holding dead on.

Most game is shot within point-blank range, say 250 yards. Beyond that, speed and drag begin to matter.

drop in C and the relatively long flight distance. The difference in remaining energy is more striking, though similar in terms of percentage: 2,256 ft-lbs for the bullet with a C of .600, and 1,929 ft-lbs for the bullet with a C of .400.

If you trim velocity by 500 fps, to 2,500 fps, both bullets drop much farther over 500 yards. The bullet with a C of .600 drops 85 inches—27 inches more than it did at a starting speed of 3,000 fps. The bullet with a C of .400 drops 96 inches—31 inches more than it did with the fast start. Remaining energy: 1,835 and 1,551 ft-lbs.

Change in C has a larger effect on remaining velocities at high muzzle velocities than at low ones, because, as bullets speed up, drag figures more heavily in throttling bullet flight. C changes markedly near the speed of sound. Knowing C and initial velocity, you can plot trajectory quite accurately.

Computer programs available to any shooter now make easy work of predicting bullet flight for just about any load. But drop and drift figures don't tell the whole story. At least, they don't *explain* it. A good share of bullet behavior can be attributed to its rotation.

Like a spiraling football, a bullet travels most directly to the target when spinning about its axis. If it remains nose-first, it also travels *farther*, because drag is held to a minimum.

A .308 bullet spun one turn in 12 inches at a muzzle velocity of 3,000 fps reaches an animal 400 yards away in about a half-second (average velocity: just under 2,500 fps). In that half-second, the bullet spins 1,500 times! Compare that turnover to the rpm's of an automobile engine powering you down the highway at 60 mph. Say the engine tachometer registers 3,000 rpm; that's only 500 rotations per second, 250 per half-second. The bullet is turning *six times faster.* Give it a 1:9 twist, and you boost rotational speed by 25 percent, to 3,750 rotations per second.

Unlike a bullet's forward speed, which slows under the influence of drag, rotational velocity remains essentially constant. It affects the reaction of bullets to twigs and other obstructions in flight, and the expansion of soft-nose bullets in game. In turn, bullet upset affects its path. Jacket petals spread far to the side add drag to both forward and rotational movement. So, besides reducing penetration, they slow rotation, reducing stability. Petals also act as lever arms to tip the bullet. Contrary to what some hunters think, however, there's no "buzz-saw" effect

Deep-driving bullets for tough game can also be accurate, with aerodynamic form and high C.

Handloading adds options. More speed is only one, and not always the most desirable.

Despite its blunt nose, the .458 Winchester has great maximum range. Credit inertia.

in bullet wounds; the .308 bullet spun 1:12 barely gets through a single revolution threading the chest cavity of a big deer.

Precessional movement is the rotation of the bullet's nose about the bullet's axis. It is undesirable, but virtually unpreventable. A bullet seldom leaves the muzzle perfectly. Any tipping of the bullet—due to a damaged muzzle, nicked bullet base, or lack of concentricity in the bullet's jacket—can put the nose into its own orbit around the bullet's axis. Like a top that "goes to sleep" after you give it a hard spin, the bullet may rotate more smoothly, with less precession, after covering some distance. That's why you can get smaller groups (in terms of minutes of angle) at long range. A rifle that shoots into 1½ inches at 100 yards might keep all the bullets inside three inches at 300. Penetration is deeper if the bullet is *not* precessing significantly.

.223 75 BTHP
Trajectory (simplified)
INPUT DATA

Ballistic Coefficient:	0.198 G7	Caliber:	0.224 in.
Bullet Weight:	75.0 gr.		
Muzzle Velocity:	2775.0 ft/s		
Sight Height:	1.50 in	Line of sight angle:	0.0 deg.
Cant Angle:	0.0 deg.		
Wind Speed:	10.0 mpg	Target Speed:	10.0 mph
Temperature:	59.0 F	Pressure:	29.20 in hg
Humidity:	78%	Altitude:	0.0 ft.

OUTPUT DATA

Elevation:	5.556 MOA	Windage:	0.000 MOA
Atmospheric Density:	0.07425 lb/ft^2	Speed of sound:	1116.5 ft/s
Maximum PBR:	329 yds	Max.PBR Zone:	280 yds.
Range of Maximum Height:	155 yds	Energy at max. PBR:	715.8 ft lbs.
Sectional Density:	0.214 lb/in^2		

CALCULATED TABLE

Range (yd)	Drop (in)	Drop (MOA)	Windage (in)	Windage (MOA)	Velocity (ft/s)	Mach (none)	Energy (ft-lbs)	Time (s)	Lead (in)	Lead (MOA)
0	-1.5	***	0.0	***	2775.0	2.486	1282.2	0.000	0.0	***
100	1.9	1.8	0.8	0.8	2549.6	2.284	1082.4	0.113	19.9	19.0
200	-0.0	-0.0	3.4	1.6	2334.6	2.091	907.5	0.236	41.5	19.8
300	-8.3	-2.7	8.1	2.6	2130.6	1.908	755.8	0.370	65.2	20.7
400	-24.3	-5.8	15.1	3.6	1937.1	1.735	624.8	0.518	91.2	21.8
500	-49.6	-9.5	24.7	4.7	1752.8	1.570	511.5	0.681	119.8	22.9
600	-86.3	-13.7	37.4	6.0	1576.5	1.412	413.8	0.861	151.6	24.1
700	-137.0	-18.7	53.8	7.3	1408.4	1.261	330.3	1.063	187.0	25.5
800	-205.4	-24.5	74.6	8.9	1249.8	1.119	260.1	1.289	226.8	27.1
900	-296.1	-31.4	100.5	10.7	1106.6	0.991	203.9	1.544	271.8	28.8
1000	-415.0	-39.6	131.2	12.5	1031.6	0.924	177.2	1.827	321.5	30.7

6.5 CREEDMOOR 140 AMAX

Trajectory (simplified)

INPUT DATA

Ballistic Coefficient:	0.293 G7	Caliber:	0.264 in
Bullet Weight:	140.0 gr.		
Muzzle Velocity:	2710.0 ft/s		
Sight Height:	1.50 in.	Line of sight angle:	0.0 deg
Cant Angle:	0.0 deg		
Wind Speed:	10.0 mph	Target Speed:	10.0 mph
Temperature:	59.0°F	Pressure:	29.20 in Hg
Humidity:	78%	Altitude:	.0.0 ft.

OUTPUT DATA

Elevation:	5.602 MOA	Windage:	0.000 MOA
Atmospheric Density:	0.07425 lb/ft²	Speed of sound:	1116.5 ft/s
Maximum PBR:	337 yds	Max.PBR Zone:	285 yds
Range of Maximum Height:	156 yds	Energy at max. PBR:	1530.0 ft lbs
Sectional Density:	0.287 lb/in²		

CALCULATED TABLE

Range (yd)	Drop (in)	Drop (MOA)	Windage (in)	Windage (MOA)	Velocity (ft/s)	Mach (none)	Energy (ft-lbs)	Time (s)	Lead (in)	Lead (MOA)
0	-1.5	***	0.0	***	2710.0	2.427	2282.6	0.000	0.0	***
100	1.9	1.8	0.6	0.5	2558.5	2.292	2034.6	0.114	20.1	19.1
200	-0.0	-0.0	2.3	1.1	2411.8	2.160	1807.9	0.235	41.3	19.7
300	-7.9	-2.5	5.4	1.7	2269.9	2.033	1601.4	0.363	63.9	20.3
400	-22.5	-5.4	9.9	2.4	2133.2	1.911	1414.3	0.499	87.9	21.0
500	-44.8	-8.6	16.0	3.1	2001.3	1.793	1244.9	0.644	113.4	21.7
600	-75.8	-12.1	23.8	3.8	1873.8	1.678	1091.3	0.799	140.7	22.4
700	-116.7	-15.9	33.5	4.6	1750.3	1.568	952.2	0.965	169.8	23.2
800	-169.0	-20.2	45.2	5.4	1630.4	1.460	826.2	1.143	201.1	24.0
900	-234.4	-24.9	59.4	6.3	1514.2	1.356	712.6	1.334	234.7	24.9
1000	-314.9	-30.1	76.1	7.3	1401.8	1.256	610.8	1.540	271.0	25.9

.308 178 BTHP

Trajectory (simplified)

INPUT DATA

Ballistic Coefficient:	0.267 G7	Caliber:	0.308 in.
Bullet Weight:	178.0 gr.		
Muzzle Velocity:	2600.0 ft/s		
Sight Height:	1.50 in	Line of sight angle:	0.0 deg.
Cant Angle:	0.0 deg.		
Wind Speed:	10.0 mpg	Target Speed:	10.0 mph
Temperature:	59.0 F	Pressure:	29.20 in hg
Humidity:	78%	Altitude:	0.0 ft.

OUTPUT DATA

Elevation:	6.075 MOA	Windage:	0.000 MOA
Atmospheric Density:	0.07425 lb/ft²	Speed of sound:	1116.5 ft/s
Maximum PBR:	321 yds	Max.PBR Zone:	272 yds.
Range of Maximum Height:	149 yds	Energy at max. PBR:	1743.2 ft lbs.
Sectional Density:	0.268 lb/in²		

CALCULATED TABLE

Range (yd)	Drop (in)	Drop (MOA)	Windage (in)	Windage (MOA)	Velocity (ft/s)	Mach (none)	Energy (ft-lbs)	Time (s)	Lead (in)	Lead (MOA)
0	-1.5	***	0.0	***	2600.0	2.329	2671.4	0.000	0.0	***
100	2.2	2.1	0.7	0.6	2437.7	2.183	2348.4	0.119	21.0	20.0
200	-0.0	-0.0	2.7	1.3	2281.4	2.043	2056.7	0.246	43.4	20.7
300	-8.9	-2.8	6.4	2.0	2131.1	1.909	1794.7	0.382	67.3	21.4
400	-25.4	-6.1	11.7	2.8	1986.7	1.779	1559.8	0.528	93.0	22.2
500	-50.8	-9.7	19.0	3.6	1847.5	1.655	1348.9	0.685	120.5	23.0
600	-86.3	-13.7	28.4	4.5	1713.0	1.534	1159.6	0.853	150.2	23.9
700	-133.7	-18.2	40.1	5.5	1582.9	1.418	990.1	1.036	182.3	24.9
800	-195.1	-23.3	54.6	6.5	1457.2	1.305	839.1	1.233	217.0	25.9
900	-272.9	-29.0	72.1	7.7	1336.4	1.197	705.7	1.448	254.9	27.0
1000	-370.2	-35.3	93.2	8.9	1221.4	1.094	589.5	1.683	296.2	28.3

.30-06 178 BTHP

Trajectory (simplified)

INPUT DATA

Ballistic Coefficient:	0.267 G7	Caliber:	0.308 in.
Bullet Weight:	178.0 gr.		
Muzzle Velocity:	2700.0 ft/s		
Sight Height:	1.50 in	Line of sight angle:	0.0 deg.
Cant Angle:	0.0 deg.		
Wind Speed:	10.0 mpg	Target Speed:	10.0 mph
Temperature:	59.0 F	Pressure:	29.20 in hg
Humidity:	78%	Altitude:	0.0 ft.

OUTPUT DATA

Elevation:	5.678 MOA	Windage:	0.000 MOA
Atmospheric Density:	0.07425 lb/ft²	Speed of sound:	1116.5 ft/s
Maximum PBR:	332 yds	Max.PBR Zone:	282 yds.
Range of Maximum Height:	155 yds	Energy at max. PBR:	1865.1 ft lbs.
Sectional Density:	0.268 lb/in²		

CALCULATED TABLE

Range (yd)	Drop (in)	Drop (MOA)	Windage (in)	Windage (MOA)	Velocity (ft/s)	Mach (none)	Energy (ft-lbs)	Time (s)	Lead (in)	Lead (MOA)
0	-1.5	***	0.0	***	2775.0	2.486	1282.2	0.000	0.0	***
100	1.9	1.8	0.8	0.8	2549.6	2.284	1082.4	0.113	19.9	19.0
200	-0.0	-0.0	3.4	1.6	2334.6	2.091	907.5	0.236	41.5	19.8
300	-8.3	-2.7	8.1	2.6	2130.6	1.908	755.8	0.370	65.2	20.7
400	-24.3	-5.8	15.1	3.6	1937.1	1.735	624.8	0.518	91.2	21.8
500	-49.6	-9.5	24.7	4.7	1752.8	1.570	511.5	0.681	119.8	22.9
600	-86.3	-13.7	37.4	6.0	1576.5	1.412	413.8	0.861	151.6	24.1
700	-137.0	-18.7	53.8	7.3	1408.4	1.261	330.3	1.063	187.0	25.5
800	-205.4	-24.5	74.6	8.9	1249.8	1.119	260.1	1.289	226.8	27.1
900	-296.1	-31.4	100.5	10.7	1106.6	0.991	203.9	1.544	271.8	28.8
1000	-415.0	-39.6	131.2	12.5	1031.6	0.924	177.2	1.827	321.5	30.7

.300 WIN MAG 195 BTHP

Trajectory (simplified)

INPUT DATA

Ballistic Coefficient:	0.273 G7	Caliber:	0.308 in.
Bullet Weight:	195.0 gr.		
Muzzle Velocity:	2910.0 ft/s		
Sight Height:	1.50 in	Line of sight angle:	0.0 deg.
Cant Angle:	0.0 deg.		
Wind Speed:	10.0 mpg	Target Speed:	10.0 mph
Temperature:	59.0 F	Pressure:	29.20 in hg
Humidity:	78%	Altitude:	0.0 ft.

OUTPUT DATA

Elevation:	4.966 MOA	Windage:	0.000 MOA
Atmospheric Density:	0.07425 lb/ft²	Speed of sound:	1116.5 ft/s
Maximum PBR:	358 yds	Max.PBR Zone:	303 yds.
Range of Maximum Height:	166 yds	Energy at max. PBR:	2352.3 ft lbs.
Sectional Density:	0.294 lb/in²		

CALCULATED TABLE

Range (yd)	Drop (in)	Drop (MOA)	Windage (in)	Windage (MOA)	Velocity (ft/s)	Mach (none)	Energy (ft-lbs)	Time (s)	Lead (in)	Lead (MOA)
0	-1.5	***	0.0	***	2910.0	2.606	3666.0	0.000	0.0	***
100	1.6	1.5	0.5	0.5	2741.5	2.456	3253.7	0.106	18.7	17.9
200	-0.0	-0.0	2.3	1.1	2578.1	2.309	2877.4	0.219	38.6	18.4
300	-6.8	-2.2	5.3	1.7	2420.1	2.168	2535.5	0.339	59.7	19.0
400	-19.5	-4.7	9.7	2.3	2267.8	2.031	2226.3	0.467	82.2	19.6
500	-39.1	-7.5	15.6	3.0	2121.3	1.900	1948.0	0.604	106.3	20.3
600	-66.3	-10.6	23.2	3.7	1980.4	1.774	1697.8	0.750	132.1	21.0
700	-102.4	-14.0	32.7	4.5	1844.4	1.652	1472.7	0.907	159.7	21.8
800	-148.8	-17.8	44.2	5.3	1712.9	1.534	1270.2	1.076	189.4	22.6
900	-207.0	-22.0	58.1	6.2	1585.6	1.420	1088.4	1.258	221.4	23.5
1000	-279.1	-26.7	74.7	7.1	1462.6	1.310	926.0	1.455	256.1	24.5

.338 LAPUA 285 BTHP
Trajectory (simplified)
INPUT DATA

Ballistic Coefficient:	0.351 G7	Caliber:	0.338 in.
Bullet Weight:	285.0 gr.		
Muzzle Velocity:	2745.0 ft/s		
Sight Height:	1.50 in	Line of sight angle:	0.0 deg.
Cant Angle:	0.0 deg.		
Wind Speed:	10.0 mpg	Target Speed:	10.0 mph
Temperature:	59.0 F	Pressure:	29.20 in hg
Humidity:	78%	Altitude:	0.0 ft.

OUTPUT DATA

Elevation:	5.413 MOA	Windage:	0.000 MOA
Atmospheric Density:	0.07425 lb/ft²	Speed of sound:	1116.5 ft/s
Maximum PBR:	346 yds	Max.PBR Zone:	293 yds.
Range of Maximum Height:	160 yds	Energy at max. PBR:	3397.9 ft lbs.
Sectional Density:	0.356 lb/in²		

CALCULATED TABLE

Range (yd)	Drop (in)	Drop (MOA)	Windage (in)	Windage (MOA)	Velocity (ft/s)	Mach (none)	Energy (ft-lbs)	Time (s)	Lead (in)	Lead (MOA)
0	-1.5	***	0.0	***	2745.0	2.459	4767.6	0.000	0.0	***
100	1.8	1.7	0.5	0.4	2617.4	2.344	4334.5	0.112	19.7	18.8
200	-0.0	-0.0	1.9	0.9	2493.0	2.233	3932.3	0.229	40.4	19.3
300	-7.4	-2.4	4.4	1.4	2371.9	2.124	3559.7	0.353	62.1	19.8
400	-21.0	-5.0	8.0	1.9	2254.3	2.019	3215.5	0.482	84.9	20.3
500	-41.4	-7.9	12.8	2.4	2140.3	1.917	2898.4	0.619	109.0	20.8
600	-69.4	-11.0	18.9	3.0	2029.7	1.818	2606.7	0.763	134.3	21.4
700	-105.8	-14.4	26.4	3.6	1922.3	1.722	2338.0	.915	161.0	22.0
800	-151.7	-18.1	35.4	4.2	1817.7	1.628	2090.5	1.075	189.3	22.6
900	-208.1	-22.1	46.1	4.9	1715.7	1.537	1862.6	1.245	219.2	23.3
1000	-276.3	-26.4	58.5	5.6	1616.3	1.448	1653.0	1.425	250.9	24.0

BALLISTICS CHART
.50 BMG (Hornady load)

CARTRIDGE DATA

Cartridge:	.50 BMG
Bullet type:	AMAX
Bullet weight:	750 grains
Ballistic coefficient:	0.474000 (Given)
Muzzle velocity:	2,800 fps
Drag factor:	G7

ENVIRONMENTAL DATA

Temperature:	59 F
Atmospheric pressure:	29.53 inches of Hg

FIREARM DATA

Sight height:	2 inches above centerline of bore
Sighting-in range:	200 yards

PREDICTED PERFORMANCE

Range (yds)	Remaining velocity (ft/sec)	Remaining energy (lb/ft)	Time of flight (seconds)	Drop (in)	Mid-range trajectory (in)	Trajectory (in)	Wind Deflection 10-mph (in)
Muzzle	2,800	13,054	0.0000	0.00	0.0	-2.0	0.0
100	2,703	12,167	0.1091	2.31	0.6	1.4	0.3
200	2,608	11,328	0.2221	9.35	2.4	0.0	1.4
300	2,515	10,534	0.3466	21.51	5.5	-6.5	4.4
400	2,424	9,784	0.4606	39.18	10.2	-18.5	5.6
500	2,335	9,077	0.5868	62.75	16.6	-36.4	9.0
600	2,247	8,410	0.7178	92.71	24.8	-60.7	13.2
700	2,162	7,783	0.8538	129.55	35.1	-91.8	18.3
800	2,078	7,192	0.9954	173.83	47.7	-130.4	24.3
900	1,997	6,637	1.1427	226.15	62.9	-177.1	31.4
1,000	1,916	6,114	1.2960	287.20	80.8	-232.4	39.5

GRAVITY, SIMPLY

Bullets don't travel flatly. Not even for one yard. As soon as a bullet leaves the muzzle, it starts to drop at an accelerating rate of about 32 feet per second. After a full second in flight, a bullet will strike 32 feet below where a horizontal barrel is pointing. Of course, bullets seldom stay aloft for a full second. A 100-grain .25-06 bullet started at 3,150 fps will strike a deer 250 yards away in a quarter-second, given deceleration that brings average velocity to 3,000 fps. During that quarter-second, the bullet drops three feet—not eight feet, because gravity has an accelerating effect, and, in the last quarter of the first second, the bullet falls several times as far as in the first quarter). A slower bullet drops the same distance during the same time, it just doesn't cover as much ground, laterally, during that time.

Say your 165-grain .300 Savage bullet clocks an average 2,400 fps over its first 200 yards. After a quarter-second, it passes the 200-yard mark, three feet below bore-line. Delay the bullet, and drop

increases at any range. Speed up the bullet and it will stay closer to bore-line longer.

Bullet speed doesn't affect gravity, but it does figure into a bullet's arc. It is true that, if you dropped a bullet from your hand and simultaneously fired an identical bullet parallel to flat ground from a rifle the same distance above the ground, the two bullets would come to earth at very nearly the same time, though far apart.

It's hard to overestimate what gravity does to any bullet at extreme range. A 168-grain .30 match bullet battles gravity better than do most pointed soft-points. Fired from a .30-06 zeroed at 200 yards, it still strikes seven inches low at 300 yards. At 600 yards, it lands more than 70 inches below point of aim! Think high velocity will pull your fat from the fire? That same sleek bullet driven at a scorching 3,300 fps from a .30 magnum falls roughly five inches at 300 and, again, 10 times that far at 600. Better, surely, but hardly as flat as a light beam! At 1,000 yards, the .30-06 load prints 328 inches low, the .30 magnum load 242 inches low. It's easier to figure that much drop in feet: 27 and 20. So much for those camp-fire champs who say they topple game routinely at half a mile by holding dead on.

Taping drop data to your rifle puts it always within easy reach. Here, a Surgeon Scalpel.

Ballistic coefficient isn't everything. Sometimes it matters much less than terminal performance.

PART 3: LONG REACH APPLIED

IT'S LIKE WATER, BUT INVISIBLE. IT HAS ITS WAY WITH BULLETS. TIP: LET WIND TAKE YOUR SHOTS TO THE MIDDLE!

Wait long enough and you'll find wind in most places. Wind is always there—sometimes idling, always ready to roar. The earth itself hunkers against a Wyoming wind. It bends thick trees and dulls the edges of big rocks. Bullets haven't a chance.

The first pronghorn I shot in Wyoming fell to my 722 Remington in 6mm. It was a long poke. I nudged the vertical wire to the buck's nose. Wind pushed that 90-grain soft-point as far as gravity pulled it from my sightline—about 18 inches. The most recent Wyoming pronghorn to wear my tag wasn't much closer. But the wind didn't interfere. My 105-grain .243 bullet dropped right in, with no perceptible drift.

A full-value wind is perpendicular to the bullet's path. It blows from nine o'clock to three or vice versa. It has more effect than wind of equal speed from oblique angles. Wind from behind you (six o'clock) or in front (12) has essentially no effect at ordinary ranges. Why? Remember

A Nebraska hunter gets his .25-06 Model 70 above prairie grass with a bipod-assisted sit.

Wyoming breeze can blow bullets off pronghorns. Vern held into the wind to kill this one.

almost every other variable you'll encounter shooting long will have a greater effect on impact point than will six-o'clock or 12-o'clock winds.

Wind far from the muzzle, where your bullet has lost speed, moves that bullet more than does the same wind close up. On the other hand, a wind-induced change in the bullet's flight angle at the muzzle is multiplied over distance. Think of drift as a trajectory. Wind and gravity move bullets in parabolic paths.

Incidentally, rifling twist can put a vertical component into drift. Right-hand spin in a three-o'clock breeze gives bullets a lift to 10 o'clock. Wind from the left sends those bullets to four o'clock.

Vulnerability to wind depends on bullet velocity and ballistic coefficient, or C. Bullets of similar C show roughly the same drift. For example, Nosler's 130-grain .270 Partition has about the same nose shape and sectional density as its 140-grain 7mm, 165-grain .308, and 210-grain .338. Their C values range from .390 to .440. Launched at 3,000 fps, all drift about six inches at 200 yards in a 20-mph crosswind. Drop the C valuation to, say, .290, and you get 50-percent more drift—*with the same starting speed*.

My introduction to wind came in smallbore rifle matches. Moving from indoor to outdoor ranges, I felt as though I'd been plucked from a wading pool and dropped into the North Atlantic. Wind flags and "windicators"—fans with tails that swung on ball bear-

that a bullet clocking 3,000 fps encounters terrific wind resistance even in still conditions. It generates its own headwind, in fact a *2,000-mph gale*. The effect of a 20-mph headwind or tailwind is negligible.

At extreme range, a strong headwind or tailwind can show up in groups from very accurate rifles. But, besides obvious change in air resistance along the bullet's axis, you must consider the bullet's angle of flight. A horizontal tailwind pressures the top of the bullet, and a horizontal headwind angles into its belly. That's because bullets travel nose-up and, unlike porpoising arrows, stay that way throughout their flight. A descending bullet is not a diving bullet. It is like a football thrown long. And more bullet weight lies behind mid-point than in front. So, while the attitude of a bullet fired at a distant target may not be off horizontally by much, or stay *absolutely* constant in flight, you can assume a mild tilt. A tailwind pushes down as it pushes forward, while a headwind gives the bullet a lift as it boosts nose pressure. In sum,

Wayne fired this 10-shot group in a prone match at 100 yards, pretty far for wind-sensitive .22s!

Wind needn't scatter your bullets. "Picking the condition" can deliver tight groups.

ings—showed us wind speed and direction. Even a light breeze could shove a .22 bullet across a couple scoring rings.

But windicators at the line didn't tell the whole story. They'd hum lazily with nary a flip of their tails, while my bullets jumped in and out of the 10-ring. The flags at 50 and 100 yards, however, affirmed that downrange conditions were unstable. Wind at the target could even run opposite that at the line! I'd see flags in full flap at 100 yards, other flags limp at 50. Or windicators would spin furiously to the left, while mid-range flags lifted to the right and 100-yard flags kicked left again. A bullet sent through that gauntlet flew a ziz-zag course; shooting during mixed signals was perilous. The patter of shots would die out as savvy marksmen waited for more favorable conditions.

Favorable doesn't necessarily mean still. It is possible to shoot well in wind, if you're zeroed for that condition or "shade" for it. Zeroed for predominate drift, you get more shooting time during a match. You can afford to hold your fire during let-offs and pick-ups, or at least reduce the number of shots you must fire under those conditions. Smart shooters make notes about the wind on a new range, so they learn its idiosyncrasies. The Spokane range, where I often competed, is on a riverbank. Wind typically angles across the line from seven or eight o'clock, then bounces off the bank and hits the targets from four o'clock. If you minded the wind only at the line, you'd make a mistake.

Centerfire rifles can drive bullets through moderate wind without significant deflection, *at normal hunting yardage*. Even a 170-grain flat-nose

.30-30 bullet drifts less than two inches in a 10-mph full-value wind at 100 yards. A 25-mph wind, strong enough to sway trees, pushes that .30-30 bullet only four inches. Pointed bullets from the .30-06 fare better. Even wind that picks up small dogs and trashcan lids has little effect at modest ranges or when the angle is acute. But, as trajectory becomes steeper the farther a bullet gets from the muzzle, so deflection becomes greater at long range.

For any distance, when wind speed doubles, you get double the drift. Halve wind speed, and you halve drift. Reduce angle from 90 degrees and you reduce drift proportionately. Change shot distance, however, and the drift may surprise you. A 130-grain .270 bullet launched at 3,000 fps drifts only about ¾-inch at 100 yards in a 10-mph wind. But, at 200 yards, it is three inches off course—four times as much! At 300 yards, it drifts seven inches, at 400, 13. Why? Well, there's little drift at 100 yards, because the bullet gets there so fast: in about $1/10$-second. It doesn't drop much at 100 yards, either. Drift and drop increase significantly between 100 and 200 yards—thank deceleration. Drift quadruples in the second hundred yards. Alas, there's no convenient constant for computing drift farther out. Drift for our .270 bullet at 500 yards is only 60-percent greater than at 400.

Anemometers like this handy Kestrel put numbers to the wind, help you predict drift.

For many popular big-game loads, a rule of thumb is to allow an inch of drift at 100 yards. Triple that at 200. Double the 200 drift at 300, and double the 300 drift at 400. Here's how that works for a 180-grain Barnes TSX bullet from a .300 Winchester Magnum:

DRIFT FOR 180-GRAIN .308 TSX STARTED AT 2,960 FPS IN 10-MPH RIGHT-ANGLE WIND

	Actual drift (inches)	Rule of thumb drift (inches)
100 yards	0.7	1
200 yards	2.8	3
300 yards	6.3	6
400 yards	11.9	12

In this case, the estimates are very close. Bullets that aren't as sleek or as fast challenge that rule, but, for popular cartridges, discrepancies are negligible until you get past 400. For the .223 and kin, use 1½ inches as the 100-yard drift figure. For "woods" rounds like the .30-30, allow two inches at 100, and triple the 200-yard drift at 300.

A bullet's rate of deceleration and its vulnerability to wind increase with drag. A bullet the shape of a soup can is not well adapted for flight. But lightweight spitzers, like 50-grain .223s, also have puny ballistic coefficients, because their sectional densities (ratio of weight to the square of diameter) are low. A sleek bullet short for its diameter can have as much trouble cleaving air as a longer bullet with a blunt nose. All else equal, fast bullets buck wind better than slow ones, and a bullet that retains its speed better keeps a truer course through downrange wind.

Rate of deceleration heavily influences long-range drift. Muzzle speed can, in fact, become all but irrelevant. Consider the following:

You can learn much about wind by shooting .22 rimfires like this CZ at 100-yard bull's-eyes.

DRIFT IN A 10-MPH, RIGHT-ANGLE WIND

range (yards)	0	100	200	300	400	500
.30-06, 110-grain velocity (fps)		3330					1240
drift (inches)		1	6	15	30	52
.308 Win. 180-grain velocity (fps)		2620					1210
drift (inches)	1	6	15	29	49	

These two bullets leave the rifles at speeds 700 fps apart, but, at 500 yards, register nearly identical numbers. Drift is the same to 300 yards, as the greater weight of the heavy bullet offsets the velocity edge of the lighter one. But, at long range, the heavy bullet better resists wind. It eventually passes the 110-grain spitzer, whose rapid deceleration erases the speed advantage. Weight alone, though, is no panacea. The heavier bullet does not necessarily perform better in wind, even if it's conical and driven about the same speed. A .223 bullet half the weight of the 110-grain .30-06 shows almost identical vulnerability to wind:

range (yards)	0	100	200	300	400	500
.223 Rem., 55-grain velocity (fps)		3240					1270
drift (inches)		1	6	15	29	50

Bullet weight, ballistic coefficient, and velocity all affect drift, because they all affect deceleration. These three bullets show how:

range (yards)	0	100	200	300	400	500
.300 Win., 150-grain velocity (fps)		3290					1810
drift (inches)		1	4	9	17	28
.300 Wby., 180-grain velocity (fps)		3250					1990
drift (inches)		1	3	8	14	23
.375 H&H, 300-grain velocity (fps)		2530					1130
drift (inches)		2	7	17	33	56
.458 Win., 500-grain velocity (fps)		2040					1160
drift (inches)		2	6	15	28	45

The .300 Weatherby's 180-grain bullet, driven as fast as a 150 spitzer from the .300 Winchester, drifts about five inches less and with 176 fps less lag at 500 yards (because of its additional weight). Given the same bullet shape and diameter, deceleration fades as you up weight. Despite their greater surface area, heavier bullets resist crosswinds better than do light ones.

The effect of deceleration shows up in the greater drift of the .375 bullet compared to the .458. Terminal velocities at 500 yards are nearly identical, but the .458 loses only about 800 fps en route, while the .375 drops 1,400 fps. (This .375 solid, incidentally, is one of the least aerodynamic of all .375 bullets.) So, here the faster bullet drifts nearly a foot farther than the slower bullet, though C values are close. The great weight of the .458 bullet hikes inertia, which extends maximum range and reduces wind drift.

Long noses with sharp tips give bullets aerodynamic shape. But it's easy to give too much credit to the bullet nose. The first .1-inch of the nose can be flat, round, or pointed without materially affecting trajectory or drift. It is the ogive, the leading curve, that matters more.

Boat-tail bullets offer little advantage at normal hunting ranges, but remain a unanimous choice

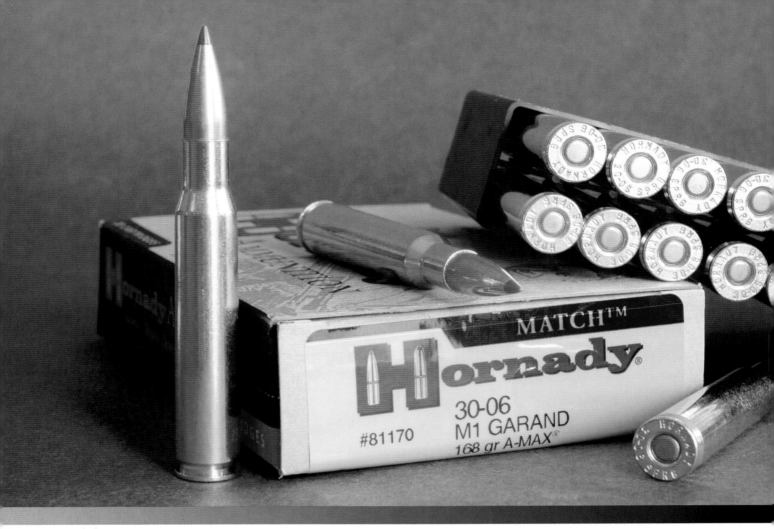

Wayne found Hornady's Garand loads buck wind quite well, despite modest bullet weight.

of long-range shooters. Example: Two 140-grain 7mm bullets, flat-base and boat-tail, started at 2,700 fps reach the 100-yard mark clocking about 2,500 fps. At 200, the boat-tail bullet is traveling at 2,320, just 15 fps faster. At 350 yards, the boat-tail bullet is leading by 35 fps; difference in drop amounts to only about half an inch. You'll get similar differences in drift in a 10-mph wind. A 30-mph wind that moves the flat-base 7mm bullet 17 inches at 350 yards moves the boat-tail bullet 15½ inches. *Percentage* difference in deflection between bullets holds regardless of wind speed. Far away, the boat-tail shows an edge, which is why target shooters favor it at 600 and 1,000 yards.

No matter how well your bullet resists wind, hitting at distance depends on your ability to predict drift. Early in my competitive shooting, rifleman Dick Nelson (who helped Boeing design the first moon buggy), put it this way: "Learn to read mirage and your bullets will hop into the X-ring like trained pigs."

Mirage is a visual distortion caused by heat waves rising from the earth's surface. Mirage doesn't move bullets; it indicates wind that does. Mirage can also show you a target that isn't there, by "floating" the target image in the direction the air currents are moving. You can't see mirage at all distances at once. You'll either see the strongest mirage or the mirage at the range for which your scope is focused. To get the most information about the wind that most affects bullets, competitive marksman focus their spotting scopes to read mirage just shy of the targets.

Mirage that's bumpy and moving slowly indicates light breeze. Flat, fast mirage shows stiffer wind. When mirage disappears with no change in light conditions, it's often because wind has picked up. Mirage that boils vertically signals a still condition—but beware, as a boil commonly precedes a reversal in wind direction or, of course, a pick-up. You're smart to zero for a light prevailing breeze, then hold fire during boils and reversals, shading and shooting during pick-ups and let-offs.

Tiny bullets seem drift-prone, but speed works in your favor to offset the effect of wind.

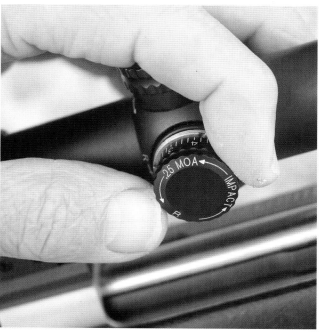

Save in rifle matches, Wayne leaves windage settings alone, preferring to "shade," lest the zero be lost.

From left: .223, 6.5 Creedmoor, 6.5x55, .308, .30-06, .300 Win., and .338 Lapua. All have been used effectively for target shooting at long range and for hunting.

At 250 yards with a 6.5 Creedmoor, Wayne aimed a foot windward of this vaal rhebok.

At 780 yards, Wayne favored left for a 12-mph eight-o'clock blow. He needed a half-minute more.

LEAN ON EQUIPMENT AND YOU'LL FALL FLAT. LONG-RANGE PRECISION DEPENDS MOSTLY ON YOU!

You wouldn't think something as big as an oven door would be tough to hit. But deer are not only more elusive than ovens, they're harder to shoot. I know. I have missed deer from just about every angle, in all kinds of weather, near and far, with a variety of rifles, on the run and standing still as a stump. If a shot can be botched, I've botched it. Such credentials are rare among hunters these days, most of whom claim a level of marksmanship far beyond mine. Many of them will advise you to buy better equipment if you want to hit deer (or anything else) more often. I'm a contrarian. In my view, marksmanship is what you need most. Especially for the long shot.

I started missing early, when you could buy McDonald's hamburgers for 19 cents and a new Ford Mustang for under three grand. It was a raw dawn, raw as only Michigan Novembers can be. A buck had given us the slip the evening before, and I was there, alone, in the dark, feeling my way along a fence, while frigid wind sang through its taut wires. I stopped at the edge of the woodlot and waited. When the

No matter your position, always grab the chance to add a support, however crude.

heavy sky got gray enough to see musculature in the clouds, I put the K4 to my eye and scoped a wheat field, the only area not still black. To my astonishment, the stubble had a deer in it! My heart was suddenly beating as fast as a gerbil's; my mouth went dry. Seconds later, the deer brought its head up and showed me a modest set of antlers.

Actually, they didn't appear modest to me. For a lad hunting where bucks appeared as infrequently as fairy godmothers, this was a spectacular rack. By the same logic, the deer itself looked big as a quarter horse. Quickly, I estimated the range at 350 yards and leveled my Mauser over a fencepost. The flat crack of the .264 did not bother the deer, which again lowered its head into the stubble. My second shot caused it to look up and stop chewing. My gerbil heart found a higher gear. The rifle was surely not shooting where I was looking—over the deer's back, so the bullet would drop 12 inches into the vitals. Had the scope been bumped? In desperation, I aimed right at the buck and yanked the trigger. The animal dropped.

Pacing 350 steps, I crossed the stubble, a farm lane, a block of alfalfa, the county line, and more stubble. Looking back, I could barely see the fencepost. Perhaps I had overestimated the distance. Backtracking took me within 160 steps of the fence, where lay the buck, as unlucky a deer as I'd ever see.

Since that day, 45 years ago, I've tried to shoot

Here, lightweight shooting sticks steady .22 rifles from the sit on a prairie dog shoot.

A typical African tripod works fine, affording quick, steady aim over tall grass and bush.

better. But, honestly, I've been lucky more often than competent. One whitetail flew by like a rocket. Patches of brown flickered through snow-splotched aspens. I swung hard and fired, as if at a grouse. Somehow the bullet found an opening. The first full view I had of that deer came as it somersaulted through a shaft of sun. Heady stuff for a young Michigan hunter on the season's last day.

In Oregon, years later, an elk sped by. Bolting from another hunter along the ridge opposite, it galloped free of the conifers, crossing. Recoil bounced my Model 70, as the crosswire sped a yard ahead of the bull's chest. He came undone over a patch of tawny grass, a head over heels tumble that raked up a rodeo of dust and piled him against a deadfall.

A truly heavy mule deer buck appeared on a cold mountaintop, in British Columbia. He had been watching *me*, while I looked in vain for *him*. The icy wind had numbed me, and I was about to move on. Then I spied a branch that looked more like antler than alder. By gum, it *was* antler! I scurried forward to close the distance, down into a cleft that separated us. But the slope got steep and slick. Clinging to iced rock with both hands, grappling with the alders, I was noisily getting nowhere. I struggled back to find another path—and glimpsed the buck sneaking away. My bullet caught him just as he vanished over the ridge. A memorable finish.

I'd like to recount more examples of fine shooting. Sadly, there aren't many more. There should

Though this shot was close, Wayne eased up to a dead tree to steady his rifle and shoot offhand.

be. In truth, I've missed a lot of shots and made too many poor hits. I've missed the chance to shoot often enough to qualify as a non-consumptive outdoorsman.

"If you can't be good, you can still be better." The old-timer was a pretty fair rifle shot and adept at consoling young shooters who came unglued in a match because they'd thrown one bullet wide. "If you let that flinch ruin your day," he said, "take up another sport." I fought back a tear. Gently, he added, "Every shooter makes bad shots. Nobody hits the middle all the time. Winners focus on good shots to come, not on bad shots they can't change." A good lesson, that, even if you don't shoot.

Shooting game is just like shooting targets, except there are more variables. You can't deal with

Shooting from field positions won't deliver one-hole groups, but it helps you kill game!

on muscles to support your body's weight. When the trigger breaks, your body wants to relax. If it is already relaxed, the rifle stays on target. If you've muscled the rifle where it doesn't want to go, it will come off-target at the shot.

PRONE, SITTING, AND KNEELING

Prone is the steadiest position, largely because your body has almost full contact with the earth. Prone's other advantage: low center of gravity. The closer you can get to the ground, the steadier you are. The lower your *prone* position, the steadier it is too, though, in practice, you may have to keep above grass to aim or ensure a clear path for your bullet. If you're using a bipod, you can grasp the fore-end with your left hand (good practice with lightweight rifles that shudder in wind, and with rifles that jump high

the variables until you've mastered the fundamentals of shooting. You've probably heard someone boast of being a great game shot. He's "death on animals," he assures you, but can't hit paper targets. That's like saying you can drive as well as anyone on the NASCAR circuit but have trouble parallel parking. Paper tells you *exactly* how good you are. On paper, you measure your progress as you master the fundamentals.

These fundamentals are quite simple. To hit, you must keep the sight on the target while you pull the trigger. To do that, you must steady the rifle, and, to do *that*, you must be still. You become still with a solid position, built from the ground up. The ground is important, because it does not move.

Another component of solid position is bone structure. Bones, not muscles, best support you and the rifle. Muscles are elastic, and they tire. Muscles contain blood that surges, nerves that twitch. Bones are like bricks: If you can align them so your muscles needn't work to keep joints from slipping, you'll build, with those bones, a platform that's as still as the human body can be.

Bone alignment must also put the rifle naturally on target. If you force the rifle on target with muscles, you'll have the same problems as if you depended

A sling-assisted sit can be very steady. Wayne fired this group—tighter than his average!

Africa's ubiquitous shooting sticks helped
Amber take this gemsbok with a 7mm-08.

A tripod is better than a bipod. Bipod legs should be
thrust well forward and leaned into.

Commercial tripods like this from BOGpod are converting African PHs accustomed to real wood.

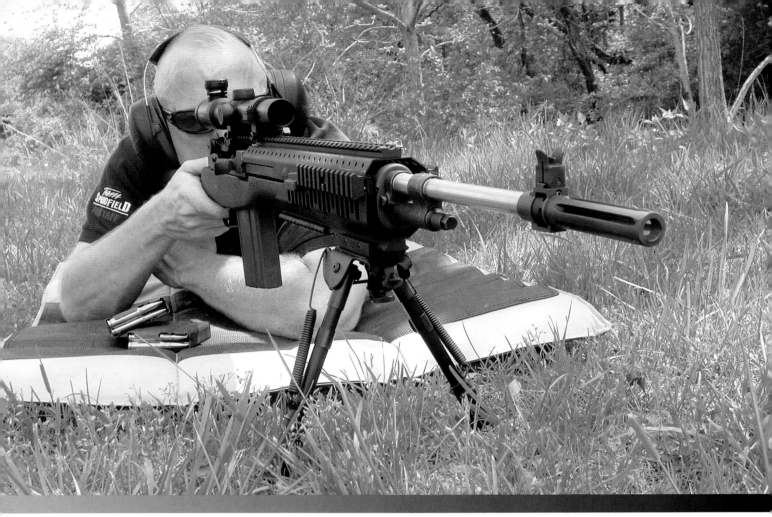

The Harris bipod is popular on sporting rifles and service models like this Springfield M14.

during recoil). Or you can steady the toe of the stock, left arm crooked under chest and chin. I prefer the toe-grip with heavy rifles.

A shooting sling can also steady the rifle. Such a sling has a loop that's adjustable independent of overall sling length. You give the loop half a turn out, then thrust your arm through that loop, bringing it up above your triceps and securing it there by sliding the keeper—a leather ring on sporting and military rifle slings, a metal clamp on target slings—into place. A shooting sling, tight from the fore-end to the loop on your upper arm, brings the rifle back into your right shoulder as it transfers weight from your left arm to your left shoulder. It deadens the nerve twitches and muscle tremors and heartbeat that make reticles dance. From your triceps to the rear swivel, the sling hangs loose—this is important, and the reason a strap (versus a proper and true sling), without an adjustable loop won't help you! A strap, slipped around your arm, pulls on both

swivels. Tension on the rear swivel pulls the rifle from your shoulder and cants the rifle. Both results are poison!

This young shooter trains, prone, for summer biathlon competition (note the special sling).

Note the Brownells sling is loose from arm to rear swivel, tight and flat across left wrist.

In a steady prone position, your left arm is almost directly under the rifle, your right knee crooked slightly to roll your belly off the ground. Reason: Transferring weight to your hip reduces the pulse bounce you'll feel when your belly contacts the ground. Your rifle points naturally at the target. If it doesn't—if you must muscle it over—your body is in the wrong relationship to the target. Move your entire body.

After getting into and out of a slinged-up prone position many times, you'll find yourself doing it quickly and comfortably, and that your body will align the rifle accurately as it meets the ground. I've shot many prone matches, have won a couple state championships, and have come to use prone often when hunting. It has come to my aid in what some hunters might consider unlikely places—in timber for elk, in African bush for buffalo, on near-vertical snow for mountain goat. Because prone is so steady, I hunt with one eye looking for game, the other seeking a convenient place to lie down. Having used a Brownells Latigo sling for four decades, I can don the loop without looking, while bent over on the final steps of a stalk. It snugs itself as soon as my elbows hit the ground. Because I shoot from prone so often afield, I've come to zero my rifles from that position

Wayne favors the Brownells Latigo sling, here steadying a McMillan rifle while the author is kneeling.

(or at least check zeros). Benching a rifle to zero is fine, but a taut sling will affect point of impact; depending on the rifle, that shift can be significant.

Sitting is the next steadiest shooting position. You can do it with crossed ankles, like high-power competitors, or with crossed legs, as is the fashion in smallbore matches. Both are useful, though the crossed-leg option is slower and gets harder as your back and thigh muscles resist stretching with age. The fastest and easiest sit for hunting—and better on uneven ground or for steep shot angles or moving game—is the "tent" sitting position. In this, your heels dig into the ground in front of you, your torso arches forward toward your bent knees. The rifle points, roughly, over your left little toe. Elbows lock against the front of your knees, flat of elbow against face of knee. This last detail is important because, without this firm contact, the tent position will come apart, your back muscles pulling your torso off your knees.

High enough to put your sightline over grass and low brush, but low enough to steady your rifle, sitting is versatile and, with practice, quick to assume. A shooting sling here helps as much as in prone. A

Wayne fires a Jack O'Connor Tribute rifle prone. Both eyes open. Latigo sling, of course.

Prone, you're less conspicuous, steadier, and can keep shots above short prairie grass.

Adam tugs the strap to steady his rifle on the tripod and pull the stock into his shoulder.

few years ago, still-hunting an Oregon ridge at dawn, I heard two deer scoot from the whitebark pine rimming the basin below. They stopped on an open rockslide for a last look back. I had immediately dropped to a sit, and the crosswire in the 2½x Lyman quickly found the shoulder of the biggest buck. The 130-grain Hornady from my .270 flattened that deer instantly. Distance: about 300 yards. A sling-assisted sit should give you three-minute accuracy under favorable conditions; make that two, with religious practice.

Kneeling is faster than sitting, but not as steady, because it's not as low and your fanny is not on the ground. Right-handed? Kneel on your right knee, your tailbone resting on the heel of your right foot, which is bent straight underneath, toes flat on the ground. Your left shin is vertical, left knee supporting left arm and rifle. The point of your elbow lies just in front of

An open, heels-in-the-ground "tent" sit excels for shots where ground falls away.

When sitting, lean well forward so that your lower back pulls your arms into the front of your knees.

the knee, not on it. Half your weight rests on the heel of your right foot, a third of it on the left foot. The right knee is simply a brace and bears the remainder of your weight. Keep your torso and head erect, so you can look straight through the sight. Do not slump forward! Secure the rifle butt high in your shoulder, to put the comb firmly against your cheek. Twist your left foot slightly so that it's parallel with your right leg, to mitigate the three- to nine-o'clock wobble you'll find with any kneeling position. Generally, it's not good to put muscles under tension when you shoot, because you can't hold that tension without quivering. But, in this case, the weight of your body and rifle press your foot against the ground, where friction holds it without effort. Again, a sling takes much of the wobble out of your rifle. (You'll find, as you adjust your sling in prone, sitting, and kneeling, that you can indeed use one sling setting for all three positions.)

Kneeling excels when you must shoot quickly and when grass or brush preclude lower positions. It's an alternative to offhand (standing) when, close to game in timber, speed becomes more important than precision. You can quickly drop below the skirts of conifers that obscure your target, to find a clear shot alley. Once, tracking an elk to ridgeline in deep snow, I saw legs move in a thicket. Instantly, I went to one knee. Antlers flickered through an opening, and I fired when the reticle found space in front of the chest. Alas, all I earned for this morning's hard effort was a big wad of hair, clipped by a bullet that went too far in front. I followed the bull for a half-mile and left him in fine fettle. The lesson: Though kneeling put nothing in my freezer this time, it gave me a shot I'd not have had from any other shooting position.

Note that this rifleman holds the tripod, not the rifle. That's a best bet except when recoil is severe.

Savage CEO Ron Coburn shot this outstanding New Mexico pronghorn from the kneeling position.

At 600 yards, small errors in position cost points in a match! Pulse bounces bullets.

Offhand is unsteady but fast. Up close, precision still matters. Aim small, carefully.

OFFHAND

"How long did it take you to learn offhand?" I asked one night, after a particularly dismal string with my match rifle.

Earl sucked pensively on the huge cigar he would light later, filling the basement range with blue haze. By that time, the rifle smoke would be so dense, nobody would notice.

"Oh, a few months," he said. I brightened. "But, after I learned how, it was years before I could hit anything."

Earl Wickman was one of those precious people who opened his home and his heart to youngsters eager to shoot. Back then, nearly half a century ago, as this is written, shooting was an honorable pastime. Earl taught me that shooting was a discipline, and to shoot well you had to be disciplined.

Offhand is the last-resort position, because it affords you just two points of contact with Mother Earth and puts your center of gravity as high as it can be. Furthermore, your sling does no good, because there's no brace to secure your left elbow. You may find your reticle gyrating like a June bug in a food processor. Your job then, is, to apply trigger pressure when the reticle is on the target, hold pressure when it is off, add pressure when it comes on again. Eventually, the rifle will fire—but getting it to fire before your muscles tire, eyes blur, or lungs implode is a challenge. Proper position helps you meet it.

Good offhand shooting starts with a solid foundation. Mine distributes my weight evenly on feet shoulder-width apart. An imaginary line across my toes meets the line of sight at about a 25-degree angle to the target. My right elbow is high, roughly parallel to the ground, to form a convenient pocket in my shoulder for the rifle butt. My left arm is not high, but almost directly under the rifle, where it can more easily support the rifle's weight. I grasp the grip firmly with my right hand and pull it gently—no white knuckles, firm is not tight! My left hand holds the fore-end (again, firmly) halfway out, to support and direct the muzzle. Depending on fore-end shape,

For offhand shots, this GreyBull rifle is supported fore and aft by a tripod and special arm.

I like to cradle it with index finger underneath, as might a shotgunner. My back and neck are straight. The comb comes to my cheek so I can look directly ahead. I stand nearly flat-footed, but prefer *slight* forward pressure on the balls of my feet. My knees are straight but not locked. It's important to keep center of gravity over your feet.

"Most successful shooters lean back and slightly to the right to counter the rifle's weight," says Gary Anderson, an accomplished shooter who won Olympic gold in 300-meter free-rifle events in 1964 and 1968. "Support the rifle by bracing your left arm against your ribs." Try that with a heavy rifle and you'll agree with Gary. But hunting rifles lack the mass to get steady with your left hand far to the rear. You'll likely fare better holding the fore-end near its midpoint. Relax. Gary advises that, on a tension scale of zero to 10, with zero being total relaxation, muscles supporting you and your rifle should register a one.

Lones Wigger, another Olympic double-gold medalist, stands straight as a corner post. "Don't hunch over the rifle. It'll put you off balance and add tension to back muscles," he points out. "Keep your head upright, even if cheeking the stock puts the rifle butt above your shoulder." Your right elbow is best horizontal. A slight wrist twist is okay. Wrist tension

offhand requires no effort to maintain; the friction of your hand on the grip does that, and such tension can help steady the rifle.

Let your left elbow support the rifle from underneath, not out to the side. Pulling that elbow left strains your shoulder muscles and tires your arm. My left elbow falls within the plane formed between shoulder and front swivel stud, just in front of my hand. That elbow is almost directly above my left little toe. Offhand, muscles in both arms come into play, but even where there's no bone support to the ground, you can use bones to advantage by aligning them comfortably underneath the load.

Point your feet before you point the rifle. Lift the gun smoothly to your cheek, as you breathe deeply to bring oxygenated air to your brain and eyes. Keep both eyes open, squinting only as much as needed to get clear aim. Contact the trigger as you exhale. Empty, but don't purge, your lungs, as the sight swings onto the target and your finger starts to apply pressure. Unless conditions change or the animal takes leave, you have 10 to 12 seconds to shoot before your eyes blur and your lungs start clamoring for air. If you can't make the shot within that window, start over. When a big buck is staring at you and the rifle won't settle, you'll feel compelled to force the shot. Almost always, a shot taken when your eyes and lungs are starved for oxygen is a bad shot. Partly that's because your muscles tire at the same time—you're losing control. Work on a cadence that puts a bullet six to eight seconds after you exhale.

Shooting at animals is easier than shooting at bull's-eyes, because most animals are much bigger. On the other hand, animals don't have concentric rings. Neither do you know the target distance. You may have to shoot uphill or down or from a spot that's wet, rocky, or steep. The wind could be gusting with enough force to splinter palm trees—or just enough to bounce your reticle gently out of the vitals when you tug the last ounce from the trigger. You'll be excited, maybe out of breath. Your hands could be cold or mittened or both. You may be too stiff for a low position, or swathed in clothes that don't let you bend or use a sling quickly. Add target movement, brush in the bullet's path, obnoxious light and, suddenly, the variables target shooters never see can make a short shot tough. Maybe so tough

it's best declined. Remember, errant bullets are as apt to cripple game as they are to miss cleanly. Depending on the circumstances, the crippling hit can be much more likely. You don't make a bad shot if you don't shoot.

No shot is lucky. You make the shot what it is. The rifle does your bidding. A bullet flies where you direct it, in a predictable path. The result of every shot you take is your doing. Practice will boost the odds you'll make lethal hits. Good judgment will keep you from crippling.

"Shoot better, and you'll have to shoot less often," said one of my mentors. I can't recall if he told me to shoot only when I was 90-percent sure of a center hit. But he could have.

A bulletin board at the U.S. Army's Marksmanship Training Unit center, in Fort Benning, Georgia, once held this reminder: *The fundamentals never change.* I can't say whether the note is still up. Because the USAMTU still teaches riflemen how to shoot, it should be.

Offhand, Wayne shows erect posture, his left arm well underneath, right elbow horizontal.

DOWNHILL

While you can't at any given moment spar with all the gremlins that might scuttle a shot, you can practice shooting fundamentals. You can practice in hunting clothes and jog before shooting so you learn how to shoot when you're short of breath. You can put yourself at the mercy of the wind on breezy days and shoot in poor light or against the sun, at unknown distances and steep angles.

Incidentally, shot angles don't affect point of impact as much as ordinarily thought. If the angle, up or down, is less than 30 degrees and the target closer than 250 yards, forget about it. Just shoot. The bullet may strike a bit high, but it won't miss deer vitals. At longer range, the effect is greater. Ditto for

steeper angles. You'll want to aim low, then, because the bullet is not traveling perpendicular to the tug of gravity and will be less affected by it than if the shot were taken horizontally. The horizontal component of a bullet's flight is the only one that matters. So a 360-yard shot with 300-yard horizontal component requires a 300-yard hold. To understand this better, visualize a bullet fired straight up into the heavens or down through the center of the earth. There is no trajectory in either case, because gravity pulls only on the nose or heel of the bullet. The horizontal component of the bullet's flight is zero. No matter how far the shot, the bullet will not cross the line of sight a second time.

If in doubt with an angled shot, shade low. Most downhill and uphill misses are high.

Wayne shot a goat halfway up this mountain face, where shot angle can affect bullet placement.

For shots to 250 yards and gentle angles, aim center. Over-compensation causes misses.

Ninth-grade geometry can help you figure proper hold for various shot angles. The triangles are all right-angle, with the bullet path the hypotenuse. Example: A 280-yard shot at a very steep 45-degree angle should bring to mind the equilateral right triangle, its legs with a value of 1 each, the hypotenuse is the square root of two, or 1.41. The ratio of 1 to 1.41 is the same as that of 200 to 282. Hold for 200 yards!

Maybe not classic, but steady! With support, improvised field positions can drop game!

TRIGGER CONTROL

"It'll come" said Earl. "Just relax."

But I couldn't relax. The blurry black dot of a target only flirted with the aperture front sight. Its insert was orange plastic. I'd see the target floating behind the orange screen, like an elusive fish beneath the surface of a lake. Then, like the fish jumping, it would explode into the bright ivory center. Now! My brain screamed it. But, by the time I yanked the trigger and the rifle fired, the target had slid behind the orange curtain—the fish back in the water. The bullet flew wild.

"Don't practice bad habits," Earl chided quietly. "As you think, so will you become."

My bad habits were legion. The worst was trying to time the shot, to pin that fish by anticipating its jump and meeting it with a bullet. That curse stayed with me for years.

To shake it, I started dry-firing. Few people I knew dry-fired. If a rifle didn't go bang and make holes, they lost interest. But they weren't Olympic-class shooters. Gary Anderson was, and he'd learned to shoot with an empty rifle. Inserting a fired case to cushion the striker, you, too, may find dry-firing a .22 useful. Bolt-action centerfire rifles can be safely dry-fired without the fired hull.

Your trigger finger should contact the trigger at the first (distal) joint. It shouldn't touch the rifle anywhere else. The idea is to tug straight back. Some pistol grips curve so close that fellows like me, with palms the size of potholders, must kink their index fingers severely. The resulting pull can then nudge the trigger to the right. I prefer slender, sweeping stock wrists set well back, so I can comfortably place my hand for a straight pull. Yes, it's a pull, not a squeeze. Squeezing implies use of the entire hand. The index finger is for firing only. With it you pull (or press or crush) the trigger. Save the squeeze for your honey's hand.

Think of your trigger finger as letting a shot go, instead of making it go. Apply pressure with the sight

Savage's AccuTrigger helps with long shots from less than solid positions and in wind.

Tempted to jerk the trigger for urgent shots offhand? Don't! Coax ignition gently.

on target, hold pressure when it wanders off. Given a solid position, the sight will spend more time on-target than off. Firing should come as a surprise. You won't know how much time will elapse before the trigger breaks. But you'll remember the pressure your finger felt when it broke on the previous shot.

Try this: Stick a dark thumbtack on your living room wall and, from 15 or 20 feet, dry-fire at it 10 times daily. Concentrate on position, sight picture, breath control, and trigger pull. Call your shots. If the trigger breaks when the sight is off the mark, or if you jerk the trigger, do that shot over. And over . . . .

This coyote presented a small target at 250 yards, head-on. Trigger control was crucial!

Hill Country Rifles tuned the trigger on this M70. A crisp, consistent break helps you hit!

A SLING STEADIES YOUR RIFLE LIKE A REST. BUT SCOTCHING THE JIGGLES HELPS ONLY AFTER A PRECISE ZERO!

DEPLOYING SLINGS

Unless you've employed sand-bags or a mechanical rest on a sturdy bench, or "gone prone" with the rifle on a bipod or over a pack or a jacket-padded rock, you'll see movement in a rifle's sight. It skips and hops to the tune of your quivering muscles and throbbing heart.

I didn't have the luxury of a natural rest when the caribou appeared, quartering off in the morning drizzle. Quebec's tundra, bare as a pool table, afforded no chance to move. I jammed my arm through the sling and swiped the ocular lens as I bellied down. While the image of the distant bull hardly qualified as clear, my rifle settled quickly. When the animal stopped walking, it was far away, but the crosswire had barely a quiver. My bullet struck mid-rib and exited the far shoulder. The bull spun and collapsed.

Shooting slings were once a common accoutrement on rifles. Most were two-part leather military versions with double brass hooks to adjust the loop and overall sling length. Target shooters used leather, too, but the slings had big cuffs and often a metal keeper with a knurled

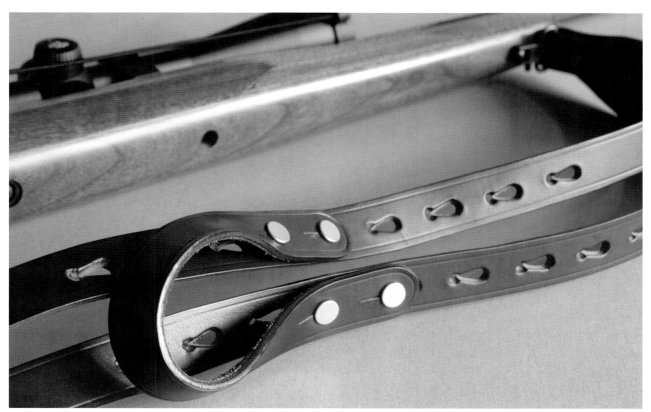

Besides superb holsters, Galco makes this ingenious Safari Ching Sling for riflemen.

Wayne bellied down to hide from this deer—and shot it from steady, slinged-up prone!

knob so you could tighten it securely after running it up to snug the cuff on your arm. Because target slings had no business to conduct with the rear swivel, i.e., they weren't used to carry the rifle, they had no "tail" behind the cuff.

Target shooters continue to employ slings. They must, if they're serious about their scores. Prone, an accomplished marksman should be able to shoot about as well with a tight sling as he or she can over a sandbag. Oddly enough, hunters have drifted away from slings, embracing carrying straps in their stead. Commonly called "slings" by people who don't know better (perhaps the same people who label detachable box magazines "clips"), "straps" lack the independent loop that identifies a shooting sling. A *strap* can't be pulled taut between the front swivel and your upper arm, unless it also tugs with the same vigor against the rear swivel. So, while it's coaxing the rifle into your shoulder and transferring weight to your upper body, the strap pulls the toe of the stock away from your shoulder and applies torque that cants your rifle.

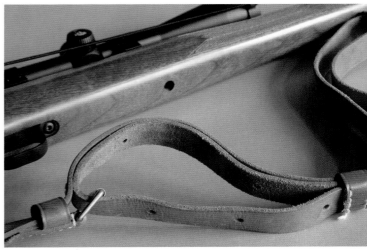

Brownells Latigo Sling excels for hunting rifles. It's lightweight, easy to use, and fully adjustable.

One reason carrying straps have gained traction at market is the new materials that give them a bit of stretch. They absorb some of the bounce that makes your rifle feel heavier than it is. Another popular feature is the "cobra" profile of many straps. Wide, and in some cases heavily padded, where the

A taut sling can shift point of impact from a benchrest zero—generally to seven o'clock.

strap meets your clavicle, these sell well to shooters toting heavy rifles. The increasing use of bipods on varminters and even trim sporting rifles has helped keep cobra straps in circulation.

My sling of choice is Brownell's Latigo. This all-leather sling, in one- or 1¼-inch widths, has a long history. I've used it since the Nixon administration. The Latigo is all leather, but, unlike the military sling, is of one-piece design. Instead of two heavy brass double-hooks, it has only a slender brass ring and a brass button to handle all adjustment. In service, the ring is shielded from contact with the rifle by the leather. No banging. No stock dings.

The Latigo's shooting loop and overall length are independently adjustable. The loop goes around your left arm just above the triceps. You snug it with a keeper, a double-stitched leather ring that slides up and down the sling when it's loose, but keeps the two sling straps from springing apart when they encircle your arm. You can use the Latigo sling to good effect from prone, sitting, and kneeling positions. No sling helps offhand, with your left arm unsupported. That arm must be anchored on the ground or your knee; if it isn't, sling tension will collapse the angle of your elbow, yielding the rifle's weight to your forearm.

Offhand, some shooters say they get help from a hasty sling. But this is a technique, not the strap itself. You can't purchase a hasty sling. You can use a carrying strap or employ a shooting sling as a hasty sling by keeping the loop flat and using the entire assembly as a strap. Poke your left arm between strap and rifle, then wrap your left wrist once around the strap's front end. If the strap is too short for the wrap, you can just cock your left elbow to snug the sling at both ends. The hasty sling *can* help deaden jiggles, but it won't prevent the rifle from dipping and bobbing offhand, because your left arm still lacks support. And putting tension on the strap means moving your left elbow from the vertical plane of the

rifle. Holding the rifle's weight with your elbow to the side, you'll soon tire—and tired muscles quiver.

The hasty sling works within a narrow range of strap lengths, which may not include the one you prefer for carry. Most of the cobra straps that distribute rifle weight nicely are too bulky and stiff to wrap around your wrist. These straps can even scuttle your shot. A pal once threw his rifle up for a quick poke at a buck and saw nothing but black! The wide strap had flopped over the barrel, blocking the scope.

A target-style stance mandates a different hasty sling: With your arm between the strap and rifle, form an upside-down pedestal with your left thumb and forefingers. Place them just in front of the trigger guard or, with thumb on the guard, fingers forward. Rest your upper left arm on your ribs and lean back. The rifle rests on its balance point. The strap tightens above your triceps, against your pectoral muscle.

Straps can work well as shooting aids when both swivels are in front of the trigger, "scout rifle" fashion. Slip your arm between strap and fore-end, then bring the strap against your tricep as you shoulder the rifle. Properly adjusted for length, the strap affords you a comfortable arm angle. As one swivel hangs just forward of the guard and the other up front, the strap tugs the rifle back from both ends. A strap on a scout rifle acts like the working end of a shooting sling without the loop or keeper. A forward-mounted sling, including the Ching Sling specifically designed for this application, forces you to carry the rifle muzzle down. It's not as bizarre an alternative as you might think, at least with relatively short barrels. With a bit of practice, you should find muzzle-down carry convenient and your rifle even faster to deploy.

The key to better shooting, with or without a sling, is practice. If sling or strap use is not second nature by opening day, you might find yourself in a tangle, when you should be squeezing the trigger!

> The key to better shooting with a sling is practice. If sling or strap use is not second nature by opening day, you might find yourself in a tangle, when you should be squeezing the trigger.

ZEROING

No matter how steady your rifle, hitting at any range presumes a proper zero. Zeroing, or sighting in, is simply aligning the sights (scope) on your rifle so the bullet hits where you aim at a certain distance. A rifle cannot be manipulated to change the bullet's path. It is the sight alone that is to be adjusted. Windage and elevation adjustments move the rear sight or a scope's reticle so it directs your eye to where the bullet hits at a given distance. You pick the range.

Because a bullet follows the bore axis out the muzzle, it will fly nearly parallel to the line of sight until gravity pulls it unacceptably off course. Bear in mind that a bullet's path is *never* perfectly straight. Gravity grabs the projectile as soon as it exits the rifle. In zeroing, you adjust the sight so your straight line of vision intersects the bullet's parabolic path not far from the muzzle, then travels below it until the two merge at the zero distance. Beyond that, the bullet drops ever more steeply away from the line of sight.

It's a common misconception that a bullet rises above line of bore during its flight. It does *not*. It *cannot*. *Sight-line is not parallel to bore line*, but, rather, at a slightly converging angle. The line of sight dips below bore line and the bullet's arc. Sightline never again meets bore line. Both are straight and, after crossing, diverge. A bullet hits *above* sightline at midrange, because sightline has been purposefully angled down through its trajectory. The bullet falls to intersect it at greater range. If the sightline were parallel with the bore, it would *never* touch the bullet's arc.

The most useful zero depends on the bullet's trajectory and on how far you intend to shoot. For most big-game rifles, a 200-yard zero makes sense. Sight in there with a .30-06 or a similar cartridge, and your bullet will stay within three vertical inches of point of aim out to 250 yards or so. A three-inch vertical error still gives you a killing strike in the ribs of big-game animals. The 200-yard zero permits "dead-on" aim as far as most marksmen can hit in the field. At 300 yards you'll have to shade high.

Why not zero at 250 or even 300? Well, with flat-shooting rounds like Weatherby's .270 Magnum, you can. A 200-yard zero puts its 140-grain bullet only 1½ inches over sightline at 100. Adjust the scope so the rifle shoots three inches high at 100, and you'll reach 300 yards with a mere one inch of

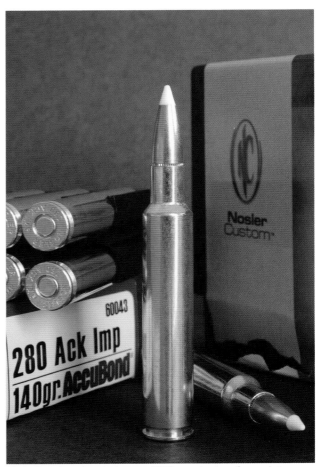

Flat-shooting loads beg a 200-yard zero, for point-blank range to 250 yards—or more.

drop! By the same logic, a zero for the likes of the .30-30 is best kept short of 200 yards, otherwise the bullet's steep arc will put it a whopping five inches high at its apex (some distance beyond 100). The best zero for a .30-30 carbine may have less to do with the limited range of the cartridge than the more limited range at which you can shoot accurately with its iron sights—or the even more limited distance you can see in typical whitetail cover! While a 150-yard zero is reasonable, a 100-yard zero may be even more practical, especially if you hunt where most of your shots come very close.

You're better off zeroing hunting rifles *so you won't ever have to hold low*. Remember that shots too long for a point-blank hold with a 200-yard zero are uncommon. Most game, even in open country, is killed well inside 300 yards. I recall a fellow shooting over the back of a magnificent bull elk at 200 because he'd zeroed his .300 Weatherby at 400.

Competitive shooters change zeros to match distances. Here, Wayne's 50-yard prone targets.

If you're firing long in competition, you'll want to change zero to match each distance exactly. An exception: In metallic silhouette matches that present targets at 200, 300, 385, and 500 meters, some shooters minimize sight changes and use fewer than four zeroes. I've zeroed at 300, shading low at 200 and high at 385, then dialing the scope to 500, where holdover would be significant.

Remember that, when choosing a zero range, your bullet's arc is parabolic. Its highest point is not in the middle, but past the middle. That .270 Weatherby zeroed at 300 yards with a 150-grain pointed bullet will print three inches high at 100 yards and *3.7 inches high at 200*, where it is nearer its zenith. Four inches is, to my mind, too much to ignore. In this case, maximum deviation occurs between 170 and 230 yards, where you can expect a lot of shooting at big game. Zeroing for long shots, which typically give you more time to refine aim, makes no sense if it requires hold-under at middle ranges, where you may have to fire quickly.

Knowing *exactly* where your bullet lands at modest ranges can be important, too: you may not have that three-inch margin! Once, after spotting a fine blacktail buck as it slipped into heavy cover, I circled downwind and still-hunted through the thicket. Moving very slowly and stopping often, I finally spotted a doe's ear. He was standing behind her, only his eye visible in a lattice of limbs. The range was perhaps 35 yards, but I had a very tight alley. Offhand, I steadied the dot in my 2.5x Lyman Alaskan and slipped a l65-grain .308 soft-point through the brush to the buck's brain.

One reason many hunters like to zero long is that they overestimate yardage in the field. One fellow told me recently that his .30 magnum could outshoot any rifle between 800 and 900 yards and that he had toppled a buck at 700 steps by holding just over its withers. Now, even a congressman would have blushed spinning *that* yarn.

The flattest-shooting cartridges land their bullets nearly *three feet low at 500 yards*, when the rifle is zeroed at 200. To keep a .270 Weatherby bullet (muzzle velocity 3,375 fps) from sagging more than a foot at 700 yards, you'd have to zero at over 600! That would put the bullet roughly two feet high at 300 *and* 400. It would be plunging so rapidly at 700 that, if you misjudged range by just 10 percent, you'd miss the deer's vitals!

When zeroing, you'll save time and ammunition separating the task into two stages, bore sighting and shooting. Bore sighting isn't necessary. It's merely a short-cut to the end of the shooting stage. Shooting *is* necessary. A rifle that's only bore-sighted is *not* zeroed!

By the way, factory technicians can roughly align iron sights, but they can't know which load you want to use or at what range you want to zero. Neither may they see the sights the way you do. You can't farm out the job of zeroing a scope either, because you're unlikely to find someone who holds a rifle quite like you do, or sees the scope field quite the same.

Before you even pick up your rifle, you're smart to find your load in a ballistics chart. Knowing the bullet's arc, you can determine the most useful zero range and holdover for longer shots. You'll also come up with a point-blank range. "Point-blank" is that distance at which the bullet lands where you aim, *or close enough to do what you want it to do*. Shooting point-blank at prairie dogs, you can't abide the three-inch vertical allowance that might please elk hunters. Maximum point-blank range shrinks as you demand greater precision from the same load.

Whatever your chosen zero, the first intersection of sightline and bullet arc is pretty close to the muzzle. The exact distance depends also on the ballistic performance of your bullet and the height of the sight above the bore. Sight height affects zero, because it determines the angle of the sightline to bullet path. Ballistics tables typically specify a 1½-inch gap between bore and sightline at the muzzle.

Before you start zeroing, make sure the scope is mounted firmly, base screws tight and the rings secured to the base. Dovetail rings are best turned into alignment with a one-inch dowel; don't use the scope for this or to check ring alignment. When the scope drops easily into the belly of horizontally split rings, slide the tops of the rings over the tube, but don't snug them. Shoulder the rifle to see that the reticle is square with the world and you have proper eye relief. You should see a full field of view when your face rests naturally on the comb. I like the scope farther forward than most shooters do, for two reasons. First, when I cheek the rifle quickly, I want the field to open up as I thrust my head forward. I don't want to waste any time pulling it back to see more through the scope. Second, I want room between the ocular bell and my eye, should I have to shoot uphill or from the sit hunkered over the rifle. My rule of thumb is to start with the ocular lens directly over the rear guard screw on a bolt rifle, then refine.

After you lock the scope in place by cinching ring screws (alternately, as you'd tighten lug nuts on an automobile hub), secure the rifle in a cleaning cradle or sandbags or a shooting rest like Midway's Lead Sled. Now you're ready to bore sight. No need to be at the range, only someplace that affords you a clear view of a small, distant object. It can be anything, from a rock to a paper target, that you can easily center in the bore. Object in the distance, remove the bolt. Then, looking through the bore, align it with your object. Without disturbing the rifle, adjust the scope until the object also falls on the aiming axis. I often bore sight on a transformer box atop an electrical pole. It's about a mile away, but the box is clearly visible. There's nothing unsafe about this, because the bolt is, necessarily, out of the rifle!

The other way of aligning sight with bore is with a collimator, an optical device you attach to the rifle's muzzle by means of a close-fitting stud that slides into the bore. The collimator's screen appears in your sight. On common versions, you adjust the scope's windage and elevation dials so the reticle centers the screen's grid. The collimator's main advantage: You can use it on lever, pump, and auto-loading rifles with solid receiver backs. Special collimators are necessary for rifles with muzzle brakes in place.

Bore-sighted rifles must still be zeroed with live fire! For targets, I prefer cardboard slabs with

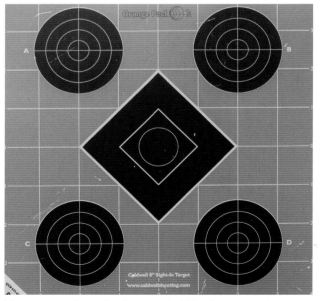

Use targets that afford easy aim! Zeroing or testing loads, small marks aren't always best!

white paper squares. With a 4x scope, I use six-inch squares, a 6x scope get four-inch squares. The white paper shows up plainly against brown cardboard, and holes are easy to see wherever bullets land. Black lines and bull's-eyes hide holes. Fluorescent stick-on dots suffice for high-power scopes. Targets designed to show a rim of fluorescent color around each bullet hole—Birchwood Casey's Shoot-N-C and Caldwell's Orange Peel—make hits easy to spot at distance. For most iron sights, I prefer a plain sheet of typing paper hung at 100 yards. Gun maker D'Arcy Echols has come up with a T-shaped alternative, black on white, that's big enough for use with the fat beads on African express rifles. It works!

An adjustable rest helps you zero, because, with it, you can position the rifle exactly, bringing its natural point of aim to the bull's-eye. You can then re-lax behind it. If you must *hold* the rifle on target, you introduce muscle tension, pulse, and nerve tremors that can kick your bullet off course. Sandbags are okay, but positioning the rifle the same, shot to shot, is more difficult with sandbags. Consistency matters!

In most cases, your rifle is best supported on firm but forgiving rests just behind the fore-end swivel and at the stock's toe. Protect rests from swivel studs during recoil with wadded washcloths. Never zero a rifle with the barrel touching a rest, as the barrel will vibrate away from the rest and throw the shot wide. I use my left hand to pull the fore-end of a lightweight rifle into a rest and keep it from hopping off in recoil. You can also tug on the sling. With heavy-barreled rifles of modest recoil, it's usually better to use your left hand to squeeze the rear bag. A little hand pres-sure here can shift the rifle enough to bring the sight to the exact center of the target.

I've drawn snickers when draping my shoul-der with towels and additional padding. "Can't take it?" Well, yes, Bubba, I *can* take it. But my purpose behind the rifle is not to see how much recoil I can absorb. It's to shoot accurately. Zeroing, you'll want to minimize the human element. To flinch is human.

First shots to zero should be at 35 yards, wheth-er or not you've bore-sighted. After each shot at 35, move the rear sight or scope dial in the direction you want the bullet to go until you hit point of aim. (Mind the dial arrows! European scope knobs typically turn clockwise to move impact up and right, while clock-

On a rest, use the left hand to steady your stock or torso—unless you need it to control recoil.

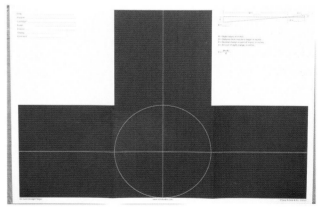

Rifle maker D'Arcy Echols designed this target for iron sights. Long shots beg big marks.

wise rotation on scopes built for the American market moves impact down and left.) Now, switch to a 100-yard target. I prefer that bullets from flat-shooting big-game rounds hit two to 2½ inches high at this range. Depending on the load, the rifle will then put its bullets close to point of aim at 200 yards.

After satisfactory results at 100 yards, move the target to 200 or your zero range. During the last stages of zeroing, make sight changes only after three-shot groups. A single shot can be misleading.

Windage and elevation dial "clicks" or graduations are engineered to shift bullet impact a precise measure at 100 yards. That's most commonly ¼-minute of angle. A minute of angle is 1.047 inches at 100 yards (but shooters know it as an inch at that range), two inches at 200, and so on. A target scope may have graduations as fine as ⅛-minute; scopes intended for long shooting incorporate coarser elevation detents—½-minute or even 1-minute clicks—to lift point of impact with less dial movement. A greater range of adjustment results, as well. When you can't turn the dial past zero, you also avoid the possibility of "full rotation" error, which can cause spectacular misses. European dials are typically marked in centimeters.

Another method as fast as counting clicks to move bullet impact, is to secure your rifle so the reticle centers the target as it did when you last fired. Then, *without moving the rifle*, turn the dials until your reticle kisses the previous bullet hole.

Even with a benchrest, it's easy to make a bad shot. In fact, a bench can give you a false sense of stability, prompting fast, sloppy shooting. No matter how steady you think you are, check your position before each shot and fire carefully. Call your shots. To learn where your bullets *really* hit at long range (and how great their dispersion), fire at 300, then 400 yards. For hunting, that's as far as you'll likely have occasion to shoot. If longer pokes are on the agenda, find a place to test your rifle and your zero farther downrange. It's worth the trouble! There's no reason to fire at game farther than you've tested your loads and your holds on paper!

Tactical rifles in .338 Lapua and .50 BMG, built to hurl match bullets at targets very far off, have been joined by sporting rifles with exceptional reach. Zeroing at long range introduces a couple special considerations most hunters needn't consider. One is the range of dial movement on the scope's elevation adjustment. Consider installing a slanted Picatinny rail, one whose front end is lower than the rear. Such a rail has "gain" and puts the scope at an angle to the bore, so that, when you center the dial in its range, the scope's axis (line of sight) crosses the bullet's path farther away. You get a longer zero without using all the adjustment. The more nearly centered the erector assembly (which holds your reticle), the better. A lens gives you the best picture through its middle. Barrett supplies rails with gain for its .50-caliber rifles.

Hunting rifles with 200-yard zeros won't do well at a 1,000-yard match, because shooters would have to aim several feet over the target frame. There's too little elevation adjustment in many scopes to get a 1,000-yard zero. If you could dial in enough lift to achieve a 600-yard zero with your .30-06, you'd still have to aim *17 feet high* to hit a 1,000-yard bull's-eye! Of course, a truly long-range

> Consider installing a slanted Picatinny rail, one whose front end is lower than the rear. Such a rail has "gain," and you'll get a longer zero without using all the scope's adjustment.

If you use a bipod afield, zero from a bipod! From prone, this Harris bipod is as steady as bags.

Afield, you'll often shoot from improvised rests. Check zeros from them at long range!

zero comes with severe mid-range penalties. Even that 600-yard zero would put '06 bullets 2½ feet high at 300 yards!

Tactical rifles with bipods are best zeroed from them, rather than from sandbags or a commercial rest. Sporting rifles can also be zeroed from a bipod or from a sling. You don't need a one-hole group. The purpose of zeroing is to align the sight with a repeatable bullet track. If you use a bench to zero a hunting rifle, follow up by getting off the bench to check zero from hunting positions. I shoot a lot with a taut sling. Typically, the sling pulls the rifle down and left. A .300 magnum put a sitting group *nine inches* below the 200-yard group I'd fired from the bench! A barrel-mounted swivel exacerbates this problem. So does a swivel on the fore-end cap of a lever rifle with its magazine tube dovetailed to the barrel. Once, after confirming a 100-yard zero at the bench, I slinged up a Marlin 1895 in .338 Marlin Express. Three shots prone formed a one-inch group six inches below point of aim! When a bench zero differs from a zero fired prone with a tight sling, I adjust the sight to the prone group.

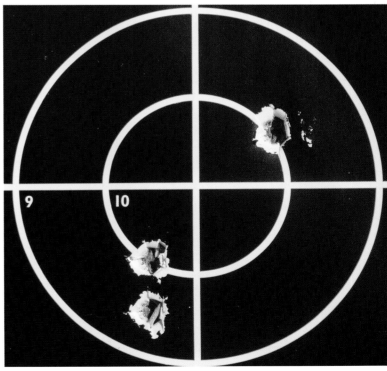

Wayne fired this 300-yard group with a Ruger American .30-06, with an eight-inch hold-over.

During extended range sessions, I fire no more than 10 shots before setting a rifle aside, bolt open to cool. If I must fire more than 30 rounds, or if groups open up, I clean the bore. Bringing two or three rifles, I can use one while letting the other(s) cool. If time permits after zeroing and a thorough cleaning, I let the barrel get stone cold. Then I send two more bullets into a fresh target at 200 yards to check point of impact. This is particularly important on hunting rifles. Cold-barrel shots are the ones that count! I save that target and, next time at the range, fire another cold-barrel shot at it. First-shot groups should be tight as those printed with consecutive bullets. They'll give you the confidence you need on opening day—especially when the game is far away!

Keith used his .25-06 offhand to shoot this buck, but that bipod is a real plus for long shots!

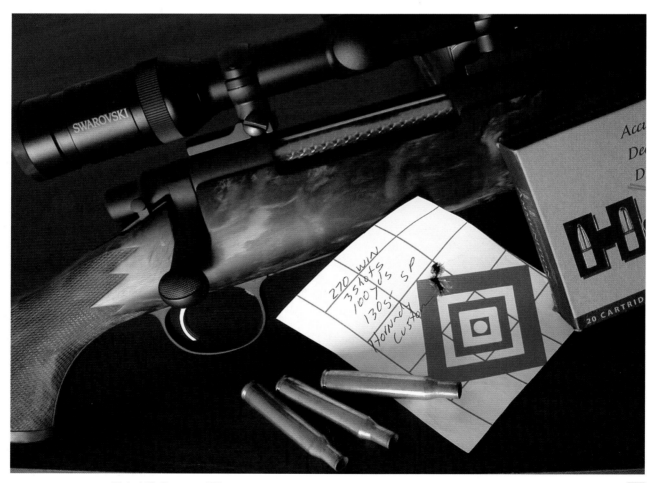

This Hill Country Rifles .270 puts bullets almost two inches high at 100 yards, a useful zero.

CHAPTER FOURTEEN
—BACK TO SCHOOL

STUDENTS LEARN FASTER THAN SHOOTERS WHO THINK THEY KNOW IT ALL—AND THEY DON'T PRACTICE BAD HABITS. ■

Quick. Your bullet drops 64 inches at 500 yards. How many minutes of angle must you dial into your scope to correct? Need more time? Try this: Your reticle brackets the 28-inch chest of an elk neatly between two mil-dots. How far is the animal? Still thinking? Well, where would you hold to kill a Dall's ram 420 yards uphill at a 30-degree angle?

Okay, you get points for attendance. Or not.

"At our school, right answers matter, because they matter when you get your only shot on a costly hunt," says Darrell Holland. "Most hunters can't shoot accurately as far as they're willing to shoot. A few days firing thoughtfully and carefully at long range can make anyone a better long-range marksman. But you have to know something about bullet arc first."

Darrell had invited me to the shooting class he hosts near his gun shop in Powers, Oregon. A rural hamlet a few winding miles up the South Fork of the Coquille from Myrtle

The most valuable product of any shooting school is the standard it imposes. You must get the answer right. Every shot matters—you either hit or you miss.

When a long shot presents itself afield, your practice at distance is your ticket to a sure hit!

Point, Powers has logging in its blood. Timber harvest reductions on the Coast Range have pinched this and neighboring communities. But the locals smile when you say you're here to shoot.

In an ancient but cozy clapboard lodge, Darrell Holland and his wife, Rosita, distribute binders thick with text. Rosita's fruit bars make the rounds, too.

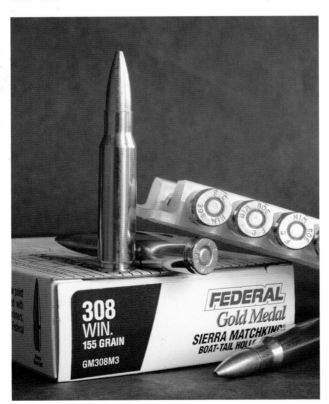

The .308 is popular at SAAM and Holland's schools. It's easy and cheap to shoot.

The couple-dozen students include past graduates here to help. One of them, David Braunies, will be my partner.

"You'll work in pairs, shooting and spotting," says Darrell. "Your spotter will help with wind doping and check your calculations of bullet drop." He elaborates: "We'll shoot as far as half a mile. From 400 yards out, you'll have to engineer shots; a little holdover won't cut it. Our workbook prepares you to hit farther than you probably thought possible."

With that, he launches into a list of procedures, with caveats on safety. Then it's on to rifles and sights.

"Most bolt rifles shoot well enough for most hunting. But an action held to closer tolerances gives you an edge at long range. You need an accurate barrel, an adjustable trigger, and a high-quality scope like Leupold's Mark 4 or a Schmidt & Bender." He recommends his ART (Advanced Reticle Technology) reticle in the 3-12x50 Schmidt & Bender scope installed on my Kimber LPT rifle. "I designed it with both minute-of-angle and mil marks, and values. But it doesn't clutter your scope field or slow you down when you must shoot fast."

High magnification isn't necessary, he says. "At 6x, you can aim well enough to hit most targets out to 800 yards." More power can help with smaller marks and extend effective range, but it comes with liabilities: less light transmission, more apparent movement, difficult aiming in heavy mirage.

While Darrell uses laser rangefinders, he warns against leaning on them too hard.

"When you're ready to shoot, you're looking through your sight. That's the best place to determine range."

Then it's on to ballistics, because, "Unless you understand how bullets behave, you can't put them in the target." We plow through the text and scramble to answer Holland's rapid-fire questions. "What's an MOA?" It's not an inch at 100 yards. It's 1.047 inches. "A mil?" It's not only a mil-radian. It is 3.438 minutes of angle. "We'll zero scopes at 100 yards," says Darrell, "then move the elevation dial to correct for drop far away. Get used to the mil and MOA. We won't talk inches on the line."

After lunch, we pile into pickups and caravan into the green spring hills, topping out on a saddle. A tarp on poles shields us from intermittent rain, but not from wind that keens through the gap as if feeding a giant carburetor. We flop mats on the ground and break out ammunition. The staccato rattle of the rifles brings ragged groups to paper faces 100 yards away. We tweak scopes, then visit Darrell's chronograph. His software will work late tonight; he'll laminate ballistic data cards for each of us, based on bullets and chrono data. My assortment of .308 cartridges from Black Hills, Federal, Hornady, and Remington feature 168-grain bullets like Sierra MatchKings. I've included a few boxes of 175 SMKs. They shoot nearly as flat as 168s up close, but battle the wind and hold velocity better at long range.

We leave the saddle at dark, most of us winding along the Coquille on a 45-minute return to the motel at Myrtle Point. As the microwave boils a cup of noodles, I recall the homework assignment: dry-fire 150 shots, cycling the bolt with trigger finger and thumb. Squeeze every shot. It is 10 o'clock, and my rifle isn't yet clean. Darrell advises a bore brush every 20 rounds.

Fog shrouds the hairpins as I take them at speed early next morning, window open to catch the throaty rattle of jake brakes. A few Peterbilts still prowl the Coast Range. I recall my days herding a

On opening day, much can ride on one shot. Learn to hit far away during the off-season.

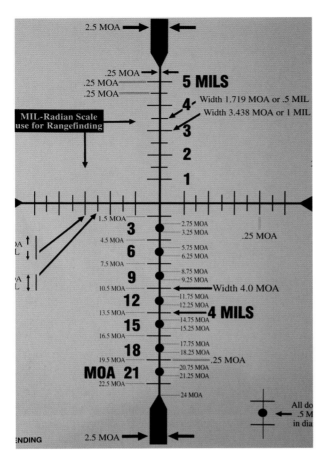

330 Cummins, 40 tons of timber snaking behind. Another life.

"Multiply target height in inches by 29. Divide the product by the number of mils bracketing the target." Darrell Holland starts fast. "An elk measures 28 inches through the chest; 28 x 29 = 812.

"Say the reticle brackets that elk with 1.5 mils; 812 divided by 1.5 is 541 yards." Too far to shoot, he adds. "A mil-dot reticle must be calibrated for one magnification. In variable scopes, it's usually the top end or 10x. Remember, a mil equals 3.6 inches at 100 yards. So the space between the ¾-inch mil-dots in a scope equals 7.2 inches at 200 yards, 14.4 inches at 400, three feet at 1,000. You can also find range by dividing target height in mils by the number of spaces subtending it. A deer three feet at the shoulder (10 mils at 100 yards) appears in your scope to stand two dots high. Divide two into 10, and you get five. That buck is 500 yards away. Or you can divide target size in yards (in this case, one) by the number of mils subtended (two) and multiply by 1,000 to get range in yards."

Then Darrell introduces us to Mil Dot Master, a slide rule shortcut to math, explaining, "It converts

Darrell Holland's school teaches mil-dots and minutes (above), how to use reticles at long range. At his range (right), in Oregon, shooters ready for a zero check before moving to 800 yards.

Lessons on drift and drop stay with you best at long range. Here, a shooter preps at 600 yards.

inches to mils and minutes and gives sight corrections based on target size and bullet drop and shot angle."

I ask why his class-work assumes a .308 zeroed at 100 yards with 168-grain MatchKings. "Not many hunters carry a .308 zeroed at 100 yards or use match bullets."

Darrell smiles. "Actually, I've shot more than 100 animals with MatchKings. They're deadly on deer. They kill elk with rib shots. Most important, they're very accurate. A 100-yard setting handles most of the shots you'll make in the field. For long pokes, you can adjust." He concedes a 200-yard zero works better for hunters who don't want to adjust elevation dials.

More important than your load or choice of zero, he continues, is marksmanship.

"Get low. Prone with a Harris bipod is best. Sit when you must. Establish a position that naturally aligns the rifle with the target. Move your body, not your arms, to adjust. Control your breathing; shoot with empty lungs. Caress the trigger. Cycle the bolt quickly after each shot."

In the classroom, Darrell puts us behind his own rifle. The trigger breaks at just under two pounds, surprising some. It has generous over-travel, "so you don't disturb the rifle by coming up against the stop as the striker falls." He recommends a lightweight, compact toe bag of his design. It supports the rifle's butt. "Just squeeze it with your support hand to fine-tune elevation." I do. It works. But Holland is no gadgeteer.

"Afield, I carry the toe bag and a card with drop and drift data. They fill a couple shirt pockets. Without them, I'm a short-range shooter." The laminated card he prepared for me shows my 168-grain BTHP at 2,700 fps falling nearly 17 MOA at 600 yards. That's close to nine feet of drop! Over the next 50 yards, that bullet sags another 15 inches, nearly an inch for every three yards of travel! Without a rangefinding reticle and a data card, a first-round hit at such distance would be unlikely.

That afternoon, we harass steel silhouettes at unmarked ranges approaching half a mile. A Kestrel anemometer helps me gauge a shifting wind.

"Zero in still conditions," Darrell had advised.

Few shooters have access to 300-meter indoor ranges, like this one in Germany. Alas ... .

"Then shade for drift, unless you'll fire many shots in a prevailing wind or drift is so great it makes shading senseless. If you adjust windage at every change, you can lose track of the setting for still air."

Adding elevation, he explains, is best done at the dial.

"Unlike wind, gravity is constant, so you can confidently repeat settings. And you'll find aiming with the reticle's center easiest. But don't make a full-rotation error." That occurs when you've added more than a complete dial revolution of clicks for a long shot, then returned the knob to zero without making the last full turn.

Each morning at Holland's shooting school brings more ballistics exercises. The math is basic, but fast replies are expected. "Wayne, how many mils high would you hold to hit a gong at 500 yards if bullet drop is 63 inches?" That would be 63 divided by 3.60 equals 17.50 divided by five equals 3.50 ... .

Daily trips to Darrell's range in the Siskiyous test our wind doping and corrections. Throttled by steep slopes, the air dives and climbs, accelerates and brakes. Flags at distant targets show different wind than do Kestrels on the line. Cool days preclude mirage that would help us decipher conditions.

"A full-value wind comes only from three o'clock or nine," Darrell reminds us. "A half-value wind from four or 10 o'clock requires less correction—about 80 percent of full-value allowance. Figure 50 percent for a quarter-value wind. A blow from the front or back is most troublesome when it subsides, because a let-off can bring a change. Shooting in a lull is a bad idea, because a pick-up or reversal can be quick."

Our final day on the range includes an exam: 20 shots at unspecified yardages, from places at which we've not yet shot, so range and wind dope from the saddle is useless. No sighter shots allowed. The steel gongs echo hits. Punching the

At the SAAM school, in Texas, Doug steadies both the rifle and his elbow for a long shot.

heart-shaped center of each brings an extra point. But only Darrell can see bullet strikes through his powerful spotting scope, so we can't adjust for center hits. Some shot angles are steep. We dismiss the corrected-cosines formula and estimate holdover with cosine multipliers: .9 for 30-degree slant, .7 for 45, .5 for 60. The 540-yard target at a 30-degree downhill pitch becomes a 486-yard target. When the final mark, a steel pig at twice the distance I've ever shot at deer, swings slowly, and the faint thump of my hit floats back, I'm relieved to be done—but would shoot again to better my score!

Darrell Holland's school is one of several nationwide that can help you shoot better. Perhaps the most valuable product of any school is the standard it imposes. You must get the right answer. Every shot matters, and you either hit or miss. Rather than trumpeting one lucky poke, you must claim all your shots. Shooting school brings egos into line as effectively as it does your bullets.

The Sportsman's All-Weather All-Terrain Shooting (SAAM) School helps hunters hit far.

After spotting distant game, two hunters circle to get out of sight, then plan a stalk upwind.

CHAPTER FIFTEEN
—MARKSMEN MOST FEARED

THE BULLETS LAND WITH NO WARNING, FROM NOWHERE. THE DEAD LIE ALONE. FAR AWAY, A SNIPER RELOADS.

He was not yet 40. But Christopher Scott Kyle was, by most measures, the most lethal marksman in U.S. Navy history, when he was shot dead. Chris Kyle fell not to an enemy bullet, but one fired from a fellow veteran soldier at a shooting range in Erath County, Texas. The killer fled in Kyle's truck, which he later crashed into a police cruiser. Deputies arrested him that evening. At this writing, no motive has been found in the Kyle murder.

A native Texan, Kyle had become a professional bronc rider soon after school, but an arm injury put him out of the arena. The pins in his arm initially prevented him from earning him a place in a Navy SEALS class, but the chance soon came to join that elite group through its underwater demolition program. Assigned to SEAL Team 3, Sniper Element Charlie platoon within the Naval Special Warfare Command, Kyle earned a fearsome reputation among the Iraqi enemy. They put a $20,000 bounty on him—and later increased it to $80,000. Known

The longest recorded kills by snipers were made with the .338 Lapua, in heavy bolt rifles.

Snipers train on paper to measure drop, drift, groups—and progress. Here, a 600-yard bull.

widely to insurgents as *Shaitan A-Ramadi*, or the Devil of Ramadi, Chris Kyle made his longest shot, in 2008, near Sadr City.

An insurgent armed with a rocket launcher was nearing a distant U.S. Army convoy. Kyle readied his McMillan TAC-338 sniper rifle, read the range and the mirage, and triggered a shot. The bullet from the .338 Lapua killed the man at a measured 2,100 yards.

During his four tours in Iraq, Kyle was shot twice and managed to escape six IED explosions. In 2009, he left the Navy to settle with his wife and two children in Midlothian, Texas. There he ran Craft International, a firm that specialized in security training. Chris Kyle's autobiographical book, *American Sniper*, was published in 2012.

Sniping is the application of the long shot in battle. Snipers not only kill from great distance, they inspire terror among the enemy ranks. Victims seldom see the shooter. Soldiers far from front-line action and sheltered from artillery salvos may still be vulnerable to snipers. There's no rest for military units in range of a hidden marksman—and these days, that range is very, very long.

Chris Kyle's furthest shot, nearly two kilometers, falls short of that confirmed for Aaron Perry, a Master Corporal in the Canadian Forces. He killed a Taliban fighter at 2,310 meters, or 2,526 yards. That record, set in March 2002, stood for only a few days.

Bigger .30s mean more speed, less drop and drift at distance—and more recoil.

Corporal Rob Furlong of the 3rd Battalion, Princess Patricia's Canadian Light Infantry, broke it with a shot in the Shah-i-Kot Valley, downing an antagonist at 2,430 meters, or 2,657 yards. Furlong was using a McMillan TAC-50 rifle with Hornady A-Max VLD bullets. Firing carefully at one of three al Qaeda fighters moving toward a mountainside position, Furlong missed with the first round, then followed quickly with another, which struck the soldier's pack. The third shot killed him. Given 2,700 fps as the muzzle velocity of that 750-grain .50 BMG bullet, it spent roughly four seconds in flight!

The longest attributable sniper kill at this writing occurred in November 2009. Corporal of Horse Craig Harrison was serving in the Blues and Royals RHG/D of the British Army, when he spotted the two Taliban fighters far beyond normal range. But the day was windless, visibility excellent. Harrison would later explain that it took him nine shots, with help from his spotter, to put his bullets on an inert target at that distance, more than 1,000 yards beyond the supersonic range of his .338 Lapua load. The air density of Musa Qala, at 1.1069 kg/m3, added nearly 200 yards to the supersonic range at sea level, 3,400 feet below. Harrison's mark was 2,475 meters, or 2,707 yards distant.

Given a 100-meter (109-yard) zero, 250-grain Lapua LockBase B408 bullets leaving the L115A3 rifle (by Accuracy International) at 3,071 fps would drop 396.8 feet in flight—48.9 milliradians or 168 minutes of angle! The corporal would have had to calculate trajectory precisely, then prove it by firing sighters. The Schmidt & Bender Mk II 5-25x56 scope was cradled in a mount with 13.09 mils or 45 minutes of gain, so long shots wouldn't require all adjustment from the elevation dial. Still, Harrison had to use hash marks in the bottom of the P4 reticle to get the holdover he needed.

According to JBM Ballistics, using drag coefficients provided by Lapua, bullet flight would have exceeded six seconds.

Neither man would have heard the first shot. The report reached them nearly eight seconds after the bullet struck—probably after Harrison had fired the second. Both men died. A third shot disabled their machine gun. A double kill at 2,707 yards.

Such an astounding feat would have been unthinkable a century and a half earlier, when Colonel Hiram Berdan organized a regiment of sharpshooters. A renowned marksman himself, Berdan evidently developed this idea in the first days of our Civil War. Political connections favored him. Shortly, the War Department approved his plan. In July 1861, he was appointed Colonel of the First Regiment United States Sharpshooters. It comprised the regulation number of 10 companies. Four came from New York, three from Michigan, and one each from Vermont, New Hampshire, and Wisconsin. Another group, the Second Regiment, formed up under the command of Colonel Henry A. Post. Its eight companies included two each from New Hampshire and Vermont, one each from Michigan and Minnesota, Pennsylvania and Maine.

Qualifications for entry into these elite companies were stringent indeed. Berdan's first recruiting announcements declared, "No man would be enlisted who could not put 10 bullets *in succession* within five

Snipers have used even the .223. The .308 has killed beyond a mile. The .50 BMG rules!

inches from the center at a distance of six hundred feet from a rest or three hundred off hand." (Italics mine.) Few hunters with modern rifles would clear the offhand bar, even with the help of optical sights.

The first Sharpshooters were required to bring their own rifles, the U.S. government promising to reimburse each soldier $60. (Evidently, this commitment was not fulfilled.) Right away, the problem of disparate ball diameters and ammunition types arose. Berdan asked the Ordnance Department for breechloading Sharps rifles, which he considered superior to all others of the day. General Winfield Scott, who headed that agency, was wary of breechloaders. Delays in procurement put Colt's revolving rifle in the hands of Berdan's Sharpshooters. The men rebelled. Only after intercession from President Lincoln, who witnessed an impressive display of marksmanship from these troops at the national Camp of Instruction, in Washington, D.C., were the .52-bore Sharps rifles delivered. The First Regiment got them in May 1862, the Second Regiment a month later. Loading a linen cartridge from the breech allowed these soldiers to re-charge their rifles from prone and

sitting positions, so they didn't have to expose themselves to fire, or even discovery, between shots. The rifles were equipped with angular bayonets.

Colonel Berdan surrounded himself with the best of officers and exceptional shooters, many from Europe. He melded guerilla fighting tactics with bugle commands, to give his troops an edge wherever the battle took them. They wore distinctive uniforms: "… a dark green coat and cap with black plume, light blue trousers (later exchanged for green) and leather leggings…." They carried calfskin knapsacks with a cooking kit. Typically, each man had 40 cartridges in his cartridge box, another 20 in his pack. But, on the eve of certain battle, the Sharpshooters increased their ammo reserves.

Berdan's Sharpshooters saw action in at least 65 Civil War engagements, starting with a skirmish at Lewinville, Virginia, September 27, 1861. These troops distinguished themselves at South Mountain, Chancellorsville, and Gettysburg. During a furious 20-minute fight in Pitzer's Woods, near Gettysburg, a small contingent of 100 Sharpshooters and 200 men of the 3rd Maine Infantry delivered such withering fire that the Confederate General Wilcox reported engaging two full regiments. Berdan's men expended an average of 95 rounds in that battle.

Though apparently Berdan preferred to keep his troops directed as substantial units, they were often deployed individually. Despite their constant contact with the enemy in unsupported positions, few Sharpshooters were taken as prisoners. One Civil War historian wrote of these troops:

They were of a high grade in physical qualifications and intelligence. They were continually in demand as skirmishers on account of their wonderful proficiency [and] undoubtedly killed more men than any other regiment in the army. In skirmishing they had no equal.

Like the repeating rifle, the telescopic sight saw its first significant use during the Civil War. The view through these early scopes was dim indeed. Adjustments and reticles were fragile. But, as the flaws of the Henry would be erased by progress in rifle design, so, too, optical sights would become more effective. By the end of the century, bolt-action repeating rifles (the Krag-Jorgensen) and smokeless ammunition (the .30-40 Krag) had replaced blackpowder muzzleloaders and lever-action repeaters. By 1917, when the U.S. entered World War I, even the ordinary infantryman had a 1903 Springfield, and short, sturdy, receiver-mounted scopes were available to snipers. Better aim at distance with the flat arc of .30-06 and, in German ranks, via 8x57 Mauser bullets, would make soldiers on both sides vulnerable to the long shot.

Sniping took a heavy toll in both the European and Pacific theatres during World War II. In the jungles of Vietnam, it became an increasingly important—and terrifying—form of warfare. Marine sniper Carlos Hathcock distinguished himself in that conflict, with an incredible 93 confirmed kills, including a shot with a modified M2 Browning .50 BMG that reportedly downed a man at 2,500 yards, a long-range record not eclipsed until 34 years later, in 2002.

Born in 1942, Hathcock enlisted in the USMC at the age of 17. He married three years later, but remained in the service, attaining the rank of Gunnery Sergeant. A rifle enthusiast since his youth

and a practiced marksman, the Little Rock, Arkansas, native started shooting competitively. At the 1965 National Matches, at Camp Perry, he won the prestigious Wimbledon Cup for his exceptional performance at 1,000 yards. A year later he went to Vietnam as an MP. His shooting credentials caught the eye of Captain E.J. Land, who was in search of qualified men to serve as snipers.

Hathcock, who wrote a book about his exploits in Vietnam, emphasized the importance of being "in the bubble," where complete concentration on the shot dominated every thought and action. He noted that, with hostiles not only the targets, but also those seeking him out, he could hardly afford to let his mind wander. As a rifleman, he recognized the role of focus in hitting precisely at long range, even when not threatened.

In Vietnam, Carlos Hathcock established such a fearsome reputation, the North Vietnamese Army placed a $30,000 bounty on him. While bounties have long been placed on snipers who've become known as being particularly skilled, the going rate in Southeast Asia at this time was well shy of $2,000. Hathcock was

Scopes like the Leupold on this Rock River rifle in 6.8 SPC make sniping rifles of accurate ARs.

Snipers train with Barrett rifles in .50 BMG at the NRA Whittington Center, New Mexico.

called *Long Trang* by the NVA: "White Feather." He did indeed wear a white feather in his bush hat. But after that feature made Hathcock a marked man, several other courageous Marines in his area donned the same, to confuse counter-snipers and take some pressure off their particularly effective comrade.

One of Hathcock's most celebrated shots came as he and his spotter, John Roland Burke, were on patrol near their station, Hill 55. They were looking specifically for an NVA sniper known as the Cobra, who had already killed several Marines. A stray reflection in the jungle caught Hathcock's attention. The rifleman brought his Winchester M70 to bear, triggering it as soon as the crosswire in his 8x Unertl scope quartered the reflection. It was the objective lens of the Cobra's scope. Hathcock's .30-06 bullet smashed through the sight and the man's eye socket. The only other way that shot would have caused such a result: if the NVA sniper had himself been aiming at Hathcock.

Another enemy soldier of particular concern was "the Apache," a woman known for her terribly cruel and always lethal torture of American prisoners of war. In the confusion of a firefight one day, she had the misfortune to be caught in Hathcock's sight.

Reportedly, Carlos Hathcock removed his white feather only once while deployed in Vietnam. A volunteer mission just days before his first tour ended put him in open country on a long crawl. His target was an NVA general. The Marine sniper spent four days and three nights inching his way to within long shooting range. Nearly discovered by a Vietcong patrol that passed within spitting distance, and narrowly escaping the bite of a bamboo viper, he lay in the sparse cover motionless until at last the general emerged from his tent. Hathcock fired a single bullet, which struck the commander in the chest. But his task was far from completed. Enemy soldiers at once fanned out in the area to find their general's killer—the crawl back was even more nerve-racking than the approach!

In 1969, after two years Stateside, Carlos Hathcock volunteered for another tour in 'Nam, where he took command of a sniper platoon. On Route 1, north of LZ Baldy, in September 1969, the LVT-5 in which he was riding struck a land mine. He sustained severe burns, pulling seven other Marines to safety. Thirty years after receiving the Purple Heart for his injuries in this event, Hathcock would be awarded the Silver Star for his actions.

Recovering back in Quantico, Virginia, Hathcock helped establish the Marine Corps Scout Sniper School. In 1975, he was diagnosed with multiple sclerosis, which would eventually kill him, 24 years later. But Hathcock worked through his debilitating illness, instructing snipers employed in police agencies and military units like SEAL Team Six.

I've spoken with Carlos Hathcock's son, who followed his father's Marine Corps path. He noted, with refreshing modesty, the sniper's contributions to the safety of U.S. troops in Vietnam. He could have reminded me that the 93 confirmed kills amounted to a conservative tally. Official confirmation at that time required a third party; the word of the sniper's spotter alone was not enough and, because snipers most often worked alone or with just one partner, many kills went unverified.

If Hathcock had an equal in World War II, it would have been Vasilyl Grigoryevich Zaytsev, a

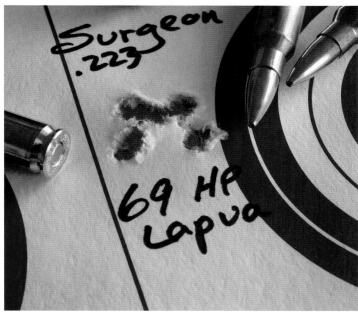

Heavy bullets matched with quick-twist rifling extend the lethal range of the .223 (5.56 NATO).

AR rifles like this Rock River rival bolt-gun accuracy at distance. The Trijicon scope helps a great deal.

The .308, here in a Rock River LAR8, is a sniper round practical well past 1,000 yards.

Pasture proof: Preston Pritchett tests his rifles, popular with snipers, from field positions.

Soviet sniper whose exploits later inspired a movie. In 1942, between November 17 and December 10, he reportedly killed 225 Axis soldiers during the Battle of Stalingrad. Included in that total were 11 snipers.

Zaytsev was hardly a rookie at the time. He'd already downed 32 of the enemy with his standard-issue infantry rifle, an 1891 Mosin-Nagant rifle firing the 7.62x54R cartridge. It launched a 147-grain bullet at 2,890 fps. By winter's end, in 1943, Zaytsev had shot roughly 400 of the enemy, some at ranges exceeding 1,000 meters.

Beginning in 1932, the Russians adapted the Mosin-Nagant rifle to telescopic sights for snipers. But it was used with great effect against them by Finnish soldiers, who eschewed scopes. Simo Hayha, a Finn who applied his considerable sniping skills to drop 505 Soviet troops, used iron sight on his M/28-30 Mosin-Nagant rifle. He explained that the high Russian scope mounts required him to lift his head off the stock, compromising marksmanship and exposing himself unnecessarily to the enemy.

THE FARTHER YOUR BULLET FLIES, THE SMALLER YOUR INVESTMENT IN THE HUNT. LONG SHOTS ARE FOR SALVAGE.

The hunter spotted him first, below us and facing away. He had wide antlers that almost wrapped around the black ooze that made the seep at his feet a target in the gloaming. I yanked the tripod legs all the way out to put the Big Eye above the alders.

"Is it him?"

The animal hadn't moved. "Can't say," I replied.

We stared across the canyon, hoping. It had been three days since the shot.

Then the bull took a step. "It's him!" We said it together, but our actions were different. I jerked the scope down, folding the tripod legs and sliding them short. My companion raised his rifle. "How far?" he asked. It took a moment to register. He was serious! But this bull was nearly half a mile distant.

Norma's new, flat-shooting Kalahari ammo is designed for thin-skinned game at distance.

ing brings ethical decisions, but those become a nuisance only after you've cleared the more pragmatic hurdles. Like hitting.

Delivering lethal energy is hardly a problem with the ammunition most popular among hunters these days. Between the world wars, sportsmen shot elk with .25-35s, and, where I grew up, legal whitetail cartridges included .22 rimfires. A 100-grain bullet in the mild-mannered .25-06 can reach 500 yards with 1,000 ft-lbs of energy, more than enough to kill a deer and more than the .25-35 brings to 100. Some .30-caliber magnums double that. Modern rifles with vertical magazines allow us to use pointed bullets that retain speed and energy more efficiently than did the blunt bullets of yesteryear's tube-fed lever guns.

Energy deficiencies at long range can have less to do with kinetic force than with its transfer. Big-

While range estimation isn't my long suit, game beyond 400 yards is just plain far. Far can be 487 yards or 874—it doesn't matter if it's *too* far. Stars in the night sky are light years away. I cannot fathom the distance even *one* light year represents, but that's okay, when I'm just marveling that some stars whose light I see may have burned out long ago. To *reach* a star, though, I'd have to do some math. It would be folly to travel in a spacecraft at the speed of sound toward a star 100 light years away.

Many hunters who shoot far don't think about what's practical, so they miss. In truth, a long shot is any shot that's almost too far for you to make every time under existing conditions.

The hunter with me on that elk hunt years ago was understandably keen to kill. But wanting to is only one element of a task. Each year, many teams want to win the Super Bowl. Only one will. Yonder elk, I told my friend, was twice as far as it had been when he'd bungled his first chance three days earlier. "We'll have to get much, much closer."

Fast bullets and high-magnification scopes conspire to focus hunter attention on the long shot. Indeed, killing game far from the rifle can become the object of a hunt, replacing the challenge of getting close. Both require skills. The long-range rifleman depends on marksmanship (and superior hardware). While the stalker need not shoot so precisely, he must have a woodsman's bag of tricks. Long shoot-

The best long-range hunting cartridges include short-coupled magnums like the WSMs.

Being ready to shoot, you'll have more time to make a careful shot. Footwork comes first!

Ken Nagel killed this bull at 390 yards, with a custom-barreled Ruger No. 1 in 7mm WSM.

game bullets are designed to open within a range of impact speeds. Hunters want bullets that stay together under the jacket-shredding impact of close-range hits, but still expand when they strike game at distance, after velocity has dropped off. Contrary to the thinking of some sportsmen, high-speed bullets do not zip through animals so fast they don't have a chance to open. You might as well claim that, if you drive a car fast enough into a brick wall, it will pass through that wall unscathed. Also, *delayed* expansion is tough to engineer. In fact, most expansion occurs during the first inch of penetration. Given similar construction, faster bullets sustain more nose damage that slower bullets, just as automobiles colliding at high speed destroy themselves. Bullets meeting flesh at low velocities are like cars in a fender-bender.

It's useful to think of an animal as a hammer hitting the bullet nose. The damage to each results from the combined velocity. If the hammer strikes the bullet sharply, the bullet will open more violently than if the hammer is swung gently into contact. At long range, when air resistance has throttled your bullet, a hit between the ribs of a deer puts little pressure on the bullet nose. Mushrooming may not occur and the

Get steady. Better a slow hit than a fast miss. At long range, you should have plenty of time.

bullet will dump little of its remaining energy. Penetration of bullets that don't open is typically greater than that of bullets whose noses rupture at impact, even when the upset bullets are moving faster. Pass-throughs at long range are common, when bullets retain pre-impact shape. Bones and muscle help bullets open, by providing solid resistance.

Energy transfer depends on deceleration in the animal. A bullet exiting the muzzle carries a finite level of energy, subsequently reduced by air resistance during its travel. When it enters an animal and expands, the bullet sheds energy more quickly, because its deceleration rate increases sharply. Animal tissue presents more resistance than air, and a mushroomed bullet acts like a parachute, as it opens a wide channel. If the bullet stops inside, all the energy it carried is absorbed by the beast.

In the West, you'll see game farther than you can shoot accurately. Stalk long, shoot short.

Though he spotted it far away, Wayne killed this deer at 100 yards, with his CZ in .30-06.

Now, full penetration means that some energy leaves with the bullet. A solid bullet whizzing through destroys tissue in its path, but that path is not very broad and, because there's no parachute effect, the bullet doesn't slow down much. Much kinetic energy remains untapped. Ditto for soft-points that lack the impact speed to upset fully. At extreme yardage, where you want the highest percentage of energy delivered, you often get limited transfer.

Bullet design, thus, includes compromises. Bullets fashioned to fly flat at high speed can, logically, be assumed to strike game most often at greater distances than heavy, big-bore, round-nose bullets. They also earn their reputations on light game. So sleek, speedy spitzers have traditionally been given jackets that yield readily at impact. Hollowpoints and thin-jacketed soft-points deliver plenty of penetra-

Winchester's E-Tip shows a current trend in bullet design, to sleek, leadless hollowpoints.

tion in deer-size game. Tough, dangerous animals warranted thick jackets bonded to the cores. At long range, the flat-flying smallbore bullets were striking about as fast as heavy big-bores stopping angry bears a few feet from the muzzle. But desired bullet action differed.

These days, both types of bullets have been fitted with sharp polymer noses. These cosmetically appealing tips come with longer bullet ogives, so even bullets built for deep penetration and high weight retention are well shaped for long shots. And hollowpoints, once thought suitable only for light game, are getting more play on animals as big as moose. The hydraulic pressure of flesh in a wide-open bullet tip can produce spectacular upset at the expense of penetration. Smaller cavities and thicker jackets are now having lethal effect by driving deeper in tough game.

"They're unpredictable," say some hunters about hollowpoints. There's basis for that claim. Once, I fired a series of wide-mouthed hollowpoint bullets into a railroad tie to compare penetration. The wood plugged the noses on impact, changing the bullets into solids. At the same time, the considerable pressure of the tie *outside* the nose as the bullet cut its channel further prevented mushrooming. Thick animal hide, even hair, can have a similar effect inside a hollowpoint cavity. Still, I've seen game as big as elk killed with VLD and other hollowpoint bullets. In some case, the deep penetration surprised me.

S&W's 460 revolver shoots flat with pointed bullets— but it's harder to shoot accurately than a rifle.

With 160-grain Swift A-Frame bullets, the 7mm Remington Magnum excels on distant elk.

But there's more to killing game than hurling a battering ram at 3,300 fps. You must direct that energy. At long range, hitting can be more difficult than delivering energy. Barrels, bullets, and optics are now so sophisticated that l,000-yard benchrest shooters cut groups miking less than a quarter minute of angle! But they're shooting at clearly defined targets at measured yardage and from solid support. Beyond point-blank range afield, you must first estimate distance:

Last fall [I shot] two bull moose ... . I hurriedly estimated the distance to be between 300 and 400 yards ... [but] found it to be 280.

W.T. Hornaday recorded that episode near the turn of the last century. His error in range estimation is a common one still. Animals often appear farther than they are, especially in broken terrain or woods. The blunt bullets from Hornaday's .303 Savage rifle would have dropped significantly between 280 and, say, 350 yards. Holding for 350 would have yielded a high hit. Luckily for Mr. Hornaday, moose are very deep through the chest.

Visible at distance, pronghorns draw fire at long range from lazy hunters. This rifleman got close.

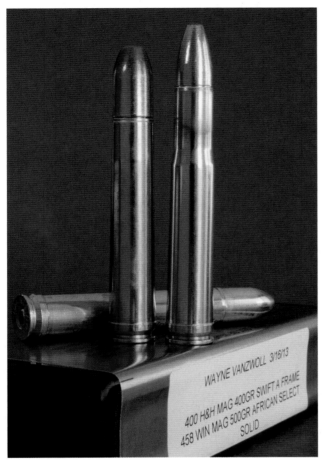

These Superior Ammo loads hit hard! The .400 H&H (right) fires sleek 400-grain Swifts.

Laser rangefinders have taken some of the guesswork from determining distance, but you won't always have one in hand before a shot. Then there's the wind and shot angle and other factors that can influence bullet placement. Shooting, even *deciding* to shoot, is more than an exercise in mathematics and marksmanship. In *Covenant of the Wild*, Stephen Budiansky excerpts from a novel by Laurens van der Post to tell of a professional hunter, Mopani Theron, who has become disgusted by bungling clients. The central character, Francois, recounts a shooting lesson from Theron, who taught "that shooting was not a matter of the will, but a kind of two-way traffic between target and rifleman, and that if one wanted to shoot accurately without hurt or unnecessary pain to animals, one must never force one's shot … . Instead, one had to keep the gun aimed truly at the target, until the target filled not only all one's eyes but activated one's imagination, until one's finger gradually tightened

on the trigger, releasing the shot only when target and rifleman were one." That may sound uncomfortably mystical to shooters who use a ball micrometer on case mouths. But accomplished handloaders and marksmen who fire only from the bench commonly fail to make easy shots at big game. Reason: They don't train under hunting conditions.

■ ■ ■

My client and I made better time down the north slope than I'd expected, perhaps because it was so steep we skidded between steps. When I stopped once to peer through a hole in the foliage, the crippled bull was still there.

"Where?" the hunter gasped. At last he saw. "Oh. Way over there!" He'd been looking too close, assuming that, since we'd come so far, the bull must be right in front of us.

Halfway to the canyon floor, I slid to a halt beside a stout aspen. Still nearly 400 yards, I guessed, but a shot alley had opened, and it was likely our best. "Figure 20 inches drop," I whispered. He steadied the Ruger against an aspen limb. Squinting through the spotting scope, I hoped my companion would not force the shot by yanking the trigger. The longer the silence, the better I felt. At last the

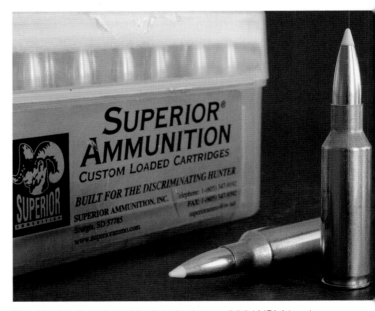

The Nosler Accubond bullets in these .300 WSM loads are only one of many options in custom ammunition.

Broken country affords long looks—and short shots. The saddle gun here won't reach far.

Long shot or short, terminal performance counts. Here, fine upset and weight retention.

You'll carry a hunting rifle more than you'll shoot it. It should wear well in either service.

rifle boomed. The aspen shook and hair winked on the quartering bull's flank. Another shot, this one a miss. The last bullet hit the elk through the chest as it turned. The great animal sank into the grass fringing the seep.

"Good shooting!" I exclaimed, and meant it. Four hundred yards is a long shot.

A Zeiss scope, precisely zeroed, helped this hunter take his first open-country mule deer.

LONG-RANGE AMMO CHOICES

Most modern hunting ammunition promises the accuracy and flat arcs that make center hits easier at distance. Most bullets in powerful .243- to .375-caliber cartridges bring lethal energy and reliable upset and penetration well beyond the limits of field marksmanship. Still, interest in long shooting has sparked a cottage industry in rifles and, now, ammunition built specifically for the task.

Nosler and Barnes, like the traditional ammo firms of Federal, Hornady, Remington, and Winchester, feature loaded cartridges with specialty bullets. South Dakota's Superior Ammunition, renowned for high-quality custom ammo, has grown its line, which stretches from the .17 Remington and .20 Tactical to the .585 Nyati and .600 Nitro Express! At Superior, you can specify your pet load or one you'd like to try. Larry Barnett offers "sample packs" that let you try several options without committing to full-box expense. He will also match your rifle to a load onsite and share loading data. You can either stock up with more loads from his bench or roll your own.

Superior catalogs both wildcat and commercial cartridges, American and metric. Want to try a 6.5-257 Weatherby? A 7mm Gibbs? A 9.3x57? They're all on the list! I just got a small batch of .400 Holland & Holland rounds. Larry offers 22 types of bullets, including North Fork and Hawk soft-points and Berger VLDs. There's no more complete source for special or custom-loaded ammunition!

DISCIPLINED PRACTICE MAKES LONG SHOOTING DEADLY. DISCIPLINE MAKES LONG SHOOTING INFREQUENT.

Extending reach remains a fundamental purpose for firearms. One shooter who has made long reach a mission is John Burns, a Wyoming gun builder who, with Coloradans Scott Downs and Don Ward, operated GreyBull Precision. At this writing, the partnership has dissolved, GreyBull reorganized. No doubt all the principals will continue in the shooting industry. They're all talented.

When I met them some years ago, Scott and Don were producing rifle scopes programmed for specific loads, so shooters could read distance on a laser rangefinder, then index the elevation dial to that distance (to beyond 1,000 yards, with some cartridges), and hold center at that range. John was building super-accurate mid-weight hunting rifles and feeding them frisky handloads developed for long shooting at big game. Chamberings: .243 and 7mm Remington Magnum.

Just two?

"They're all you need in North America," shrugged John. "We load 105-grain bullets in the .243, and 180s in the 7mm. They're VLDs." John and Scott had taken game at

Powerful and scoped, the S&W 460 is lethal hardware. Shooter skill limits effective reach.

Alberta's prairie yielded this fine buck to a hunter who made one long, careful shot.

extreme range. "But that doesn't mean we shoot irresponsibly," John added. "Every hunter must know his limits and hew to them."

Truly. Maximum effective range depends on conditions that affect your precision. A close offhand shot can be tougher than a long poke with

Bears are hard to follow after bad hits. Fat and hair plug wounds; water and thickets hide blood.

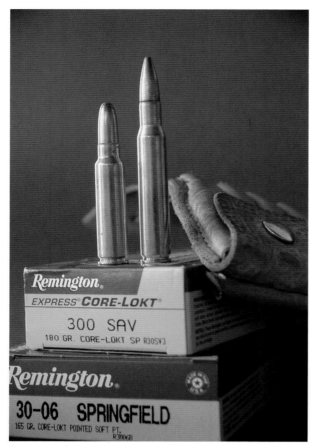

The .300 Savage (left) arrived in 1920, helped short-action lever rifles challenge the .30-06.

"Calibrating a dial to match the arc of a bullet requires accurate data," explained Don Ward. "For every load, we must know starting velocity and 700-yard drop to calculate the ballistic coefficient (C) and accurately mark the dial."

He told me some published data by bullet makers aren't accurate enough for the precision he and Scott demand.

"If that C number is off a little, you won't notice it at under 400 yards. But the farther a bullet travels, the steeper its trajectory and the more important the accuracy of the data." John builds in 1/3-minute clicks to replace standard 1/4-minute detents on the elevation dial. That's so he can milk more distance from one dial revolution. "Then you won't get a full-rotation error."

Numbers scribed above distance marks on the elevation knob show minutes of lateral correction needed in a 10-mph crosswind. Later, using GreyBull

Bullet designs change, but the .270 still ranks among top deer rounds, after 90 years.

bipod or sling. Wind complicates a shot. So does a small shot alley. Your physical state matters, too; hitting gets hard when you're catching your breath after a climb.

You can learn much by shooting steel gongs and paper bull's-eyes at half a mile. It's both fun and fine practice! But even with a steady position and the best equipment, the risk of a crippling hit at extreme distance argues against shooting game far away. Besides, the pivotal part of any hunt lies in the approach. Shooting from many hundreds of yards can be humane—but it does not test hunting skills.

Optics are a key component of GreyBull rifles. The firm contracts with Leupold to install its own reticle in Leupold's 4.5-14x VX III sight. It's essentially a Duplex with a series of fine horizontal lines for range estimation, and one-minute tics to help you shade for wind. The elevation dial, tall and capped only when you're not intending to use it, is meant to be turned for every shot.

scopes on a variety of rifles, I found yardage and windage marks astonishingly accurate. Of course, a laser rangefinder is all but necessary to get the most from Don's efforts. You must know the target distance to dial to it!

Before you can benefit from a sight that tracks trajectory, you need ammo that delivers precision where arcs get steep. High-performance handloads help. Those from the bench of John Burns don't start bullets much, if any, faster than ambitious factory loads with same-weight missiles. In fact, the faster the exit, the greater the drag and the higher the deceleration rate! A 180-grain 7mm bullet lies at the heavy end of the weight range, so, too, 105-grain .243s. They can't be driven nearly as fast as lighter bullets. But VLD bullets *retain* velocity better than ordinary spitzers. Reducing the *rate* of deceleration at distance is a key element of long-range shooting. Driven by Hodgdon's Retumbo powder, John's handloaded VLDs "fly very flat and with enough precision for 1,000-yard hits."

Long ogives (the curved surface between bullet nose and shank) make seating a problem in short actions, so John prefers the roomy Remington 700

Some cartridges—often old ones with heavy bullets— seem to kill better than they should!

Even rifles of modest power are deadly, when held to modest ranges and well-aimed.

This bull fell at long range to Wayne's Magnum Research/GreyBull rifle in 6.5 Creedmoor.

Wayne's prone shots with this Marlin—one each at 100, 200, 300, 400, 500, and 600 yards—all hit.

GreyBull's load-matched dials are range-marked for center aim, show MOA drift for 10-mph wind.

long-actions, even for the .243. Seating bullets out also increases case capacity. John cuts relatively long throats in his barrels, because, he explained, "Short bullet jump hasn't produced the best accuracy. Besides, bullets seated into the rifling can become a problem in the field. One cartridge a tad too long may stick the bullet when you close the bolt." Instead, John guides bullets with a lengthy throat the thickness of a mosquito's wing over bullet diameter. "Bullet alignment is crucial. Many factory chambers are too generous."

GreyBull rifles wear 26-inch medium-heavy barrels from custom makers like Kreiger, Schneider, and Lilja. John floats the barrel and glass-beds actions in a synthetic (hand-laid) stock he and his partners designed. Its has a steep, full grip and ample fore-end. A special stud accepts a Stoney Point flexible bipod. The GreyBull team has also used Harris bipods.

Like me, John thinks stiff recoil and harsh muzzle blast can offset benefits afforded by accurate loads, costly barrels, and sophisticated optics. "If you're

Wayne shot this eland with a 6.5 Creedmoor, but considers the cartridge light for such a big beast.

Skirting a Wyoming canyon just below ridgeline, these hunters are equipped for long shots.

A tripod is a huge help at distance, especially with handguns like this scoped S&W 460.

afraid of the rifle, you can't shoot well," he said. A range session near our camp confirmed that observation. I watched several hunters fire powerful rifles. Softball-size groups predominated—at 100 yards! One fellow had trouble hitting even big targets with his .338 Magnum. No wonder! At each pull of the trigger he shut his eyes and ducked away from the comb!

"Ring that gong." John handed me his Grey-Bull Precision rifle in .243. Good grief! The 16-inch steel plate was so far it appeared a mere dot in the Wyoming sage. "It's as big as a deer's chest," he said matter-of-factly. "Dial to 800 yards. It's actually 780, so take a click off." I indexed the knob and settled onto the bipod. A sharp wind quartered toward us at about 15 mph. "Give it four minutes left windage." At 780 steps, that's 31 inches! Lots of air gaped between crosswire and plate!

The two-pound Jewell trigger broke cleanly. No impact sound floated back. John took his eye from the spotting scope. "Add a minute left," I did. Seconds after my next shot, we heard the distant pop of a solid hit. I repeated. And again. Graciously, the wind didn't change. "When you can shoot into a minute of angle far away, 300-yard shots become easy and 100 looks like a putt," he smiled.

Seeing game is a first step to killing it. Smart hunters get as close as possible before firing.

This buck fell to a 105-grain .243 VLD bullet at 320 yards. GreyBull rifle, Leupold scope.

Even at modest ranges, a tripod makes sense. Precise hits bring clean kills with .223s.

Trusting the dial was harder than I'd thought. "We loaned a rifle to a neighbor," recalled Scott. "At 780 yards, he shot high. I was perplexed until he admitted he'd shaded high. Of course, adding a few inches of elevation is laughable. Were it not for the dialed adjustment, he would still have planted bullets several feet shy of the steel!"

More shooting at gongs and a one-shot kill on a distant deer convinced me the GreyBull system works. Hit on the shoulder, that buck (and others killed by my campmates), demonstrated the lethal effect of VLDs.

"Of course," Don reminded me, "you must aim at the right spot. You must also steady the rifle and break the shot without disturbing your sight picture."

Several months and many steel gongs later, I'd be putting those imperatives into practice.

■ ■ ■

Wyoming can stretch your reach, but Adam downed this buck at less than 150 yards.

Scant minutes of legal light remained. The elk sifted through tall sage half a mile distant. They were moving away.

"We can get closer. A little."

Ray Milligan tried to inject optimism. He'd had plenty of practice. Milligan Brand Outfitting hosts many elk hunters in northern New Mexico, each year. Dozens go home with bulls.

"Let's do it fast," I hissed, picking up the pace.

Phil, John, and Ray stayed close on my heels through the pinions. We scooted up the spine until it fell off abruptly, the sage a sea below us, the elk edging toward a ridge on its far shore.

"Six hundred." Ray had a positive read with his Leica Geovid binocular.

"Too far." I shook my head, gulping wind.

"Get ready," Ray urged, "okay? This five-point might be our only chance. Whatever the range, you make final decisions after you're ready to fire, not before."

Sliding the sling up my arm, I flopped prone and chambered a round, then spun the elevation dial to

This fine kudu, Leslie's first big-game animal, dropped to a perfect shot, thanks to shooting sticks!

Tom took this outstanding buck, while shooting prone at 410 yards with a GreyBull rifle in 7mm Magnum.

six. Dead-still air promised zero drift. Confident in the Magnum Research rifle after its fine performance on distant steel, I was also certain the GreyBull dial had accurately corrected for my bullet's drop. Still, I hesitated. This elk was twice as far as any I had shot at in 35 years of hunting. I had passed shots at many closer bulls, one just this morning. The smallest errors in hold and execution become problems at extreme range. What if the bullet strayed? A follow-up shot would be almost impossible if the elk moved. Surely they would. And trailing a hit animal would be difficult at best. I didn't *have* to shoot this elk … .

But my position was solid, the air dead-calm. I felt my excuses slipping away. If ever there was a time to shoot long, this was it.

"Trust the dial," John whispered. "Remember, you kept all the bullets in a 12-inch gong at 500."

The raghorn bull was quartering to, almost entirely exposed. Not yet. My finger came taut against the trigger. The crosswire quivered in the shoulder crease. The bull turned slightly.

Still uncommitted, I saw him stop, tawny ribs aglow in the orange, slanting light of dusk. Of such images are memories made.

Finding game before daylight makes an approach easier, long shooting less necessary.

RECOMMENDED READING

Much has been written about rifles, cartridges, ballistics, shooting, and hunting. Avid riflemen have big libraries. Here are three more must-have books if you're keen to hit at long range!

Ammo and Ballistics 5, by Bob Forker, Safari Press 2013, Long Beach CA, 518 large-format pages … ballistics data for multiple loads for a staggering number of commercial rifle and handgun cartridges, including 1,000-yard drop, drift, velocity and energy figures for more than 190 rounds.

Shooter's Bible Guide to Rifle Ballistics, by Wayne van Zwoll, Skyhorse Pub. 2011, New York NY, 216 large-format color pages … condensed ballistics tables with lively, in-depth writing on ballistics history, ammo manufacture, bullet arc, rifling pitch, wind drift, gear and shooting techniques for long-range hits.

The Rifle Shooter, by David Tubb, Zediker Pub. 2003, Oxford MS, 429 pages … proven advice on rifles, ammunition, handloading and shooting techniques from an 11-time National High Power Rifle Champion—with a section on long-range shooting and notes on development of Tubbs' own 6 XC cartridge.

▪ ▪ ▪